Praise for *A Most Glorious Ride*

"While many superb biographies of TR have utilized these diaries, this is the first time they have been published in their entirety. To finally have this material available for one of our most important American Presidents is no small achievement, and one long overdue. As a student of Theodore Roosevelt for over 30 years, I was astonished at the insight these chronological diary entries allow into this period of TR's life that has never been conveyed effectively in the hands of even the most talented biographer."
— Greg Wynn, *Long Island History Journal*

"…[Kohn] provides scholars and history buffs alike with a much-needed, accessible, annotated, and expertly footnoted one-volume collection of Theodore Roosevelt's personal diaries from 1877 through 1886 … Highly recommended."
— *CHOICE*

"…Kohn is not just a layout artist, tossing the entries down on paper and leaving the reader adrift in outdated terminology and the occasional confusing misspelling. He has gone much further. He is present as an instructor; the entries are respectfully enhanced with abundant annotations, clarifications and sic marks as necessary … *A Most Glorious Ride* ties up many loose ends in a way normally reserved for the conclusion of a life story. In this case, the story has only just begun. The book will alter and expand perspective for those who only maintain a solid textbook knowledge of Theodore Roosevelt."
— *Watertown Daily Times*

"This is a great book for those who simply cannot get enough of Theodore Roosevelt ... an excellent book as well as an easy and enjoyable read."
— *Bismarck Tribune*

"I thought there was nothing new under the sun to be done on Theodore Roosevelt, given the thousands of books already published, but Edward P. Kohn has discovered, and admirably filled, a major gap in books on the life and times of TR. By bringing these diaries together in one place for the first time and providing expert annotation and footnotes, Kohn makes an extremely valuable contribution to understanding Roosevelt."
— Paul Grondahl, author of *I Rose Like a Rocket: The Political Education of Theodore Roosevelt*

"*A Most Glorious Ride* is an outstanding addition not only to the scholarship on Roosevelt but also to the study of the Gilded Age, capturing the social norms of the times and offering insights into a long-gone era of family life."
— Michael Patrick Cullinane, author of *Liberty and American Anti-Imperialism: 1898–1909*

A MOST GLORIOUS RIDE

A MOST GLORIOUS RIDE

The Diaries of Theodore Roosevelt,

1877–1886

EDITED BY

Edward P. Kohn

AN IMPRINT OF STATE UNIVERSITY OF NEW YORK PRESS

Cover: Photograph of Theodore Roosevelt in his first year in the
New York State Assembly, 1882. Courtesy of the Theodore Roosevelt Collection,
Houghton Library, Harvard University (call number 520.13-003).

Published by
STATE UNIVERSITY OF NEW YORK PRESS, ALBANY

© 2015 State University of New York

All rights reserved

No part of this book may be used or reproduced in any manner whatsoever without written permission. No part of this book may be stored in a retrieval system or transmitted in any form or by any means including electronic, electrostatic, magnetic tape, mechanical, photocopying, recording, or otherwise without the prior permission in writing of the publisher.

Excelsior Editions is an imprint of State University of New York Press

For information, contact
State University of New York Press, Albany, NY
www.sunypress.edu

Production and book design, Laurie Searl
Marketing, Anne M. Valentine

Library of Congress Cataloging-in-Publication Data

Roosevelt, Theodore, 1858–1919.
 [Diaries. Selections.]
  A most glorious ride : the diaries of Theodore Roosevelt, 1877–1886 / edited by Edward P. Kohn.
      pages cm — (Excelsior editions)
   Includes bibliographical references and index.
   ISBN 978-1-4384-5513-6 (hc   )—978-1-4384-5514-3 (pb   )
   ISBN 978-1-4384-5515-0 (e-book)
   1. Roosevelt, Theodore, 1858–1919—Diaries. 2. Presidents—United States—Diaries. 3. Presidents—United States—Biography. I. Kohn, Edward P. (Edward Parliament), 1968– editor. II. Title.
   E757.A3 2015
   973.911092—dc23
   [B]   2014013125

10 9 8 7 6 5 4 3 2

Contents

Preface: Theodore Roosevelt as Diarist   vii

Introduction: Theodore Roosevelt's Life until 1877   ix

    Harvard: Volume I (1877)   1
        Diary Entries   4

"Trust in the Lord, and Do Good": Volume II (1878)   13
        Diary Entries   16

    Chestnut Hill: Volume III (1879)   69
        Diary Entries   72

    Married: Volume IV (1880)   121
        Diary Entries   124

photo gallery follows pages 176

    Politics: Volume V (1881)   177
        Diary Entries   180

    Albany: Volume VI (1882)   205
        Diary Entries   209

1882 Legislative Diary:
Diary of Five Months in the New York Legislature   213

Albany and "Dakotah": Volume VII (1883)   219
DIARY ENTRIES   221

"The light has gone out of my life": Volume VIII (1884)   225
FEBRUARY 14 ENTRY (IMAGE)   228
DIARY ENTRIES   228

"E.K.C.": Volume IX (1886)   245
DIARY ENTRIES   248

Conclusion: Theodore Roosevelt's Life after 1886   257

Glossary of Latin Names of Wildlife
Observed and Collected by Theodore Roosevelt   269

Works Consulted   271

Index   273

Preface

Theodore Roosevelt as Diarist

Theodore Roosevelt was a compulsive list-maker and journal-writer. The Theodore Roosevelt Collection at Harvard University is full of notebooks with titles such as "Notes on Natural History," "Zoological Record," and "Remarks on the Zoology of Oyster Bay." In addition to diaries Roosevelt kept during two tours of Europe as a boy and young adolescent, he also kept a diary as lieutenant colonel of the Rough Riders during the Cuban campaign of 1898.

The diaries from 1877 to 1886 cover a key time in Roosevelt's life and reveal how Roosevelt changed from a homesick and frequently ill adolescent at Harvard, to a strapping and confident young man. The diaries recount Roosevelt's many love interests before he finally won the hand of Alice Hathaway Lee. As well as love, the diaries recount loss. Heartbreaking entries cover the death of Roosevelt's father, mother, and wife. In addition to Roosevelt's personal life, the diaries offer a glimpse of Roosevelt's start in New York politics and of his three terms in the New York State Assembly. Finally, the diaries also describe his first trips out West and a large part of his two-year Western sojourn before returning to New York in 1886 after he became secretly engaged to Edith Carow, his childhood friend and adolescent love interest.

Biographers of Roosevelt have necessarily relied on the diaries to gain insight into Roosevelt. In the 1950s Carleton Putnam drew heavily on the diaries when they were still in the possession of Roosevelt's eldest daughter, Alice, and the resulting biography, *Theodore Roosevelt: The Formative Years*, is probably the best treatment of Roosevelt's early life until 1886. In his Pulitzer Prize-winning *The Rise of Theodore Roosevelt*, Edmund Morris calls the diaries "the most revealing documents to survive." David McCullough also relies heavily on the diaries for the relevant chapters in his National Book Award-winning *Mornings on Horseback*. The diaries obviously helped bring to life Theodore

Roosevelt in a way that pleased readers and critics alike. Since these volumes, most biographers have tended to quickly slide past the years covered by the diaries. As a result, the diaries have arguably been underused in exploring Roosevelt's early life, or, as Putnam correctly called them, his "formative years."

Such lack of utilization of a valuable biographical source may result from the fact that until now the diaries have never been published. The question is: Why? The failure to publish the diaries may result from several factors. First, unlike many of the thousands of letters published in Elting Morison's *The Letters of Theodore Roosevelt*, all diary entries are handwritten rather than typed. Deciphering Roosevelt's writing, spelling, penmanship, and use of colloquial and specialized language is a daunting challenge. The second factor may be simple logistics. The diaries are not held in a single place. The first and last volumes are part of the Theodore Roosevelt Collection, Houghton Library, Harvard College, and the other volumes are part of the Library of Congress's Theodore Roosevelt Collection. Finally, Roosevelt was not a consistent diarist. The 1877 volume contains about fifty entries, while the volumes covering 1878–1881 contain more comprehensive entries. The diaries from 1882 to 1886 are once again sparser, with no diary at all for 1885. Moreover, Roosevelt had a tendency to rip out entries. This was particularly the case in his 1884 diary after the death of his first wife, Alice, in February of that year. After her death Roosevelt also destroyed many of her letters and photographs. As a result there exists a great lack of personal information about Roosevelt for the years 1884–1886—a "lacuna," as Morris notes.

This volume presents the diaries published in their entirety for the first time. Annotations seek to explain the people, places, and events Roosevelt noted. Entries are presented as Roosevelt penned them, complete with misspellings and grammatical mistakes. The notation "sic" has been used sparingly, usually when the mistake is particularly egregious or potentially confusing, while the correct spellings of names and places are given in footnotes. As Roosevelt used a fountain pen, inkblots have rendered some entries illegible. An introduction and conclusion summarize Roosevelt's life before and after the years covered by the diaries in order that this volume might serve as a single source covering his entire life. At the center are Roosevelt's personal diaries from 1877 to 1886, covering his life from age eighteen to twenty-seven. They provide a fascinating and intimate glimpse into the life and early political career of the young man who would one day become one of America's most important presidents.

Introduction

Theodore Roosevelt's Life until 1877

Theodore Roosevelt was born in New York City on October 27, 1858, in a luxurious brownstone house near Gramercy Park. His father, Theodore Roosevelt Sr., was a partner in Roosevelt and Son with the Roosevelt family patriarch, the future president's grandfather Cornelius Van Schaack Roosevelt. Theodore Roosevelt Sr. was a great philanthropist in his day, helping found the Newsboys' Lodging House and Orthopedic Dispensary Hospital, as well as the American Museum of Natural History and the Metropolitan Museum of Art. During the Civil War, Roosevelt Sr. had paid a substitute rather than risk being conscripted into the army, a common practice among men of his class. Instead, he became one of three allotment commissioners, responsible for persuading soldiers to set aside part of their monthly pay for their families back home.

Theodore Roosevelt Sr.'s strong pro-Union sentiment inevitably clashed with his wife's sympathy for the Confederacy. Martha "Mittie" Bulloch Roosevelt had grown up on a classic Southern plantation in Georgia called Bulloch Hall, and had regaled her children with stories of slaves and the Old South. Mittie even had two brothers, Irving and James, who served in the Confederate Navy. Having been transplanted from rural Georgia to New York City, Mittie was something of an alien in such an urban setting. She lived in terror of dirt and of the contaminated food and water that could lead to typhus, a common and deadly malady of the nineteenth century.

Theodore Roosevelt was the second of four children born to Theodore Sr. and Mittie. Anna or "Bamie" was born only three years before him, but acted almost as a second mother to her younger siblings, always sitting and conferring with the "big people," as Theodore remembered. Elliott Roosevelt, born eighteen months after Theodore, was his brother's closest friend and playmate during their childhood. Sister Corinne was born a year after Elliott, meaning that the three youngest children were born within a span of only three years. Illness plagued the children. Anna suffered from a spinal defect that required her wearing a painful harness. Elliott suffered seizures that, as he grew older, would make him turn to alcohol in an effort to control them. Theodore and Corinne both suffered from asthma and headaches. Theodore's frequent illness left him smaller than Elliott and turned him into something of an introvert. He spent many solitary hours observing insects, learning the Latin names of birds, and practicing taxidermy. Once Theodore's father implored his young son, "You must make your body." The boy took the order to heart, and it served as a guiding principle for the rest of his life.

For the Roosevelts, summers meant the countryside. Eventually Theodore Roosevelt Sr. acquired a summerhouse at Oyster Bay, Long Island, near the house of his father. Roosevelt remembered the time spent there with great joy. In the countryside the children rode horses, swam in and rowed on Long Island Sound, and tramped through the woods. On Long Island the young Theodore fed his growing interest in natural science, and his lifelong love of the outdoors.

The Roosevelt children did not attend school, so they were deprived of the social instruction afforded by the classroom and playground. Throughout Theodore's childhood his siblings and many cousins remained his only playmates, and the presence of strange boys—often bigger, stronger, and more aggressive—caused him great anxiety. Roosevelt drew great enjoyment and support from his close-knit family. Roosevelt's father was the dominant figure of the boy's life, and the younger Theodore remained close to his siblings—his sisters in particular—until the day he died.

The Roosevelt family took two grand tours of Europe, the first in 1869–70 as Theodore turned eleven, the second in 1872–73 when he turned fourteen. The first trip was troubled by Theodore's near-constant bouts of headaches, asthma, and homesickness. Later, in his memoirs, Roosevelt himself would note that this trip was colored by his immature "chauvinism and contempt" toward Europe, while the second trip reflected growing maturity, a sense of "discernment and appreciation," and a love of Germany cultivated during a long stay with a German family in Dresden. Roosevelt's direct boyhood contact with Europe was certainly important in the development of his ideas, both about America and the world. Roosevelt admired the art, history, and landscapes of England, France, Switzerland, Italy, and Germany.

For all of his appreciation of European art and scenery, young Theodore decried the poverty and filth he saw. This was ironic, as New York's lower wards were notorious for their abject poverty and mountains of garbage. During his childhood in New York, aside from trips with his father to the Newsboys' Lodging House, at the corner of Fulton and Nassau streets, Roosevelt had been largely shielded from such sights. Before Roosevelt had similar contact with New York's "other half" in the 1880s, the European trips probably were the boy's first close observations of real poverty.

During the family's second tour, Theodore and Elliott spent the summer of 1873 living with the Minckwitz family of Dresden, where they were immersed in German language and culture. This was when Roosevelt began a love affair with all things German that would last until the Great War. The choice of Germany, and Dresden in particular, was no accident. In the nineteenth century, German was the language of literature, history, and science. In New York, the German people were considered sober, cultured, and industrious. Unification having taken place two years before, Germany was an important European power. Finally, while Berlin was the political capital of the new country, Dresden was the German capital of art, music, science, and education. A beautiful city often compared to Florence, Dresden boasted some of Europe's best galleries, museums, and libraries. If Theodore Roosevelt Sr. was looking for a city to provide his children intellectual stimulation, he found it in Dresden.

Upon returning from the second grand tour, young Theodore began preparing for entrance into Harvard. In the winter of 1873, he began receiving tutoring from Harvard graduate Arthur Cutler with the single goal of passing the university admission exams. At the time, Harvard was undergoing expansion and curriculum changes. President Charles Eliot had instituted a controversial system of "electives" that allowed students to choose courses that simply interested them, such as botany and history. Such subjects might not have seemed to prepare America's top young men for careers in law, medicine, or business, but that was the point. The United States needed more than mere specialists. The country also needed men who could think.

The elective system also emphasized educating the individual student, rather than imposing a one-size-fits-all curriculum. Eliot rejected the idea that schools should be merely factories of homogeneity. This seemed to reflect Roosevelt Sr.'s attitude toward raising his own children by cultivating their individuality and responding to each child's unique needs. His elder son's talent clearly lay with the natural sciences, and under Professor Louis Agassiz, Harvard had become the leading university in the field.

Harvard was more than just the university and the town of Cambridge. In Gilded Age America, Harvard meant Boston. The city of Boston and its ruling class must have figured prominently in the Roosevelts' decision that Theodore should attend Harvard. One reason was probably Boston's reputation as the "Athens of America," as *North American Review* founder William Tudor put it. For its small size, Boston boasted an enormous array of authors, poets, historians, artists, and scientists. Roosevelt's father perhaps viewed Boston as he regarded Dresden in Germany, not as the political or financial capital of the country, but as the cultural capital. Just as the European grand tours were meant to broaden and enrich his children's view of the world, sending his son to Boston was meant to make Theodore a refined and cultured gentleman.

The Boston Brahmins also shared the elder Roosevelt's sense of *noblesse oblige*, the understanding that wealth and power conferred responsibility for one's community. The elite Bostonians were also reformers. At the Republican

National Conventions in 1876 and 1880, the Massachusetts delegates stood against the choices of the party leaders and instead secured the nominations of Rutherford B. Hayes and dark horse James Garfield. By 1881 they had helped found the National Civil Service Reform League, backed by the quintessential Boston intellectual journal, *The North American Review*. For Theodore Roosevelt Sr., then, Harvard provided the perfect environment to educate his namesake. There he would rub elbows with the sons of the Boston elite and ingest their ideas on morality, culture, patronage, charity, and reform.

This was far from evident, however, as seventeen-year-old Roosevelt arrived at Harvard in September 1876. To a New Yorker, Cambridge, Massachusetts, in 1876 appeared little more than a village. Three miles from Boston, Harvard Square was almost somnolent, the absolute quiet of the area disturbed only by the infrequent bells of the horse-drawn carriages. "Once in a while," a contemporary observer wrote, "its dust is stirred by some mortuary procession of cattle on their way to the abattoirs." The university and its buildings on their surrounding twenty-two acres dominated the town, just as the massive tower on the new Memorial Hall dominated the skyline. On Sundays the streets were even emptier than usual, as most of the Harvard men went into Boston to spend the Sabbath with their families. Roosevelt would usually spend these days teaching a Sunday school class, writing letters to his family, and collecting specimens of birds and toads.

At Harvard he fell in with some of the Boston crowd, joining a dining club for meals rather than partaking of the "uneatable" food in the student Commons. In addition to throwing himself into his studies—all required classes the freshman year, including Greek and Latin—he began boxing and wrestling. Although Roosevelt was frequently knocked down, he undertook these sports as ways to continue to "make his body," as he had promised his father. During the first winter break at the end of 1876, he began a tradition of hosting some of his Boston chums in Manhattan. For Roosevelt, still something of an outsider in Boston, this must have proved a particularly enjoyable experience. Now Roosevelt could play guide in America's greatest city, showing Bostonians the towers of the Brooklyn Bridge and taking them sleighing in Central Park. And at some point during that holiday break in New York, Roosevelt decided to again take up a habit he had not followed since he was fourteen. He began keeping a diary.

Harvard

Volume I (1877)

Theodore Roosevelt's first adult diary contained only about fifty entries. The entries are largely emotionless, dedicated to chronicling the largely solitary life of an eighteen-year-old Harvard undergraduate. Yet they provide a marvelous contrast to the later volumes that reveal Roosevelt as a maturing young man, increasingly involved in the social life of Cambridge, Boston, and Chestnut Hill. At the beginning, though, young Theodore began Harvard suffering from asthma and various other maladies, including a bout with the measles; and as a New Yorker, he did not immediately find a place within the closed ranks of the sons of the Boston Brahmin elite. His father's connections and those of his sister Anna—or "Bamie," as Roosevelt called her—helped ease his way socially. Theodore Roosevelt Sr.'s friend William Minot immediately checked on the newly arrived freshman and introduced him to his son Henry Davis, a fellow freshman. After a couple of summers up at Bar Harbor, Maine, Bamie had become acquainted with the Hoopers and Saltonstalls, two more families who would figure prominently in young Theodore's time at college.

Within two weeks of arriving, Roosevelt had joined a dining table with some of the "Boston men" who would become his closest friends. They would provide entrée into the best social clubs on campus, and would welcome Roosevelt into their homes. Through them Roosevelt met a number of young women, including his future wife. Roosevelt also made social inroads by way of the boxing and wrestling rings of the Harvard gymnasium. There he sought to follow his father's advice to make his body as strong as his mind. Through boxing matches and long summertime rows on Long Island Sound, Roosevelt grew increasingly fit and physically confident.

Much of this first volume is dedicated to Roosevelt's "expeditions" looking for wildlife and bird specimens. These were undertaken either alone, or with one or more of his classmates Russell Hooper, Henry Davis Minot, and Christopher Minot Weld. A number of diary entries are dedicated to Roosevelt's noting the Latin names of common birds, turtles, and toads found in Cambridge, Forest Hills, and Newtonville, Massachusetts. At this point Roosevelt was preparing for a career as a natural scientist. Harvard president Charles Eliot's elective system allowed Roosevelt to try two natural history courses his sophomore year, including one with William James. With this common interest Roosevelt became closest to "Harry" or "Hal" Minot, another avid amateur naturalist, who at age seventeen had published *The Land and Game Birds of New England* (Boston 1877). Roosevelt and Minot often went birding together in the Adirondacks, and after their trip in the summer of 1877 the two of them published *The Summer Birds of the Adirondacks in Franklin County, N.Y.* Roosevelt's first published work, the slim "catalogue" of roughly one hundred bird species received a glowing review from famed biologist C. Hart Merriman. Roosevelt now seemed primed to launch his career as a natural scientist. Such a decision, though, first had to be run by his father.

Theodore Roosevelt Sr. cautiously encouraged his namesake to follow a scientific career. He told his son that he if took up science he must pursue it seriously, and not as a dilettante. The father told his son that the Roosevelt family had enough money to support the pursuit of a scientific career, but that Theodore would have to adjust his lifestyle accordingly. "If I went into a scientific career," Roosevelt recounted later, "I must definitely abandon all thought of the enjoyment that could accompany a money-making career, and must find my pleasures elsewhere." Recalling the conversation thirty-five years later in his memoirs, Roosevelt noted that the talk with his father confirmed his intention to make science his lifework. Ultimately, Roosevelt was turned off by Harvard's treatment of biology as purely "a science of the laboratory," while ignoring the outdoors, observational work conducted by biologists such as Merriman. Roosevelt himself admitted that this probably reflected his lack of "intense devotion to science." In fact, his observation and collection of wildlife likely resulted more from a love of the outdoors than a love of science.

With his solitary expeditions came a longing for home and his teenage sweetheart, Edith Kermit Carow. The highlight of his freshman year was a visit by Roosevelt's father, brother, Elliott, and sisters, Anna and Corinne. Accompanying the family was cousin Maud Elliott and Edith Carow. "I do'n't think I ever saw Edith looking prettier," Roosevelt wrote Corinne after the visit, "everyone, and especially Harry Chapin and Minot Weld admired her little Ladyship intensely, and she behaved as sweetly as she looked." He made a point of concluding the letter, "When you write to Edith tell her I enjoyed *her* visit *very* much indeed."[1] Their departure a few days later left Roosevelt, in his words, "disconsolate."

---

1. Morison, TR to Corinne, 3 June 1877, 28.

Roosevelt's father so dominated the young man's life that any incident involving the elder Roosevelt proved significant. One such incident occurred at the end of 1877, in the middle of Roosevelt's sophomore year. Theodore Roosevelt Sr. had recently become active in Republican reform circles. He had joined with New Yorkers such as Joseph Choate, J. Pierpont Morgan, and John Jay to form the Republican Reform Club, an early movement to press for good municipal government. In the summer of 1876, Roosevelt Sr. had traveled to the Republican National Convention in Cincinnati to secure the nomination of reform candidates to the national ticket in lieu of the corrupt James Blaine of Maine. The eventual nomination of Rutherford B. Hayes marked something of a triumph for the reform forces that June, especially as the New York delegation initially supported the state party boss, U.S. Senator Roscoe Conkling. After the election, President Hayes took direct aim at Conkling's power in New York. The new president ordered an investigation of one of the richest plums in Conkling's basket, the New York Customhouse, headed by Conkling lieutenant Chester A. Arthur, who held the official title "Collector of Customs." Loyal Republicans had long been rewarded with choice appointments in the customhouse, which in turn became a powerful political base for the machine. As it was a federal institution, Hayes ordered all political activity at the customhouse to cease.

The president was not finished. Against the New York boss's wishes, Hayes nominated Theodore Roosevelt Sr. to replace Chester Arthur. This was tantamount to a declaration of war by the president on the New York Republican machine. The elder Roosevelt was caught in the crossfire. Hayes's efforts were complicated by the fact that Roosevelt's appointment had to be approved by the Senate's Committee on Commerce—a committee chaired by Conkling. From Harvard the younger Roosevelt followed the drama as best he could. "Tell Father I am watching the 'Controllership' [sic] movements with the greatest interest," he wrote his sister Anna that fall.[2] On December 3, Conkling prevented Roosevelt's confirmation from coming to a vote in the Senate, and the issue died. For Theodore, it was a valuable education in Republican Party politics and the conflict between the machine and the forces of reform.

Young Theodore had been home for Thanksgiving at the time of his father's rejection by Conkling's committee, and he returned to Cambridge the next day. Roosevelt did not know that his father had been suffering severe intestinal pains for weeks. By mid-December, Theodore Roosevelt Sr. was very ill. Days before Christmas, the son received a telegram summoning him back to New York. Over Christmas, however, his father seemed to revive, and Roosevelt returned to Cambridge in early 1878. Unknown to Roosevelt, his father was suffering from a tumor of the bowel, an ailment that would soon prove fatal.

---

2. Morison, TR to Anna, 14 October 1877, 29.

Volume I
1877 Diary

Sunday January 7

Returned to Cambridge, to my studies, after the weeks vacation. Took up my Sunday school class.

Saturday February 10

Beaten by Dick Grimble, boxing.

Sunday February 18

Sick with measles.[3]

Monday February 26

Partially recovered. Went on to New York.[4]

Monday March 12

Went out to Oyster Bay, for a little shooting.[5]

Friday March 16

Came back from Oyster Bay. Only procured a couple of ducks.

Saturday March 17

Returned to Cambridge.

Thursday March 29

Wrestling. Threw Billy Hooper, Learned, Peters & Nickerson. Thrown by Davis.[6]

---

3. "An amusement I always considered as belonging, together with rattles and teething purely to babies." TR to his mother, 18 February 1877. TR mistakenly wrote "January" for the date, a mistake picked up by Morison, 22.

4. Now at Harvard's mid-year, Roosevelt had just completed "a spell of examinations," and traveled home for a short break. Morison, TR to his parents, 11 February 1877, 25.

5. The future site of Roosevelt's Sagamore Hill estate, Oyster Bay had become the summer residence of both his father and grandfather, Cornelius Van Schaack Roosevelt.

6. William Hooper, William Pollock Learned, George Gorham Peters, Thomas White Nickerson, and Charles Stevenson Davis. One of Harvard's best football players, Nickerson would go on to be rector of St. Stephen's Church in Pittsfield, Massachusetts. William Hooper later called Roosevelt at Harvard "a freak, a poseur, and half crazy."

Sunday April 1

Forest Hills, Mass.[7] Eutaenia sirtalis.[8] Chrysemys picta.[9] With Minot Weld.[10]

Saturday April 7

Newtonville, Mass. Arvicola riparia. Hesperomys leucopus. Melospiza palustris. Loxia curvirostra.[11] Salamandra. Rana damitans and palustris. Accipiter fuscus.[12] Expedition with Russell Hooper.

Monday April 9

Cambridge, Mass. Rana halecina [crossed out]. Bufo americanus.[13]

Tuesday April 10

Forest Hills, Mass. Colaptes auratus, abundant.[14]

Sunday April 15

Forest Hills, Mass. Accipiter looperii. Denedraoica pina. Plethodon erythronotus.

Monday April 16

Forest Hills, Mass. Dendroica palmarum. Aramochelys odoratus.

Friday April 27

Cambridge, Mass. Emys guttata.[15] Rana halecina.

---

7. The home of classmate and fellow avid amateur naturalist Henry Davis Minot. Minot became a successful railroad man, in 1888 becoming the youngest railroad president in the country at the helm of the Eastern Railroad in Minnesota. He was killed two years later in a railroad accident.

8. Common garter snake.

9. Painted turtle, the most common native turtle in North America.

10. Christopher Minot Weld, another close Harvard classmate with whom Roosevelt shared an interest in nature, including collecting such specimens as the snake and turtle. "Minot" would go on to be a successful Boston financier. Roosevelt often spent holidays and weekends with one of these two friends and their families. Of Minot Weld, Roosevelt wrote his sister Corinne, "I like his family very much, and he himself is a peculiarly manly and gentlemanly fellow." Morison, TR to Corinne, 5 February 1877, 23.

11. Common crossbill.

12. Pigeon.

13. Common American toad.

14. Northern flicker woodpecker.

15. Spotted terrapin (turtle).

Thursday May 10

Father, Bamie, Conie, Cousin Maud and pretty Edith came on to visit me. Elliott also, full of Texan adventures.[16]

Monday May 14

The family all went home, leaving me disconsolate. The last three days have been great fun.

Monday May 21

Grinding like mad for the semi [crossed out] annuals.

Tuesday June 19

I have done well in my examinations so far. (Got on the Rank list in all but one).[17]

Wednesday June 20

Poor Aunt Mary died. I left Cambridge for New York, to attend the funeral.[18]

Thursday June 21

Started for Adirondacs.[19]

Friday June 22

Reached St. Regis Lake Adirondacs. Staying at Paul Smiths, with Harry Minot.[20]

---

16. This party included Roosevelt's entire immediate family, except his mother: his father, sisters, Anna and Corinne, and brother, Elliott. Cousin Maud was Maud Elliott, just about Roosevelt's own age. While living in Dresden in 1873 they had spent much time together along with Maud's brother John. Only the following year, at age 12, Maud wrote of her cousin, "Well my dear little friends I must tell you something about Theodore you know he was a naturalist on a small scale, he was a very amusing boy but he had a great fault he was very absent minded so much so that whenever his Mother would tell him to go and do something for her he would say 'Oh yes you pretty little thing' but instead of doing it directly he would go and skin his birds or something that he took into his head to skin, and then he always thought that he could do things better than anyone else." "Pretty Edith" is Edith Carow, with whom Roosevelt had started a relationship before departing for Harvard.

17. Roosevelt attained an honor grade in all of his classes except Greek.

18. Mary West Roosevelt, wife of Silas Weir Roosevelt.

19. Beginning in August 1874, Roosevelt began keeping a "Journal of a Trip to the Adirondacks," containing his observations of the area's wildlife and topography.

20. Paul Smith's Hotel was a fashionable wilderness resort in the Adirondacks. Despite its intentionally primitive state—including no indoor bathrooms—it was a favorite of late-nineteenth-century elite looking for a wilderness experience. Future presidents Grover Cleveland and Calvin Coolidge also stayed there. The hotel burned down in 1930.

Saturday June 30

St. Regis Lake, N.Y. Quisqualus purpureus.[21] A colony near a stream. Not shy. Tringoides macularius.[22] Common Loxia curvirostra.[23] Common in small parties. Flies high and keeps to the tops of the tallest pines, on whose seeds it feeds. Ardea Herodias,[24] Botaurus mugitans,[25] Mergus serrator,[26] Anas obscura,[27] Aex sponsa,[28] Colymbus torquatus,[29] seen. 3 skins.

Sunday July 1 [This entry continues through July 2 into July 3.]

St. Regis Lake. Loxiacurvirostra. Frequently comes around the hunters shanties, to pick up crumbs &c. Otherwise rarely approaches the ground, keeping to the top of the pines, among whose branches it climbs about like a parrot, even hanging head downwards from the branches. It is tame and unsuspicious. Its ordinary note, given while flying, sounds like "kip kip." It also chatters occasionally, and has a sweet, powerful song, like that of the purple finch. It flies strong & high, "dipping" slightly. If wounded it clings tightly to [the tops of—crossed out] the branches, even when dead, not falling. Although it feeds chiefly on seeds it also snaps up any insect it happens to come across.[30]

Tuesday July 3

Started into the woods to camp out, today.

Wednesday July 4

St Regis Lake. Quisqualus purpureus. Found in small colonies, each one usually many miles from its neighbours. They are found by ponds, in tamarack swamps or among the alders that fringe the streams. I saw several feeding among the lily pads, walking on them & catching small frogs.

---

21. Crow blackbird.
22. Spotted sandpiper.
23. Red crossbill.
24. Great blue heron.
25. Bittern.
26. Merganser.
27. Black duck.
28. Wood duck.
29. Loon.
30. This entry is representative of Roosevelt's observations in *Summer Birds*, which also includes descriptions of behavior, habitat, and birdsong. Roosevelt's first published work, it received a glowing review from famed biologist C. Hart Merriam and seemed primed to launch Roosevelt on a career as a professional naturalist.

Thursday July 5

Potters Pond, 25 miles from Paul Smiths. Shot my 1st deer, a buck. Also a couple of black ducks and three ruffed grouse.

Saturday July 7

Came out of the woods today. Good fun, but not much fishing.
Weeks bag
    1 buck
    2 duck
    3 grouse
    52 trout (about 15 lbs)
Have had no tent. Eatables—bread & tea.

Tuesday July 10

Reached Oyster Bay in the afternoon.

Monday July 16

Am leading the most thoroughly out of door life. Riding and walking every day, and rowing in my little boat almost as often.

Wednesday July 25

On a "frogging excursion" saw Ranatemporaria, damitans, pipiens, halecina & palustris.

Thursday August 2

Emlen, Elliott and I started on a sailing trip in the Sound (which occupied 3 days).[31]

Friday August 10

Got 6 herons at a heronry.

Saturday August 11

Jack Elliott arrived today.

Friday August 24

Jack Elliott & I in my little 11 foot boat rowed down to Whitestone 25 miles.[32]

---

31. William Emlen Roosevelt, Roosevelt's first cousin, son of James Alfred Roosevelt, was a frequent childhood companion and later Roosevelt's financial adviser.
32. Roosevelt's aunt Mrs. Gracie lived in an old farmhouse at Whitestone.

Saturday August 25

Coming back from Whitestone got caught in a heavy nor-easter, got home 1 a.m.

Wednesday September 5

Spent the day seineing for fish in a panny.

Saturday September 8

Jack Elliott and I rowed round Loyds Neck, portaging the "isthmus."[33]

Monday September 10

Jack and I rowed to Loyds neck, shooting several herons with rifle.

Tuesday September 11

Jack and I rowed round Centre Island getting ½ dozen snipe.

Wednesday September 12

Shot 2 sea-coots[34] in the mouth of the Harbour.

Thursday September 13

Jack and I started in our little boat and rowed to Hempstead Harbour.[35] Camped out at night.

Friday September 14

Early in morning got 4 coots & 6 snipe. Returned to Oyster Bay.

Saturday September 22

Rowed to Loyds neck to see Miss Boden.[36] Heavy sea, got very wet, had to dry myself by lying naked on the dock for an hour. Big sea running as I came home.

Wednesday September 26

Rode over to see Miss Boden at Loyds Neck; came home at 10 p.m. & horse fell down on way back.

---

33. Lloyd Neck used to be part of the town of Oyster Bay, connected to Long Island only by a small strip of land—an "isthmus."

34. Scoter duck.

35. A considerable row of perhaps fifteen miles, much of it out on Long Island Sound.

36. Although apparently still devoted to Edith Carow, Theodore had a running flirtation with Miss Boden.

Thursday September 27

Left for Cambridge

Friday September 28

Cambridge. Am elected 5th man of 2nd ten of Institute (Δ.K.E.)[37] Started with my Sunday School again.

Thursday October 4

Threw Davis wrestling.

Monday October 8

The work is much pleasanter than last year. I like the zoological course very much.[38]

Friday October 12

Threw Ellis wrestling.[39]

Thursday October 18

Boxed with Arthur Hooper. Even. Beat Ellis wrestling.

Monday October 22

Beat Hooper boxing, and also Ellis.

Saturday October 27

19 years old today. Rode over and spent night with Minot Weld.

Saturday November 3

Hooper beat me badly boxing. I beat Ellis & Brooks.[40]

Wednesday November 28

Went on to New York for Thanksgiving.

---

37. Delta Kappa Epsilon.

38. Roosevelt was taking two natural history courses: a class on botany and a course on vertebrates with William James. Roosevelt wrote his sister Anna that James's class was "extremely interesting." Morison, TR to Anna Roosevelt, 14 October 1877, 29.

39. Ralph Nicholson Ellis.

40. Arthur Anderson Brooks.

Tuesday December 4

Returned to Cambridge after Thanksgiving.

Saturday December 15

Gave red-haired Coolidge a tremendous thrashing in the gymnasium, boxing.[41] Have done better than last year in my studies so far.

Friday December 21

Suddenly called to New York. Dear Father very sick.

Sunday December 23

Father very much better.

Tuesday December 25

Xmas. Father seems much brighter. Received a double barreled shotgun.

MEMORANDA
[printed title of page]

COLLECTIONS FOR YEAR

Mammals	16
Birds	68
Reptiles	17
Batrachians	61
Fishes	10
	172

GAME BAG

1	buck
10	duck
12	snipe (shore snipe)
3	grouse
6	plover
4	gray squirel [sic]
10	herons
46	

---

41. William Williamson Coolidge.

"Trust in the Lord, and Do Good"

VOLUME II (1878)

The year 1878 began with Roosevelt much more socially active. His dining table continued to be a key source of social connections, with one exception: Dick Saltonstall missed his sophomore year due to diphtheria. Another member of the table was Robert Bacon, considered the most attractive and popular of Roosevelt's Class of 1880. Belonging to Bacon's "set" immensely aided Roosevelt socially. By October, at the beginning of his junior year, Roosevelt was asked to join two of the most exclusive clubs at Harvard, the A.D. and the Porcellian. Having to choose between the two, Roosevelt chose the Porcellian, not Bacon's A.D. But the two remained friends, and Bob Bacon would one day serve as assistant secretary of State to President Theodore Roosevelt.

The diary entries of early 1878 differ from 1877 especially in their frequent mention of young women. Of the twelve entries between January 9 and 29, nine of them mention dinners or dances. Letters home mention a number of women, including Bessie Whitney and Jeannie Hooper. "Some very sweet girls in Boston," Roosevelt wrote in his diary on January 12, "as Carrie Goodwin, Bessie Whitney and the Miss Roaches. Also Pauline Revere." In August, while at the Roosevelt summer home at Oyster Bay, Long Island, he and Edith stopped into the summerhouse and an incident occurred that led them to end their relationship. Possibly the seventeen-year-old Edith rejected Roosevelt's romantic advances, or turned down a marriage proposal. There followed a period of several days when Roosevelt's unhappiness manifested itself in a number of incidents, including riding his horse to near lameness and shooting a neighbor's dog. Only two months later, however, Roosevelt met Alice Hathaway Lee, the object of his attentions until their marriage almost exactly two years later.

Before Roosevelt could begin a particularly happy junior year in the fall of 1878, however, he would suffer one of the greatest blows of his life. On February

10, Theodore Roosevelt Sr. finally succumbed to his bowel tumor. Theodore was summoned home by telegram, but missed his father's passing—for which he could not forgive himself. He heard from his siblings how they had tended to their suffering father. From Corinne, in a letter to Edith: "I have sat with him some seven hours. He slept most of it but at time was in fearful agony." She described how the pain caused her father's hair to turn gray, when before falling ill the forty-six-year-old Roosevelt had not had a single white hair. Elliott's own diary recorded the father's "cries for ether" as the doctor came and put him into a drugged sleep from which he would awake in excruciating pain.

His father's death plunged Roosevelt into a depression that would not lift for months. Roosevelt took solace in his faith, noting in his diary psalms, Bible verses, and hymns. He reread his father's letters and his childhood diaries of their trips to Europe and the Middle East. Even visits home did little to alleviate his grief, as every memento and member of his family only brought his father to mind. Only on May 1 did Roosevelt note that thinking of his father caused him only pleasure instead of pain. His father's death also forced Roosevelt to contemplate a future as the head of his family and his father's namesake. Following Roosevelt Sr.'s death, New York newspapers lauded his many civic and charitable activities. What path could Roosevelt take to live up to his father's name? "O, how little worthy I am of such a father," Roosevelt noted in his diary in December. "I feel such a hopeless sense of inferiority to him." By the end of the year, however, Roosevelt was still planning on a career as a naturalist.

Such thinking was only underscored by a trip to the Maine woods in the early fall, just before the start of his junior year. It also foreshadowed a time when grief would again propel Roosevelt into America's wild places. In July he had noted that Psalm 55 was one of this father's favorites: "My heart is severely pained within me, and the terrors of death have fallen upon me . . . Oh, that I had wings like a dove! I would fly away and be at rest. Indeed, I would wander far off and remain in the wilderness." The three-week trip featured Roosevelt and his companions—including cousins West and Emlen—tramping through the woods in search of game, which consisted mostly of partridges. The trip also introduced Roosevelt to Maine woodsmen Wilmot Dow and Bill Sewall, with whom Roosevelt would later enter into his Dakota ranching venture. Unlike Roosevelt's previous birding trips to the Adirondacks, this was the first trip he undertook solely for the sake of hunting. While he would again return to Maine, within a few years Roosevelt would shift his hunting expeditions out West.

That Roosevelt eventually opted for the West was made all the more surprising by his love of the water. If a single feature of American geography ever captivated Roosevelt, it was not the Badlands or the Elkhorn Mountains. Roosevelt appeared most at home rowing or sailing on Long Island Sound. During the summer of 1878, when not riding his horse or tramping through the woods, Roosevelt could be found on the water. His most common practice was to row around Center Island, which jutted into Oyster Bay Harbor and was attached to the mainland by a narrow, low-lying isthmus. Low tide would force Roosevelt to portage his boat from the sound back into the harbor. His mastery of sails and use of nautical terms ("running sea," "shipped water") foreshadowed his love of all things nautical. He would go on to write a naval history of the War of 1812, serve as assistant secretary of the Navy, and build his own family estate at Oyster Bay, Sagamore Hill.

Roosevelt began his junior year by making two important social connections. He was admitted into the prestigious Porcellian Club, and much of his final two years would be spent inside the club playing billiards, feasting on partridge, and imbibing wine and champagne. With Dick Saltonstall returning to Harvard that fall, Roosevelt began spending more time out at the Saltonstall home in Chestnut Hill. The Saltonstall house was adjacent to that of their cousins the Lees, a household that included young Alice Hathaway Lee and her younger sister Rosie. Roosevelt was immediately smitten with the gray-eyed Alice and her sunny disposition. Over the coming year he pursued Alice energetically, spending as much time as possible out at Chestnut Hill.

At the end of the diary Roosevelt kept a ledger of his expenses for the year. His growing expenditures reflected both his inheritance from his father, and his changing social life. Roosevelt spent less each year on "science" and more on his social life. This took the form of club dues, "amusements," and increasingly gifts to Alice and Rosie Lee, and Dick's sister Rose. The following year Roosevelt would add an important item to his expenses: he began keeping a horse and small carriage in Cambridge, essential items for courting Alice out at Chestnut Hill.

Volume II
1878 DIARY

Tuesday January 1

New York. Made about 20 calls. A particularly pleasant one on Annie Murray; she is a singularly sweet girl, and one whom I wish I could serve. Little Fab Smith is also a great favourite of mine—a pure, religious, bright girl, well read and I think a true friend. Edith C. makes up my trio of "Freundinnen."[1]

Wednesday January 2

The vacation has now come to a happy end, although it opened so gloomily; but I wish my dearest Father were better. Today he told me I had never caused him a moment's pain; I should be less than human if I ever had, for he is the best, wisest and most loving of men, the type of all that is noble, brave, wise & good.

Thursday January 3

Cambridge. I have returned to my work today.

Friday January 4 [Entry continues into January 5.]

Have naturally been thinking a good deal of home, especially of Father and of my darling mother and sweet sisters. Elliott is a noble fellow, wonderfully grown up in every way. I suppose, after him, Jack Elliott is my best friend, one who would do *anything* for me. But West is a very decent fellow, and I am very fond of him. Alfred I like extremely; and so I do Em, but he grates on me a great deal, and is too selfish or egotistical, I scarcely know which to call it.[2]

Of my college friends I should say, at present, that Hal Minot, Will Blodgett, Minot Weld and Harry Chapin, were likely to become friends, and very possibly George Pellew, Arthur Hooper and Charley Washburn.[3] The other boys are very good as acquaintances; Jack Tebbetts (and Dick Trimble?) as a little more.[4]

Sunday January 6

Took up my Sunday School class as usual.

---

1. "Friends."

2. Jack Elliot is John Elliott, brother of Maud; the two of them were friends of Roosevelt's from Dresden. Alfred is TR's cousin Alfred Roosevelt.

3. William Tilden Blodgett, Henry Bainbridge Chapin, William George Pellew, and Charles Grenfill Washburn, all Class of 1880. Washburn and Roosevelt remained friends for life, and Washburn later served in the Congress as a Republican, 1906–1911.

4. John Sever Tebbets and Richard Trimble, both Class of 1880.

Monday January 7

Studies now fairly under way again. I think I shall do well in all except French 4, and very well in the Natural History courses.[5]

I am boxing with my "Tutor" five times a week; I am going to try hard for the light weight cups in boxing and wrestling.

Tuesday January 8

The Natural history Professors are very pleasant and obliging.

Wednesday January 9

Dined with Agassiz. Very pleasant dinner.[6]

Thursday January 10

Dined with "Piggy" Everett.[7] Charming and remarkably cultured man—but very dirty.

Saturday January 12

Dancing class in the evening. Some very sweet girls in Boston—as ["the" crossed out] Carrie Goodwin, Bessie Whitney and the Miss Roaches. Also Pauline Revere. Spent the night with Arthur Hooper. (Not coming back till Monday).

Sunday January 13

Spent a lovely evening; Miss Jeannie Hooper, reading aloud. She is a singularly sweet girl.[8]

---

5. Roosevelt was right; at the end of the year he barely passed French 4, "French literature in the XVII century," and received honor marks in the two natural history courses. His highest grades, though, came in German and rhetoric.

6. Alexander Emanuel Agassiz, son of famous natural historian Louis Agassiz. Alexander made a fortune in Peruvian copper in the 1870s, donating $500,000 to Harvard's Museum of Comparative Zoology, of which he was the curator from 1874 to 1885.

7. Dr. William Everett, eccentric professor known to Harvard students as "Piggy," and son of Edward Everett, famed orator, politician, and ambassador. A Massachusetts Mugwump, William Everett ran as a Democrat in 1890 for the seat in Congress held by Roosevelt's close friend Henry Cabot Lodge.

8. Sister of Arthur Hooper and Roosevelt's love interest.

Monday January 14

Went to the Nutall Ornithological club with Hal Minot.[9] I like Brewster and Allen very much.[10]

Wednesday January 16

Went to a party at the Hoopers and had a pleasant time.

Friday January 18

Went to the theatre in the evening with a set of them.

Saturday January 19

Dined with Harry Shaw, going to a party afterward.[11]

Tuesday January 22

Party in the evening. Went with the Hoopers.

Wednesday January 23

Boxed with little Briggs and beat him.[12]

Saturday January 26

Got 100 p.c. in an examination in Nat. Hist. 3.

Spent the afternoon with Minot Weld, staying at his house (Did not return till Monday).

Dancing class in the evening.

Tuesday January 29

Went to a party with Minot Weld, Harry Chapin, Bessie Whitney and the two Miss Lanes. Very nice girls are the two Miss Lanes.

---

9. The club, which was founded in 1873, still exists and meets at Harvard.

10. William Brewster, prominent ornithologist who would later become curator of birds at Harvard's Museum of Comparative Zoology, a position he would hold for nearly 35 years. Joel Asaph Allen, another prominent ornithologist who would later head that department at New York's American Museum of Natural History.

11. Henry Russell Shaw, Class of 1880.

12. Frederic Melancthon Briggs, Class of 1879. Would become professor of clinical surgery at Tufts University.

Wednesday January 30

Was rather beaten in a boxing match [by] Bob Bacon; not much though.[13]

Friday February 1

Threw back Tebbetts in a wrestling match.

Saturday February 2

Made calls with Arthur Hooper.

Sunday February 3

Have been spending Sunday with Hoopers—of course pleasantly. My opinion of Miss Jeannie grows more and more.

Tuesday February 5

"Anticipated" my second half year's required History, 83%.[14]

Thursday February 7

Semi-annual in history 91%.[15]

Saturday February 9

My dear Father.

Born Sept 23 1831.[16]

Tuesday February 12 [Entry continues into February 17.]

He has just been buried. I should never forget these terrible three days; the hideous suspense of the ride home; the dull, inert sorrow during which I felt as if I had been stunned, or as if part of my life had been taken away; and the two moments of sharp, bitter agony, when I kissed the dear, dead face and realized he would never again on this earth speak to me or greet me with his loving smile, and then when I heard the sound of the first clod dropping on the coffin holding the one I loved dearest on earth. He looked so calm and sweet. I feel that if it were not for the certainty, that as he himself has so often said,

---

13. Robert Bacon, Class of 1880. Would become assistant secretary of state under Roosevelt and briefly secretary of State in early 1909, just before Roosevelt left the presidency.

14. "Anglo-American constitutional history," the only history class he ever took at Harvard.

15. At the end of the year Roosevelt received an 87 in this class.

16. Roosevelt received a telegram that afternoon calling him home to New York, where his father lay dying from a painful tumor of the bowel. Taking the overnight train, Theodore arrived Sunday morning to find his father had already passed away.

"he is not dead, but gone before,"[17] I should almost perish. With the help of my God I will try to lead such a life as he would have wished.

He was the most wise and loving father that ever lived; I owe everything to him. It is terrible to think I have never done anything for him, not even during his sickness. I never had an unkind word from him; though I was always promptly punished if I did wrong. For the last five years he has scarcely spoken to me reprovingly. He was so unselfish, and was so continually making others happy that he was always happy himself; his 46 years of life were, excepting the last two months, very happy ones.

He was as wise and good in public as in private life. He was a great personal worker among the poor; some of his old "patients" whom I visited have been very touching about him.

By the way, it is very pleasant to see my old Mission scholars again.

Monday February 18

The family have all been simply wonderful during his illness, especially Elliott and Bamie. It was no more than their duty towards such a man and such a Father, but they have nobly done it.

Tuesday February 19

It seems impossible to realize I shall never see him again; he is such a living memory.

Truly "he was eyes to the blind, feet to the lame, and a father to the poor."[18]

Wednesday February 20

Every one has been very kind. I never shall forget Uncle Jimmie Gracie's sweet sympathy at the two times I most needed it.[19]

---

17. From Aristophanes, "Your friends are not dead, but gone before, advanced a stage or two upon that road which you must travel in the steps they trod."

18. Job 29:15.

19. The same day Roosevelt wrote his close friend Hal Minot, declining an invitation to stay with his family upon his return to Harvard. Many of the phrases Roosevelt used are repeated in his diary. "Dear old boy, your sweet letter cheered us up a great deal. As yet it is almost impossible to realize I shall never see father again; these last few days seem like a hideous dream. Father had always been so much with me that it seems as if a part of my life had been taken away; but it is much worse for Mother and my sisters. After all, it is a purely selfish sorrow, for it was best that Father's terrible sufferings should end."

Thursday February 21

It is much worse for Mother and the girls than for me; but it is very terrible for us all.

Friday February 22

Every now and then it seems to me like a hideous dream.

Saturday February 23

I came back to Cambridge today.

I am left about $8000 a year; comfortable although not rich.

Sunday February 24

Oh my father, what loving, living memories you have left in my heart!

Monday February 25

Hard at work again.

Quite touched by my boxing teacher.

Tuesday February 26

All the fellows have been wonderfully kind, especially dear old Hal Minot. Harry Shaw very thoughtful.

Wednesday February 27

Will Blodgett has rather disappointed me.

Thursday February 28

Got well through two of my semi-annuals—80 p.c.

Friday March 1

All the Professors very kind and considerate.

Saturday March 2

Been dissecting a seal most of the day.[20]

Sunday March 3

Have been thinking about Father all the evening, have had a good square break down, and feel better for it.

---

20. In his 1913 *Autobiography*, Roosevelt remembered his passion for natural science first being aroused as a small boy by the sight of a dead seal in a market along Broadway: "That seal filled me with every possible feeling of romance and adventure." *Autobiography,* 14.

Monday March 4

It was as if I could only begin to realize it now.

Tuesday March 5

Had the first meeting of the glass ball club.[21] I broke 11 out of 25.

It seems brutal to go about my ordinary occupations, but I must keep employed. I can not bear to mix with the fellows yet.

Wednesday March 6

Every now & then there are very bitter moments; if I had very much time to think I believe I should almost go crazy. But I think I can really and honestly say, "Thy will be done."

Thursday March 7

Looking back on his life, it seems as if mine must be such a weak useless one in comparison.

I should like to be a scientist: oh, how I shall miss his sweet, sympathetic advice!

Friday March 8

Meeting of G.B.C.[22] Shot 11 out of 22.

Saturday March 9

The light weight wrestling occurred today. It is funny to look back and remember how I had trained for and anticipated it. It seems as if it was years ago.

It is just one month since the blackest day of my life.

Sunday March 10

Sunday School as usual.

Have been thinking over the many, many lovely memories I have of him; had another square break down.

Monday March 11

It has been a most fortunate thing for me that I have had so much to do that I have not had much time to think.

---

21. A shooting club.
22. Glass Ball Club.

Tuesday March 12

It is really wonderful, what sweet, unselfish letters the dear ones at home send me. It seems so strange never to write to him.

Wednesday March 13

Have been tutoring Billy Gaston for his second wrestling bout.[23]

Thursday March 14

I have not been able to make up my mind to call on any of my friends in Boston yet.

Friday March 15

Looked over his sweet, affectionate letters. They will always be to me a talisman against evil.[24]

Saturday March 16

Looked at the sparring contest. Took a long walk with Dick Morgan.

Sunday March 17

S.S. as usual. Have been reading one of his favourite chapters, John xiv.[25]

Communion Sunday.

Monday March 18

Had a one hour examination in German. 98%.

Tuesday March 19 [Entry continues into March 20.]

Have been looking over my Egyptian journal[26]; every incident is connected with him.

---

23. William Alexander Gaston, Class of 1880.

24. Earlier that month he had written to Corinne, "I am going to bring home some of his sweet letters to show you; I should always keep them, if merely as talismans against evil." Morison, TR to Corinne, 3 March 1878, 32.

25. Sunday School. John 14, as Jesus comforts his disciples, begins, "Let not your heart be troubled: ye believe in God, believe also in me. In my Father's house are many mansions: if it were not so, I would have told you. I go to prepare a place for you." And later, "Peace I leave with you, my peace I give unto you: not as the world giveth, give I unto you. Let not your heart be troubled, neither let it be afraid."

26. Diary of the Roosevelt family's trip to the Middle East and the Holy Lands from late 1872 to early 1873. This included a long stay in Cairo and a houseboat trip along the Nile.

Sometimes when I think of my terrible loss it seems as if my heart would break; he shared all my joys and in sharing them doubled them, and soothed all the few sorrows I ever had. But it is worse for mother and the girls than for me; I wish so that I could be with them now.[27]

Thursday March 21 [Entry continues into March 22.]

Sometimes when I by accident think of him, it seems utterly impossible to realize that I shall never see him again, till we meet in that Better Land. It is as if part of myself had been taken away. Every event of my life is bound up with him; he was as pure and unselfish as he was wise and good. But I have very much left to be grateful for. Truly in all my family relations I have been blessed far beyond the lot of most men.

Saturday March 23

Had a 3 hour examination in Natural History. Saw the third meeting of the Athletic club.

Sunday March 24

S.S. as usual. Have been writing to the dear ones at home, and thinking of the dear one to whom I shall never again write.[28]

Monday March 25

Am tutoring Arthur Hooper in his german; he has quite a strong taste for poetry, and is a decidedly moral young man (except in getting tight); also a great athlete. Boxed with Teschmaker, and I think I beat him.[29]

Tuesday March 26 [Entry continues into March 29.]

I remember so well, all his dear little peculiarities and originalities; his "warlike curl" that never would stay brushed, the quick way he would dress, and all his

---

27. Two days earlier he had written Anna, "I so long to be with you, my own precious sister, to try to comfort you; I know only too well the dull, heavy pain you suffer, and I know too that it is even harder for you than for the rest of us." Morison, TR to Anna, 17 March 1878, 32. The eldest child and suffering from a spinal defect, Anna was regarded as their father's favorite.

28. That day he wrote to his mother, "I have just been looking over a letter of my dear father's in which he wrote me 'Take care of your morals first, your health next and finally your studies.' I do not think I ever *could* do anything wrong while I have his letters; but it seems very sad never to write to him." Morison, TR to his mother, 24 March 1878, 33.

29. Hubert Engelbert Teschemacher, Class of 1878. Although born in Boston, Teschemacher made his way west and became a cattle rancher in Wyoming, served in the Territorial Legislature, and helped draft the state constitution.

other traits. I do not think I shall ever realize he is really gone. I love all the rest of the family, especially darling Muffie, more than words can tell, but my, but my [sic] love for him was something even greater.[30] I have been astonished at the quiet way I have gone about my occupations and even amusements as if nothing had happened; and yet I really think that I would at any moment have died to save him pain. I have not been nearly as miserable as I expected; but every now and then when something occurs to bring him vividly before my memory, there come moments of terrible, dull heart pain. He was everything to me; father, companion, friend. I do not know whether I most valued his advice or his sympathy. He was so fond of all amusements and outdoor sports, as riding, sailing and shooting, and, without a particle of cant, was so deeply religious.

Saturday March 30

Had a three hour semiannual in German. 90%

Bought Bonaparte's Fauna Italica; it is a rare work.[31]

Sunday March 31

S.S. as usual. I do not think there was a man in New York who did as much good as Father; and there certainly was no one who was so much loved and respected in his own family.

Monday April 1

Bacon rather used me up in a sparring match. Shot glass balls with Minot Weld and beat him—6 out of 10; bad.[32] Went to Nuttall Ornithological Club in evening.

Tuesday April 2 [Entry continues into April 5.]

I am looking forward with an intense pleasure and longing to seeing all the dear ones at home, and yet I dread very much the arrival. It will seem so utterly unnatural for him not to be there. I can hardly conceive of a home without his presence; in looking back to all my happy, family memories he is associated with every one. No evening was ever complete if spent without him. We have been a most happy and united family, and oh how we all loved him! Now there is a terrible, sad gap in our midst; but still I am most deeply blest in the love the remaining dear ones have for me.

---

30. "Muffie" was one of several nicknames Roosevelt had for his mother.

31. Between 1832 and 1841, French naturalist Charles Lucien Bonaparte published his *Iconografia della Fauna Italica* on the animals of Italy.

32. All his life the nearsighted Roosevelt remained a bad shot.

I remember as well as if I had seen him but a moment ago every expression of his face every one of his actions and gestures. Sometimes when I fully realize my loss I feel as if I should go wild.

Saturday April 6

It is raining so I have been in the house all day; and have had rather a gloomy time, thinking over our loss.

Sunday April 7 [Entry continues into April 8.]

S.S. as usual. After all, it is merely selfish grief, I know this thoroughly, but it is very terrible sometimes.

It is curious, how different my scholars are in character; the only one that asks me questions is Watson, who is also very good; Ward is very good but frightfully stupid; Blennerhasset just as good, but much brighter; Kinney bad and bright; Phillipot bad and stupid, and much the worst case of all. It is very sweet to think how he liked my taking a Sunday School class.

Tuesday April 9

‖ Two months ago ‖

I left for New York in the night boat, in company with Harry Chapin.

Wednesday April 10

Was greeted with the most heartfelt joy by all but Bamie, who is away in Denver.

Thursday April 11

The coming home has been much harder than I expected; for the memories are frightfully vivid. I realize now that the days of unalloyed happiness are now over forever. But oh how much I have left to be thankful for!

Had a very pleasant dinner with Aunt Annie and Uncle Jimmie.[33]

Friday April 12

Darling little Pussie has been just so sweet for everything.[34]

I am getting back my good opinion of Emlen.

---

33. Anna Bulloch Gracie, sister of Roosevelt's mother, Martha; Anna lived with the Roosevelts and helped raise the children before marrying James K. Gracie.

34. Roosevelt called his younger sister Corinne "Pussie" or "Conie."

Saturday April 13

Went down to see Cassin, the poor, bedridden cripple. He is one of the many who will miss Father terribly.

Sunday April 14

Had a theological discussion with the boys. As my motto I take, "Trust in the Lord, and do good."[35]

"Lord, I believe, help thou mine unbelief."[36]

Monday April 15

Went out with Mother and Conie for 3 days at Oyster Bay. It was very hard at first, for everything was connected with the dear one we so loved.

Tuesday April 16

Rowed around Centre Island in my skiff. Killed a duck, shot two muskrats in a brackish pond.

1 duck (old squaw)[37]

Wednesday April 17

Shot a muskrat in a small brook, not two feet wide and six inches deep; went back to the city. Bamie has just returned from Denver.

Thursday April 18 [Entry continues into April 21.]

Have just come across a lovely hymn, which little Pussie has copied for me;—

> "Come unto me while shadows darkly gather,
> When the sad heart is weary and distressed,
> Seeking for comfort from your heavenly father,
> Come unto me and I will give thee rest.
>
> "Ye who have mourned when the spring flowers were taken
> When the ripe fruit fell richly to the ground,
> When the loved slept, in brighter homes to waken,
> Where their pale brows with spirit-wreaths are crowned;

---

35. Psalm 37:3.
36. Mark 9:24.
37. "Oldsquaw," the long-tailed duck.

> Large are the mansions in my Father's dwelling,
> Happy the homes which sorrows never dim,
> Sweet is the harp in holy music swelling,
> Glad are the tones which raise the heavenly hymn.
>
> There, like an Eden blossoming in gladness,
> Bloom the fair flowers this earth too rudely pressed,
> Come unto me all ye who droop with sadness
> Come unto me, and I will give you rest."

It is lovely to think of us meeting in heaven, and how we shall be united with the dear one who has gone before.

I have lost the only human being, to whom I told everything, never failing to get loving advice and sweet sympathy. In return, no one but my wife, if ever I marry, will ever be able to take his place.

I so wonder who my wife will be! "A rare and radiant maiden,"[38] I hope; one who will be as pure and innocent as she is wise. Thank Heaven, I am at least perfectly pure.

Monday April 22

In the afternoon I took the night boat for Boston. Darling, beloved Motherling came down and saw me off.

On the boat I felt awfully homesick; and, oh, so heart sick for Father.

Tuesday April 23

Cambridge

Am back in my little room once more, and enthusiastically greeted by all the fellows.

Wednesday April 24

Only four more weeks of grinding; hard german.

Thursday April 25 [Entry continues into April 27.]

I am now getting over the first sharpness of grief, but now and then, especially at night, I feel that the pain has entered into my soul. It seems so terrible to

---

38. Lenore was Edgar Allan Poe's "rare and radiant maiden," from "The Raven."

have lost the one who helped me, if only with advice, in everything, and from whom I concealed nothing.

It is much easier here at college than at home, for there every little thing is connected with him, while here it is not so; the only difference, but oh such a sad one, is that I never write to him on Sunday afternoons, and never receive any letters from him. Reading some of the chapters in the bible that he was especially fond of (such as John XIV), always brings him before me so vividly that it gives me both happiness and sadness; it is lovely to have such memories, but so sad to think they are only memories.

Sunday April 28

Went into S.S. for, I expect, the last time till October.

Monday April 29

I have been getting many good marks in my studies, he took such pride in my progress.

Tuesday April 30

Shaved off my whiskers and have in consequence been endlessly chaffed by the boys.

Wednesday May 1

As usual, May opens with most gloomy weather. Was rather unwell and kept to the house; of course I have been thinking a great deal of Father, but, I do not know why today it has only given me pleasure.

Thursday May 2

Dear Old Hal Minot has left college.[39] I am awfully sorry. I had intended to room with him next winter. He was just too sweet to me in the hour of affliction.

Friday May 3

In the evening I went over to Minot Weld's and shall not return till Monday.

Saturday May 4

We walked about the barn yard in the morning looking over cows and chickens. In the afternoon Minot and I drove over to see Dick Saltonstall.

---

39. Minot left because of mental exhaustion and his father's desire that he study law.

Sunday May 5

Heard a most capital and practical sermon. It is wonderful to see how Father was beloved and respected by every one.

Monday May 6

Returned to Cambridge early.

Tuesday May 7

Am working away pretty hard, but I do not care so much for my marks now; what I most valued them for was his pride in them.

Wednesday May 8

Our table was photographed.[40]

Thursday May 9

// Three months ago //

In the evening I went on (in company with Hal Chapin) to New York, by the Fall River boat.[41]

Friday May 10

Arrived in New York at 7.00 a.m. and took the train for Oyster Bay, where I found sweet Muffie. The country is looking beautifully.

I shot a Helminthophaga chrysoptera.[42] Stayed night at Oyster Bay.

Saturday May 11

The Helminthophaga pina[43] very plentiful. Came in town 4.00 p.m., and immediately came out here to Orange, Uncle Corneil's place, where all the family and Aunt Annie and Uncle Jimmie are. Of course I was awfully petted up.

2 squirrel

---

40. Roosevelt's dining club. An 1880 photo exists of the eight members. An undated photo of Roosevelt and five friends—Richard Saltonstall, Minot Weld, John Tebbets, Harry Chapin, and Harry Shaw—might also be of the same "table."

41. The Fall River Line connected Boston to Fall River, Massachusetts, by railroad, where passengers would board steamboats for the trip through Narragansett Bay and Long Island Sound to the company's dock in Manhattan.

42. Swamp warbler.

43. Blue-winged warbler.

Sunday May 12
Orange N.J.

Had a lovely, quiet Sunday. I have not been here for many years; then my loved Father was with me.

All the family seem to be looking very well. It does me positive good, morally and mentally, to be with them even for a short time.

Monday May 13
Came in town early and took the night boat for Boston.

Tuesday May 14
Cambridge. Arrived early in the morning.

Wednesday May 15
Am grinding like a Trojan.

Thursday May 16 [Entry continues into May 18.]
Walked in town with Jack Tebbets. He is a very rough diamond; but still, I think, a diamond. He was really touching about Father; no one who came in contact with Father could possibly help loving and admiring him. I have been accustomed to so implicitly rely on him that I sometimes feel as though the aim and purpose of my life had been taken away. While always giving me the most complete freedom, I had been so accustomed to go to him for advice that I hardly know how to decide by myself some of the things that come up. No words can tell how I shall miss his advice as to what I shall do when I leave college.

But oh, infinitely sadder, is the thought of how I shall miss his love!

Pellew by the way seems to be rapidly going to the dogs.

Sunday May 19
Am passing Sunday with George Minot. Heard a very good sermon on the duty of putting a complete finish on whatever we undertake. Took a very long walk in the afternoon.

Monday May 20
Back to Cambridge. Am studying hardest on that villainous French; but I have to work on everything.

Tuesday May 21

For exercise I have been relying on lawn tennis, and occasionally going out in the river in a shell.[44]

Wednesday May 22

Dick Saltonstall came into the ΔKE theatricals; he is an old trump and I am glad he is going to be at our table next year. A good many fellows—among them Pellew—were awfully drunk.

Thursday May 23

Rather unwell and feverish; had a terribly distinct and vivid dream about Father. It has made me feel very sad. Now and then sudden memories of him are so vivid I can almost feel as if he were by me; but it is only almost, and when I fully realize this I feel, oh so lonely! "The Lord is my comforter."

Friday May 24

The H.A.A.[45] held foot races at Beacon Park. Bob Bacon made wonderful time.

Saturday May 25

Semi Annual in French.

Our nine was disgracefully beaten by the Yales.

Sunday May 26

Broke through my rule and studied today; I feel ashamed, but my examinations come all in a heap.

Monday May 27

Annual in Anatomy.

Tuesday May 28

"Tutoring" about six men for tomorrow's examination.

Wednesday May 29

Annual in Rhetoric.

Thursday May 30

Annual in German.

---

44. Racing boat used in crew.
45. Harvard Athletic Association.

Friday May 31
The weather has luckily been very cool and good for studying in.

Saturday June 1
Annual in French.

Have been feeling rather under the weather this week, unluckily.

Our freshmen nine beat Yale '81 disgracefully.

Sunday June 2
Thank fortune all the hard work for this spring is over. Very often when I have done well in something, I find my self thinking "How proud Father will be!" It seems perfectly terrible sometimes to think of not seeing him again; I long for him so.

Monday June 3 [Entry continues into June 4.]
All my Bostonian friends have been very hospitable and kind, and by so doing have added wonderfully to the enjoyment of my college course. Jack Tebbits has just asked me to spend a month with him at Schooner Head[46] and Harry Shaw wishes me to stay with him next Sunday.

Our Club Table having temporarily broken up I am now at Memorial Hall[47] with haphazard little Gorham Peters.[48]

The weather has become much warmer and hard to study in; but my three remaining examinations need very little preparations.

Wednesday June 5
Annual in Botany.

In evening left Cambridge for New York.

Thursday June 6
Oyster Bay

---

46. "A rugged little curve of coastline sticking out into Frenchman Bay" south of Bar Harbor, Maine. Andrew Vietze, *Becoming Teddy Roosevelt: How a Maine Guide Inspired America's 26th President*, Down East Books, 2011, 72.
47. The neo-Gothic building honoring Harvard men killed in the Civil War had just been completed in 1877.
48. George Gorham Peters, Class of 1880.

Arrived about mid day.

Coming back here has recalled Father very vividly and very sadly to my mind. Every nook and corner about the place, every piece of furniture about the house is in some manner connected with him. It is impossible to tell in words how terribly I miss him.

Friday June 7
Spent the morning in Fleets Woods; shot Parula americana[49] & Coturniculus passerinus.[50]

Had a splendid ride on Lightfoot. Annie Murray has come to spend a few days with Conie.

Aunt Annie & Uncle Jimmie are at Oyster Bay.

O, Father, Father, how bitterly I miss you, mourn you and long for you!

Saturday June 8
Spent the morning in sandpapering and varnishing my boat.

All the family are wonderfully lovely to me; but I wish Mother and Bamie would not quarrel among themselves.

There comes a dull pain at my heart whenever I think of the dear lost one.

Sunday June 9
/ Four months ago /

All through the sermon I was thinking of Father. I could see him sitting in the corner of the pew as distinctly as if he were alive, in the same dear old attitude, with his funny little "warlike curl," and his beloved face. Oh, I feel so sad when I think of the word "never."

Monday June 10
Made a long tramp in the morning, rising with the sun and coming back at nine. Then built my boat house for the rest of the day.

---

49. Warbler

50. Yellow-winged sparrow.

Tuesday June 11

Rainy but I divided my day pretty equally between my horse, gun and rowboat. I am afraid if I should stay long at home I should get spoiled and conceited; the family pet me up so.

Wednesday June 12

Rode with Annie Murray to Syosset and down Laurel Hollow; and took her out in the row boat. She is a singularly sweet and lady like girl, and very pretty and clever. She goes away tomorrow.

Thursday June 13

Rowed over to Rim Island where I shot Dendroica pina.[51] Had my first swim.

This is the first summer that all the Roosevelt boys (except myself) have been in business.

Friday June 14

Fanny Smith arrived yesterday afternoon, and West came over to tea. Poor fellow! He is really deeply in love with her and has been so for three years.

I rowed her over to Cooker Bluff, down which we ran like children.

Saturday June 15

Fanny, Conie, West & myself went on a picnic to Yellow Banks. In the afternoon I took Fanny out for a long ride; we had a very pleasant ride. I like her very much.

Aunt Annie and Uncle Jimmie have come to spend some weeks with us.

Sunday June 16

Church in the morning.

In the afternoon went back to Harvard (via New York) to pass my two remaining examinations.

I took tea at 6 W 57th St.[52] The house was very gloomy and desolate, and thinking of Father made me feel so sad and lonely.

---

51. Pine warblers.
52. The Roosevelt family home in New York.

Monday June 17
Semi-annual in Botany.

I made a miserable failure in my crack examination, three weeks ago, owing to being forced to sit up all the previous night with the asthma. It was terribly hard luck; thank heavens I am not of a nature to take things harshly.

Tuesday June 18
Annual in German 5.

Funnily enough I was elected into the A.D. club[53]—a totally unexpected social success.

So ends my second year at Harvard; and a most pleasant and, I think, useful year it has been.

I took the night boat to New York.

Wednesday June 19 [Entry continues into June 20.]
Oyster Bay L. I.

Came out here in the afternoon & in the morning I visited poor Cassin.[54]

I owe everything I have or am to Father; he did everything for me, and I nothing for him. I remember so well how, years ago, when I was a very weak, asthmatic child he used to walk up and down with me in his arms, for hours together, night after night, and oh how my heart pains me when I think that I never was able to do anything for him during his last illness.

Made hideous scores with the rifle in the morning; rowed to Plum Point, and had a horseback ride.

Friday June 21
Am leading the most intensely happy & healthy, out of doors life. Spending my time riding on horseback, making long tramps through woods and fields after specimens or else on bay rowing or sailing—generally in a half naked condition and with my gun along. I could not be happier, except at those bitter moments when I realize what I have lost. Father was himself so invariably cheerful

---

53. Known among members as "Haidee," a final club like the Porcellian, A.D. Club derived from the Alpha Delta Phi fraternity.
54. Elderly and ill former Roosevelt servant.

that I feel it would be wrong for me to be gloomy, and besides, fortunately or unfortunately, I am of a very buoyant temper—being a bit of an optimist.

Had a glorious 20-mile ride on Lightfoot; cantering the whole time.

Saturday June 22
In the morning rowed to Plum Point & back. Then Alfred[55] and I sailed to Loyds Neck,[56] where we took our lunch, shot a little, and returned. Rode in the afternoon with the two girls.

Monday June 24
Rowed to Pine Island, where I found a chickadee's nest.

Took Miss Nellie Beckman out riding in afternoon.

My face is beginning to look like an underdone lobster.

I wish old Chuff had a better set of friends.

Tuesday June 25
Rowed round Centre Island, shooting on the way, in 2 hours. There was quite a sea running and I shipped a good deal of water.

Had a long ride; I am very fond of galloping over these level Long Island roads, and there are some beautiful ones around here.

2 sandpipers [shot]

Wednesday June 26
Rode in the morning to Brookville & Glencove. Walked in Fleets Woods with Muffie. Drove Pussie to Cold-spring to pick waterlilies. Rowed to the marsh. Sailed in evening with Chuffie, taking our dinner on board the boat.

Thursday June 27
New London.

Came on here to see the race. Am staying in company with Minot Weld and Jackson at Harry Chapins.

---

55. Cousin Alfred Roosevelt, killed in 1891 by falling under the wheels of a moving train.
56. Lloyd Neck.

Friday June 28
Harvard won easily.

Am perfectly hoarse from shouting.

In evening took night boat for New York.

Saturday June 29
Oyster Bay.

Came out here in the afternoon. Bought a Sharps rifle.[57]

Harvard won the baseball championship.

Sunday June 30
Had a very good sermon, I was much struck with one remark, that Christianity gives us on this earth, rest in trouble, not from trouble. Nothing but my faith in the Lord Jesus Christ could have carried me through this, my terrible time of trial and sorrow.

We passed the evening largely in singing hymns, as usual.

Monday July 1
Tried the new rifle and made 67 out of 100; it works very well, but I am an awful shot.

I am getting to be deep mahogany color from the waist up, thanks to the rowing.

My horse went a little lame today.

The bathing is perfectly delicious.

Tuesday July 2
Tried the rifle; 70 out of 100.

Went in town in the afternoon to see off Annie Murray, who sails for Europe tomorrow. Paid her a very pleasant visit in the evening.

---

57. A long-bore rifle that was known for its long range and accuracy. It is possible this was the 1878 Sharps-Borchardt model that was the last rifle the Sharps Rifle Company produced, and which Roosevelt took with him on his trips west.

Wednesday July 3

At 7 am was down on the Russia[58] to see Annie Murray, whom I found very sweet and pretty and a little wee bit out of temper.

Took Aunt Susie[59] out to Oyster Bay.

Elliott and I in his 21 foot sail boat the Daphni started out at 9.30 p.m. with a light but steady southerly wind, and cast anchor in Rye Harbour at 1.30 a.m.

Thursday July 4

Spent the morning at Mrs. Buckleys, where we took dinner.

At 4.15 started back and did not make our buoy till 11.00 p.m.

Enjoyed the sail most thoroughly. It reminded me of the many cruises Chuff and I have taken together formerly.

Friday July 5

Had a long and very sweet but sad talk with mother over our beloved lost one. Uncle Jimmie Grace stayed up from the city, and we went out sailing and rowing together.

Saturday July 6

Rowed around Centre Island. 8 miles

Started 8.51; Plum Pt. 9.15; Pine Centre Island neck 10.00; returned 10.33.

The portage took 14 minutes, and the tide was so low I had to make a circuit of half a mile.

Shot the rifle with Alfred in the afternoon, beating him by 54 to 18.

Sunday July 7

Have been feeling very heart sick for Father; when singing tonight, we none of us could sing "Safe in the arms of Jesus"; we sang it together on that terrible Sunday.[60] I read today at prayers one of his favourite chapters—Ps.

---

58. Cunard steamship running between Liverpool and New York.

59. Susan Elliott.

60. The day after Theodore Roosevelt Sr. died.

LV.[61] I can never thank God sufficiently for having given me such a lovely affectionate family.

Monday July 8

Beat West and Emlen in rifle match—57 to 48 & 49.

My horse now goes very well and is almost entirely free from lameness.

Tuesday July 9

/ Five months ago /

It seems to me that I have aged very much since that bitter day; now I must rely on myself in difficulties, while before I had always carried everything to him. The vividness with which I can recall his words and actions is sometimes really startling.

Wednesday July 10

Rowed around Loyd's Neck, portaging the isthmus, in which operation I got stuck in the mud flats and had hideous work getting out. Rowing home there was a strong southwesterly wind and I was caught in a bad thundersquall. (15 miles)

2 plover (& 2 gulls)

---

61. Psalm 55 includes lines 4–8:

> My heart is severely pained within me,
> And the terrors of death have fallen upon me.
> Fearfulness and trembling have come upon me,
> And horror has overwhelmed me.
> So I said, "Oh, that I had wings like a dove!
> I would fly away and be at rest.
> Indeed, I would wander far off,
> And remain in the wilderness.
> I would hasten my escape
> From the windy storm and tempest."

Also lines 16–17:

> As for me I will call upon God,
> And the Lord shall save me.
> Evening and morning and at noon
> I will pray, and cry aloud,
> And he shall hear my voice.

Thursday July 11

Went out sailing with West and Alfred, taking our lunch along. Divided the remaining of the time pretty equally between my horse and row boat.

I often feel badly that such a wonderful man as Father should have had a son of so little worth as I am.

Friday July 12

Rained all day, and so, for the first time this summer, I had to stay indoors. Of my five intimate friends, Chuff and John Elliott over-, West and Emlen underestimate me; while Alfred takes me for about what I am worth.

Saturday July 13

Ran a mile through the woods at speed, shall probably repeat this every day.

Sunday July 14

Communion Sunday.

Was rather struck in reading Pascal, by the following: "Deux excès: Exclure la raison, n'admettre que la raison."[62] (Apologie de la religion, VIII, (VII)). Materialism and superstition are equally repugnant to me.

During service today I could not help reflecting sadly on how little use I am, or ever shall be in the world, not through lack of perseverance and good intentions, but through sheer inability. I realize more and more every day that I am as much inferior to Father morally and mentally as physically. But "Trust in the Lord and do good!"

Monday July 15

Rowed around Centre Island, high tide and dead calm, but hotter than Tophetts.[63]

Started 10.45; Pine Neck 11.20 (portage takes 5 minutes); Plum Point 11.50; returned 12.13.

Had a long gallop with Emlen beyond and around Wheatley.

---

62. "Two excesses: excluding reason, accepting only reason."

63. Tophet or Topheth, where the Canaanites sacrificed children to Moloch by burning them alive. Representing the "roasted place," in literature, authors such as John Donne, John Milton, John Bunyan, and Nathaniel Hawthorne used the name as a synonym for hell.

Wednesday July 17

West and I started on horseback for Lake Ronkonkomi.[64] The day was cool and cloudy. Started 8.00 a.m.; reached Smithtown 10.45 a.m., took lunch, and in afternoon rode to the lake where we took supper, and returned to sleep at Smithtown.

In all about 35 miles, and the horse as fresh as when he started.

Thursday July 18

Started in the morning for Oyster Bay, which we reached in two hours and a half.

Very hot.

Friday July 19

Rowed to Rye beach and back. Perfectly calm but very hot. Started 5.15 a.m.; Rocky Point 6.10; Oak Bluff 6.40; Rye Beach 8.15. Started back 4.45 p.m.; Centre Island buoy 6.15; home 7.15. In all I rowed rather over 25 miles. Saw stormy pestrel.[65]

Sunday July 21

Lord, I believe, help thou mine unbelief![66]

Monday July 22

Took a long tramp through the woods and fields with my gun.

1 woodcock 2 doves

Thursday July 25

Went in town; called on poor Cassin. In evening came out here to the Dickeys; I like them ever so much, they are so sweet and homelike. Dickey is coming to Harvard next year, and I shall do the best I can for him.

Friday July 26

Returned to Oyster Bay.

---

64. Lake Ronkonkoma. From Oyster Bay a good ride east of about thirty miles.

65. Seabirds who got their names from sailors who believed their appearance foreshadowed a storm.

66. Mark 9:24.

Saturday July 27

Rigged a leg of mutton sail[67] on a seven foot mast, with six foot boom, in my little out rigger, lapstreak skiff, and went out sailing. She beats[68] very badly, but is stiff and sails pretty fast off the wind.

Monday July 29

Rowed to Loyds Neck, shooting through the marsh. At high tide it is good fun to paddle through the lagoons and among the winding channels, with an occasional shot at a heron or snipe. In the afternoon a strong southerly breeze came up, so I rigged my sail and went out three or four miles into the sound. Chuff has left for a three weeks holiday.

3 sand snipe[69]

Tuesday July 30

Rainy, but I strolled through the woods with my gun during the morning, and had a splendid ride in the afternoon.

1 dove 1 wild pigeon

Wednesday July 31

Rowed round Centre Island in Alfred's boat in 1 h 24 m.

Friday August 2

Rowed round Loyd's Neck. Started 10 a.m.; Point 11.15 [space before "Point" left blank]; Huntington Harbour Lighthouse 12.15; Neck 1 p.m.; home 1.45. Portage took but four minutes, tide being dead high. Southerly wind.

Saturday August 3

Emlen and I sailed across the sound, intending to go to Greenwich but struck the wrong side of Shippan Point[70] and got into Darien; we had a fresh, full sail breeze.

My horse has done wonderfully this season; I have not missed riding him a single day when at home; his back and legs have both stood beautifully.

---

67. A simple, triangular sail with a high boom, good for small boats.
68. The procedure by which a boat follows a zigzag course in order to sail upwind.
69. Sandpiper.
70. They went east when they should have gone west.

Sunday August 4

I like very much the text over the door of our Church: "Be ye doers of the word and not hearers only." I am no believer in faith without works.

Have been reading the beautiful "Memorial of Theodore Roosevelt."[71] With God's help I shall try to lead such a life as Father would have wished me to.

Monday August 5

Went out woodcock shooting, tramping about twenty five miles through awful places, for the cock are only now found in very thick cover. I shot wretchedly, missing over half my birds. As the day was pretty hot I and the dog are pretty well done up.

7 woodcock

Tuesday August 6

It being Edith C.'s 17th birthday, I sent her a bonbonierre.[72]

Wednesday August 7

Dear old Jack Elliott arrived today, to stay five or six weeks.

Thursday August 8

Jack Elliott and I went in my boat to Loyds Neck; the wind was three quarters aft, so we rigged the mast, & with sail, oars and paddle managed to make pretty good time. We shot through the lagoons, took lunch, had tough work getting out of the marsh, as the tide was dead low, rowed home against a head wind.

2 yellowlegs[73] 2 heron

Friday August 9

Jack and I went out sailing; the breeze was almost a reefer, but we kept all our canvass up and had a glorious time.

Oyster Bay is the perfection of a place for fellows; I often wonder if any one could have a happier time than I am having.

Six months ago—it seems so much longer.

---

71. This is likely the privately printed "Memorial Meeting of the State Charities Aid Association, New York, February 15, 1878," to commemorate the death of Theodore Roosevelt Sr.
72. Bonbonniere: fancy box of bonbons.
73. A long-legged shorebird with yellow legs.

Saturday August 10

The Harvard rank list arrived today; my marks for last year were French IV, 51; Themes 69; Nat. Hist 3, 79; Hist., 87; Nat. Hist 8, 89; Germ IV, 92; Germ V, 96.[74] My average is about 85, 10 per cent better than last year. I am well satisfied; my dearest Father would have been so pleased.

Funnily enough I am rather laid up by an attack of cholera morbus.

Sunday August 11

For almost the first time this year I did not go to church, thanks to the cholera morbus.

As usual when I have nothing to do (a rare event, thank fortune) I have been thinking a great deal of Father.

Monday August 12

Jack and I rowed to Plum Point, paddled up the marsh on this side of it, portaged for 200 yds over awful ground, with clouds of mosquitoes, into the great marsh on the north side of Centre Island, shot through it, rowed to the neck, lunched, shot through the pine woods & sailed home.

Edith C. has written me a very sweet little note of thanks for the bonbonierre.

1 sand snipe

Tuesday August 13

Jack and I rowed to Loyd's Neck, shooting through the marsh at flood tide and coming out with the ebb.

A strong south wind arose so we did not get home till quite late in the afternoon.

1 yellowlegs 1 sand snipe

Thursday August 15

Went out woodcock shooting, tramping from 8 a.m. till 5 p.m. (9 consecutive hours) through awful ground, without food or rest; going of course at slow pace. I tried my new knickerbockers, gaiters, and hunting shoes, which worked to a charm. The cover was fearful, so I missed two thirds of my shots; but had glorious sport, &, funnily enough, feel fresh as a lark.

6 woodcock

---

74. Roosevelt also took Rhetoric, 94. For a complete Harvard transcript see Morison, I, 25–26.

Friday August 16

Edith C. has come to spend two weeks with Corinne.

Emlen, Jack & I sailed over to the Connecticut shore, & coming home in the afternoon got caught in a bad rain storm.

Monday August 19

Edith, Corinne and Jack, Emlen and I went out sailing and took our lunch at Yellowbanks.

Am teaching Jack to spar; had a little match with Em and rather used him up. He beat me rifle shooting.

Tuesday August 20

Rowed Edith out towards Loyds Neck.

Sparred with Jack and West; while out riding with the latter was made the recipient of confidences respecting his devotion to the much worshipped Fanny. Poor old boy! It is really touching to see how much in love he is.

Wednesday August 21

Drove Edith to Coldspring to pick waterlilies, spending a lovely morning with her.

In the afternoon Nell arrived on the Waterwitch,[75] with Jack Roosevelt, from his three weeks cruise.

Thursday August 22

Elliott, Jack & I took Mother, Edith & Corinne out sailing; in the evening we all, together with Uncle Jimmie & Aunt Annie and Alfred & Emlen, took tea at West's. Afterwards Edith & I went up to the summer house.[76]

---

75. After James Fennimore Cooper's 1830 novel *The Water-Witch* was published, many ships were christened Water-Witch, including a Confederate gunboat during the Civil War and a Lake Champlain Ferry that wrecked in 1866. This *Water-Witch* was part of the Vanderbilt fleet.

76. It is at this point that Roosevelt and Edith seem to have broken off their courtship. Biographers speculate that Edith turned down Roosevelt's marriage proposal—she had just turned seventeen—and that Roosevelt's unhappiness manifested itself in the episodes he notes in the following days: riding his horse to near lameness, and shooting a neighbor's dog.

My ride today was so long and hard that I am afraid it may have injured my horse.

Saturday August 24

The other day a dog annoyed me very much while on horseback, and I told the owner I should shoot it; which threat I fulfilled while out riding with West today, rolling it over with my revolver very neatly as it ran alongside the horse.

Sunday August 25

I like our custom of having family prayers in the morning and evening of Sunday very much.

Monday August 26

Early in the morning, which was clear & cool, I had a magnificent twenty mile gallop with Emlen.

Towards midday Emlen, West, Jack & I started off on the Addie[77] for a short yachting cruise; Emlen leaves us early tomorrow morning. The wind was light and we made New Haven about 10 p.m.

Tuesday August 27

The wind was very light and we sailed till 8 p.m. before reaching New London. We divided our time between swimming, reading the New Symposium, clambering about the rigging and playing whist with a good deal of sheer doing nothing. It is very lazy, but very pleasant.

Wednesday August 28

We sailed into Greenport, the wind being light and puffy. Having several hundred cartridges aboard we practise [sic] with our revolvers at everything that comes up, from bottles or buoys to sharks and porpoises.

I never slept better or ate better in my life.

Thursday August 29

There was a fair steady breeze and we got under weigh early in the morning and all day long we sailed in a straight course by the low & sandy bluffs of the Long Island coast; I passed a good deal of time in the cross trees,[78] whist and discussions about materialism and politics occupying the remainder.

---

77. Cousin Cornelius Roosevelt's sailboat.

78. The crossbar near the top of the mast.

Friday August 30

We reached Oyster Bay early in the morning (1 a.m.) & came ashore for breakfast. Have most heartily enjoyed the cruise.

In afternoon Jack, Alfred & I went out sailing.

Saturday August 31

Jack & I went out after sea coots[79] but did not see one, though we rowed nearly 20 miles.

George Minot has come to spend a few days with us.

Sunday September 1

I had a long talk with Uncle Jim about my future life; I have absolutely no idea what I shall do when I leave college.

Oh, Father, my Father, no words can tell how I shall miss your counsel and advice!

However, for the next two years my duty is clear—to study well and live like a brave Christian gentleman.

Monday September 2

Elliott & Alfred stayed up for the day, and as there was a strong, steady westerly wind, we sailed over to Rye and back—Alfred and I in the Meteor, Elliott, Jack, George & Minot in the Daphne. We had a very pleasant lunch at the Barkleys where I met Miss Lee of Derry.

Tuesday September 3

Jack and I went out in our skiff, intending to pass the night out, but it rained in torrents, so towards evening we came home. We lunched at Matinnicock Pt., and on our way back, while off Oak Bluffs were struck by a heavy squall from the North West, which soon kicked up a very big sea; so we hoisted our sail and drove with the wind on our quarter, at a furious speed, to Rocky Pt.; staunch though the little boat is, we shipped a good deal of water.

Wednesday September 4

Poor, dear Harry Minot: George M. just told me that he has totally lost his mind and is in an insane asylum. What a terrible thing it is to have insanity

---

79. Sea duck, also called scoter.

in a family. Oh, how sorry I feel for him; he is as sweet and gentle a fellow as I have ever seen, and very bright; and a true friend to me. How I sorrow for his family.

Uncle Hill and Aunt Susie have come to dinner.

Thursday September 5
Went in to New York, where I pass the night. Called on poor Cassin; he is dying by inches.

Cousin Sam Roosevelt is dead; it is terrible for his poor daughter.[80] I have been feeling very sad about dear old Hal Minot.

In the evening Jack Roosevelt, Emlen & I had a very pleasant dinner at the Union League Club.[81]

Friday September 6
West, Emlen & myself took the 8.15 train for Boston, en route for the Maine woods where we intend to pass three weeks. I can hardly realize about old Hal Minot; but Father's death has taken away much of my capacity for grieving.

Saturday September 7
We traveled all last night, reaching Matawaumking[82] at 10.30, and from there took a buckboard and reached here ([Highland crossed out] Island Falls) at 8 p.m.

Whenever I think about old Hal Minot I feel very sad; he was such a loveable man.

Have a pretty bad attack of asthma; I miss riding my horse; he has not been unwell a day this summer.

---

80. A distant cousin, Samuel Roosevelt was a prominent New York businessman. He had several daughters, but Roosevelt likely meant the youngest, Virginia, who was only about a year younger than he was.

81. Founded in 1863 during the Civil War, the Union League Club was one of the most important and influential of New York's social clubs. It was founded, according to its charter, to "discountenance disloyalty to the United States, and for the promotion of good government, and the elevation of American citizenship." Theodore Roosevelt Sr. was a member when the club helped found the American Museum of Natural History and the Metropolitan Museum of Art. With a reformist bent, the staunchly Republican club often battled with the machine bosses and would serve as a valuable base of support for Theodore Roosevelt Jr.'s political career. Not to be confused with the older Union Club.

82. Mattawamkeag, Maine.

Sunday September 8

In the morning took a walk & read the bible, learning by heart the XIX Psalm—a most beautiful hymn of praise.[83] There is no church here, but in the afternoon I went to a Methodist meeting in the school house. Thinking about poor Hal Minot has again made me think much and oh so sadly of Father's death; I try whenever I can only to recall his grand and beautiful life. Oh, Father, Father!

Monday September 9

Seven months ago

Spent the day hunting partridges but did not even see one.

Tuesday September 10

West, Emlen, Will T.,[84] one guide (Sewell),[85] & I are in a batteau[86] started down stream to a large lake Mattawamkeag [name inserted between lines] at whose foot we are camping out; I preceded them in a canoe with another guide (Dow).[87] I had good fun paddling, and tramping through the woods, but though I had several shots at pigeons & ducks I missed them all.

Wednesday September 11

In the morning Emlen and I paddled about Mattawamkeag lake in the canoe; I had two or three shots with the rifle at a loon which was over a hundred yards off and came pretty close to him. In the afternoon Em & I tramped about ten miles through the woods after partridges; we saw only one bird but enjoyed the walk very much; he and I are great companions, and he is a true friend.

1 partridge. (ruffed grouse).

Thursday September 12

Rainy, so we stayed in camp, reading, playing whist and cleaning our guns. We have quite a varied diet—duck, partridge, trout, pickerel &c.

---

83. The psalm begins, "The heavens declare the glory of God; the skies proclaim the work of his hands," and ends, "May these words of my mouth and this meditation of my heart be pleasing in your sight, Lord, my Rock and my Redeemer."

84. Sewall later identified him as Dr. W. Thompson.

85. Tutor Arthur Cutler introduced Roosevelt to Bill Sewall, with whom Roosevelt would later enter into the cattle business.

86. Flat-bottomed boat. Roosevelt spelled the word correctly as the English derivation of the French *bateau*. Oddly, the English-language plural of batteau—batteaux—follows the French.

87. Wilmot Dow would also join TR and Sewall in ranching.

In the afternoon Em and I watched (from behind some bushes) the river, in hopes of some ducks passing by; but after sitting about three hours in the rain we returned with nothing.

Friday September 13
Rained all day so we stayed in camp—reading, playing euchre and whist and practising with our rifle. I again waited a couple hours for ducks, getting one long and unsuccessful shot. I killed a bat and a nighthawk.

Saturday September 14
Rained till noon, then it cleared and I took a fifteen mile tramp through the woods with Sewell, but got nothing. I had two shots with the rifle at a couple foxes about sixty yards off across the river, but missed both; I do'n't think I ever made as many consecutive bad shots as I have this week. I am disgusted with myself.

Sunday September 15
Read my bible in the morning; in the afternoon, for lack of better occupation, cleaned guns, labeled specimens and we bathed in the race of the damn [sic].

Monday September 16
There was a frost last night, and today I took a thirty mile tramp through the woods with Sewell, keeping near the Mattawamkeag river most of the time. Except half an hour for lunch we were on the go steadily from 8 a.m. till 7 p.m. I got out four shots and saw no game whatsoever during the last 20 miles. But enjoyed the walk greatly.

1 red rabbit 1 merganser[88]

2 ruffed grouse

Tuesday September 17
West and I, with Dow, took the canoe and paddles to the upper end of the lake and shot through the slews and bogs—with very indifferent success. We three camped out in a wigwam near the far head of the lake, taking a very frugal supper.

1 dipper duck[89] 1 wood duck

---

88. Large duck.

89. A duck that dips its head into the water looking for food as fast as once every second.

Wednesday September 18

The three of us got up at four in the morning, and started after ducks before daylight, but saw nothing. When we got back to the old camp I took Will Dow and tramped about ten miles through the woods, getting four shots. I like moccasins to walk through the woods with very much.

1 merganser 3 ruffed grouse

Thursday September 19

Walked about fifteen miles through the woods; about three miles were through a succession of alder swamps and cedar swamps, where the walking was about as difficult as any I have ever been through. I killed a spruce partridge in a cedar swamp and a birch partridge on a hemlock ridge.

1 canada grouse[90] 1 ruffed grouse

Friday September 20

Took a ten mile tramp with Sewell; I saw nothing in the woods, but after a rather neat stalk killed a duck in a small lake.

Was nicely sold by the boys with a dead duck placed in a life like attitude in a pond. Have had beautiful baths in the dam race every day.

1 partridge 1 duck

Saturday September 21

Emlen and I went out shooting in the afternoon, but he never fired of [sic] his gun; I had two shots, missing a duck and killing a partridge. The leaves are now beginning to turn and the woods are perfectly beautiful. I have enjoyed this week very much; the trip so far has been a great success.

1 ruffed grouse

Sunday September 22

Spent the day much as last Sunday.

Monday September 23

Broke camp and started for Island Falls in the batteau—a clumsy looking craft Sewell paddled, Dow and I rowed, Thomson trolled, and West and Emlen,

---

90. Also known as spruce grouse.

with rifle and shotgun, watched from the bow for loons and ducks. We made very good time; I spent the afternoon tramping through the woods with West.

1 ruffed grouse

Tuesday September 24

Took a twenty five mile tramp through the woods with Dow, shooting a log cock[91] and two partridges. I have had wonderfully bad luck as regards shooting, finding very little game; but never the less have enjoyed the trip greatly. There has been absolutely no disagreement between any members of the party.

2 ruffed grouse

Wednesday September 25

Spent the day driving around in a buckboard with Will Dow, getting out whenever we saw a partridge—which occurred five times. I saw a fox.

5 ruffed grouse

Thursday September 26

Drove in a wagon to Mattwamkeag where we took the night train for Boston; tomorrow the other three fellows go on to New York, while I go out to Harvard.

Friday September 27

All the fellows greeted me with enthusiasm. To my great surprise I was offered the Porcellian; of course I could not accept, being a member of the A.D.—but I wish I could. It is very pleasant to get back among all the fellows again; but I can't help feeling a little home sick.

Saturday September 28

I find that my recitations, lectures and labratory [sic] will occupy about 20 hours a week. I have a recitation every day, including Saturday, at 9 a.m.[92]

Harry Shaw and Dick Saltonstall both asked me to spend tomorrow with them. Our club table is at Mrs. Wilson's,[93] where the food, service & attendance are excellent.

---

91. Large North American woodpecker.

92. Roosevelt had his heaviest course load at Harvard during this, his junior year. He took nine classes, five of which were electives.

93. On Brattle Street, today's no. 62.

Sunday September 29

Went to Church as usual, I shall not take up my Sunday school till next Sunday or the one after.

Monday September 30

Have begun studying regularly. I joined the rifle club; I am going to practice pretty regularly with the rifle this year.

Tuesday October 1

Was elected into the glee club.

Wednesday October 2

Went up to the first meeting of the Δ.K.E.; I get rather tired of seeing such a drunken club as a regular thing, but once in a while it is good enough fun to go up there—though I never drink anything up there. I shall not begin smoking till I am twenty one; as it is, I drink very little.

Thursday October 3

Attended the first meeting of the Art Club, and found it very pleasant.

Friday October 4

Of my studies this year I like best the philosophy and political economy; my natural history courses are also very interesting, though less so than last year; for the others I do not care so much.

Saturday October 5

Spent the morning at the rifle range.

Sunday October 6

Communion Sunday

Monday October 7

I am working pretty hard now; but as I have optional recitations, thanks to my high average last year, I expect to get about three weeks holiday during the course of the winter.

Tuesday October 8

Started with my boxing teacher again.

Wednesday October 9 [Entry goes into October 10.]

Last night a Porcellian and an A.D. man, both drunk, were discussing me, and in the quarrel the former let it leak out that I preferred his club. The A.D. men held a meeting and voted to give me my choice of the two clubs—as I had never been in the A.D. rooms, had not signed the constitution, possessed no voting powers and in fact was not a member. Of course by this arrangement I have to hurt somebody's feelings, and I have rarely felt as badly as I have during the last 24 hours; it is terribly hard to know what is the honorable thing to do.

Friday October 11

Have finally decided to go into the Porcellian; my classmates who are in it are Minot Weld, Harry Shaw, Dick Trimble, Charley Morgan and George Griswold. The A.D. men from my class are Bob Bacon, Billy Hooper, Billy Blodgett, Charley Ware, Harry Jackson and Freddy Allen & Johnny Samson.

Saturday October 12

Arthur Hooper has left college; Brooks and Peters are dropped. Charley Ware is a capital fellow and a thoroughly good one too; I have grown to like him very much. The same is true of swell old Harry Shaw.

Harry Chapin is also a perfect trump.

Sunday October 13

It makes it very homelike to have old Charley Dickey in the same house with me. I think I have been able to do a good deal for him.[94]

Monday October 14

One of my Natural History courses this year needs a great deal of labratory work, which I like but which takes up an awful amount of time.

Tuesday October 15

Have been sparring with several of the fellows.

The A.D. men have behaved like trumps.

---

94. On this day Roosevelt penned a letter to his sister Bamie: "I walked in town day before yesterday to call on Miss Jeannie Hooper, but unfortunately she was out so I had to console myself with a game of billiards with old Arthur instead. I enjoy having Charley Dickey underneath me very much; I almost every evening spend about an hour with him, sitting and talking over the day. It seems funny to think that now over half my college career is done; I have enjoyed it extremely so far—although not quite as much as I do home. I must try to see Mr. [Joseph Hodges] Choate this year; it is time for me to think what I shall do when I leave college." Choate was a New York lawyer and family friend. Later he was American ambassador to Great Britain during Roosevelt's presidency. Morison, TR to Anna, 13 October 1878, 34.

Wednesday October 16

Our table is composed of Minot Weld, Harry Chapin, Charley Ware, Charley Washburn, Ralph Ellis, Gorham Peters & Dick Saltonstall.

Thursday October 17

Had a very pleasant dinner at the Hoopers; I was very glad to see Miss Jeannie again.

Friday October 18

Sparred with Tucker Burr, using him up.

In the afternoon Dick Saltonstall drove me in a buggy over to his house on Chestnut Hill, where I am now, enjoying myself to the utmost. All his family are just too sweet to me for anything, and the whole house is so homelike.

Saturday October 19

I spent the morning walking through the woods with Dick, his sister Miss Rose, and their cousin, Miss Alice Lee—a very sweet pretty girl.[95] About midday we drove over to the Whitneys where we spent the evening dancing and singing, driving back about 11 oclock.

Sunday October 20

Church in the morning; in the afternoon I went chestnutting with Miss Alice Lee.

Monday October 21

Drove back to Cambridge in the morning.

In the evening went to the glee club and heard some really beautiful singing.

Tuesday October 22

Quite a little town and gown row apropos of a Butler[96] and Kearney[97] political meeting. It was good fun to see the crew wade in.

---

95. Alice Hathaway Lee, of the Boston Brahmin Lee banking family, Roosevelt's main love interest for the next 18 months and his first wife. Alice also had a sister named Rose, usually called "Rosie," to distinguish her from the Saltonstall cousin next door.

96. Benjamin Butler, the Civil War general and Massachusetts congressman, was running for governor as an independent.

97. Denis Kearney was a labor leader known for his violent nativist views. In his fiery speeches he also targeted businessmen and politicians, but always ended every speech by saying, "And

Wednesday October 23

I am very much interested in the Political Economy, although I by no means altogether agree with Mill.[98] I am getting rather disgusted with Ferrier's Philosophies.

Thursday October 24

Took long tramp with Jack Tebbets, who has improved wonderfully, I like him very much indeed.

Have just received a letter telling me that Cornelius[99] has distinguished himself by marrying a French actress! He is a disgrace to the family—the vulgar brute. P.S. She turns out to be a mere courtesan [sic] ! a harlot!

Friday October 25

Took the evening boat for New York.

I have not hitherto been studying as hard as I ought to have—at least in some subjects; but as soon as I come home from this holiday I shall set to with a will.

Saturday October 26

Breakfasted with West; poor old Doc is awfully cut up about Corneil's insane marriage. Spent the morning with darling little Aunt Annie, lunched with West and Alfred and came out to Oyster Bay in afternoon. It is just lovely to be back with the family again. All look beautifully except dear old Nell.

Sunday October 27

My twentieth birthday. Lovely though it is to be spending it with darling Muffie, Bysie and Pussie, I can not help having some very sad thoughts about my beloved Father. Oh, Father, sometimes I feel as though I would give half my life to see you but for a moment! Oh, what loving memories I have of you!

2 gray squirrel

---

whatever happens, the Chinese must go." The *Harvard Crimson* noted, "Dennis [sic] Kearney will speak here to-night, if a suitable 'sand-lot' can be found; the price of eggs has risen rapidly in anticipation of this event." His name is frequently misspelled "Dennis."

98. John Stuart Mill, *Principles of Political Economy* (1848). A revised seventh edition appeared in 1871.

99. Cousin Cornelius Roosevelt, son of Silas Weir Roosevelt.

Monday October 28

In the morning rowed around Centre Island. There was a stiff Norther blowing, and so heavy a sea running in the sound that the curlers[100] filled the boat half full. I sailed home from Pine Island at a tremendous speed. In the afternoon took a brisk walk through the woods with my gun, but saw nothing.

Tuesday October 29

Went out sailing for ducks. The wind was light and baffling and we saw but few birds, but had capital fun. We got into a flock of coots and I knocked down two; I killed a checkerback loon after a long chase; and missed a shot at an old squaw; we saw some grebes but could not get near them.

1 loon 2 surf ducks

Wednesday October 30

There was a southeaster blowing, with continual heavy rain squalls. I went out sailing for ducks, but after getting drenched through returned with nothing; missed a good shot at a grebe.

Thursday October 31

Rainy again! I have had most awful luck in weather this time. Monday so rough we couldn't go out; Tuesday so calm we couldn't get anywhere; yesterday and today rainy.

Friday November 1

Went on to Cambridge.

Saturday November 2

Was a steward of the field meeting of the athletic association which took place today.

In evening was initiated into the Porcellian Club, and was "higher" with wine than I ever have been before—or will be again. Still, I could wind up my watch. Wine always makes me awfully fighty.

Sunday November 3

Rather under the weather, owing to last night's spree. Took up my Sunday school class again; the scholars were all delighted to see me.

---

100. Large waves.

Monday November 4

Am going to give an accurate abstract of my doings this week, as a sample

7.45 prayers 8.00 breakfast
8.30–1.00 study, 1.00 lunch
1.30–4.30 study, 4.30–6.00 walk, 7.00 went to dinner to University Crew. Came out towards 12.00 and lounged in Club for a couple of hours.

Tuesday November 5

7.45 Prayers. 8.00 breakfast. 8.30–12 studies. To my utter astonishment Nell & Mother turned up, on for the day. I took Nell up to the Club, and lunched with Darling little Muffie in town.
Studied 3.00–5.00.
5.00–6.00 boxed. Dinner at 6.00. Played whist till 9.00; studied till 11.00.

Wednesday November 6

7.45 Prayers 8.00 Breakfast
8.30–4.00 studied.
4.00–6.00 walked with Dick Saltonstall and Jack Tebbetts. Spent evening in Club till nine; studied till 11.00

Thursday November 7

Prayer 7.45
Studied 9.00–4.50 & 8.00–10.00. Boxed & played billiards.

Friday November 8

Prayers 7.45
Studied 9.00–5.30

In the evening had a supper, with 8 or ten of the fellows, in the club—partridges & burgundy.

Did not get to bed till towards two a.m.

Saturday November 9

Took breakfast at the club at about 10 a.m.

Drove over to see football match with Harry Chapin.

In afternoon drove over to Minot Welds, where I shall stay till Monday morning.

Sunday November 10

Church in morning; walked home with Miss Wheelright. In afternoon drove over with Minot in his tilbury[101] to Dick Saltonstalls, where we took tea and came home at 10 oclock by moon light. Miss Alice Lee was there, as sweet and pretty as ever; and I enjoyed myself most heartily.[102]

Tuesday November 12

Had a sparring match with Billy Saxton.

Saturday November 16

Political Economy examination.

In afternoon went out to George Minots, where I spend the night.

Sunday November 17

After dinner drove back to Cambridge in time for my Sunday School.

Monday November 18

Have 3 exams. this week; have been studying like a Trojan lately.

Saturday November 23

There was an alarm of scarlet fever among the Richardson children so I turned out promptly and for the present am "chumming" with Harry Jackson, Bob Bacon having gone home with a sore throat.

Sunday November 24

Went in to Harry Shaws for dinner, and had a very pleasant time.

---

101. A small two-wheeled carriage with large wheels. Known as fast and sporty, the Tilbury carriage was also dangerous, as the many accident reports in nineteenth-century newspapers attest.

102. In an informative letter to Corinne this day, Roosevelt mentioned Alice Lee, but also Rose Saltonstall and two other girls. He noted he would start a finance club, the members of which included Charles Washburn, Josiah Quincy, and Albert Bushnell Hart. Roosevelt ended his letter with a reference to his New York girlfriends: "Remember me to Annie and Fanny, and give my love to Edith—if she's in good humor; otherwise my respectful regards. If she seems *particularly* good tempered tell her that I hope that when I see her at Xmas it will not be on what you might call one of her off days." Morison, TR to Corinne, 10 November 1878, 35–36.

Monday November 25

Took dinner at the Hoopers; Miss Jeannie Tuckerman was there.

Wednesday November 27

After lunch drove over with Dick Saltonstall to his place (at Chestnut Hill) where I shall spend Thanksgiving. I like the whole Saltonstall family very much; I really feel almost as if I were at home when I am over there. Mr. Saltonstall is one of the best examples of a true, simple hearted "gentleman of the old school" I have ever met.

Thursday November 28

Spent the day with Alice and "Rose" dancing, walking, playing lawn tennis &c. I have gotten very well acquainted with both of them; Rose is a very good, pleasant girl, and as for pretty Alice Lee, I think her one of the sweetest, most ladylike girls I have ever met.

They all call me by my first name now.

Sunday December 1

Breakfasted as usual at the Porcellian, these Sunday breakfasts are a great institution, taking place about 9.30. The food is capital, and it is pleasant to be with the fellows.

Monday December 2

Shifted my quarters to Ware's & Washburne's room; where I shall probably remain till Xmas. All the fellows have been very kind about asking me to share their rooms.

Teddy Bayliss came of age and gave a Porcellian breakfast in the club; it was great fun.

Thursday December 5

Sparred for over a half an hour steadily with Sharon,[103] getting the worst of it of course; but I gave him his work.

I have gotten pretty high marks in my hour examinations so far.

---

103. Frederic William Sharon.

I enjoy the Porcellian more and more every day; I like almost all the fellows—especially Otho Williams.[104]

Sunday December 8

Several "honoraries" were out at the Porcellian breakfast. After Sunday School went in town and had a very pleasant dinner at Jack Tebbets.

Monday December 9

This being out of my own room has broken up my regular habits a good deal, and cut into my studying and exercise. Kind though the two Charlies are, I find it difficult to get my hours arranged to suit me; and spend more time in the club than I ought to, playing whist and billiards, and at partridge suppers.

Tuesday December 10

We have started a Finance Club which bids fair to do very well; it will be of great benefit to us. Bob Bacon & I are preparing a piece on municipal taxation.[105]

Wednesday December 11 [Entry continues into December 14, but large section blotted out by ink.]

It is strange how much I am pressed at Harvard; I have absolutely no time to think, except about my studies. Sometimes however, at night especially, I get thinking about my loved Father, and then I feel very desolate and heartsore. It seems so terrible to think that he will not be with us at Christmas. It often does not seem possible that he is really dead. I can recall all his speeches and actions very vividly. It is so sweet and yet so very sad to remember one of his last speeches to me; where he said that after all I was the dearest of his children to him. O, how little worthy I am of such a father; I feel such a hopeless sense of inferiority to him; I loved him so, and yet I could do so little for him! He was such a very large part in my life, and yet I am [blotted out] I feel such a dull terrible, dull pain at thinking that never in this world shall I see him again. But with the help of my God I shall try to lead such a life as he would have wished, and to do nothing I would have been ashamed to confess to him. I am very [blotted out]

Sunday December 15

This week everything seems to conspire to remind me of Father. The whole Sunday School went to the funeral of one of the children. When the coffin came

---

104. Otho Holland Williams [died 1896].

105. The Finance Club was supervised by Professor Dunbar of Roosevelt's political economy course. Perhaps more than any of TR's actual Harvard courses, the club prepared Roosevelt for a political career in New York City. Not only did he and Bacon give a paper on municipal taxation, but among the invited speakers were Democratic Congressman Abram Hewitt and land tax advocate Henry George—both of whom Roosevelt would run against in the New York City mayoral election of 1886.

into church, it recalled the day when I saw the body of him I loved dearest carried so, with such vividness that it almost unmanned me. I was afraid I should break down in church. It has made me feel very homesick.

Wednesday December 18

Went up to Δ.K.E. Theatricals which were really remarkably good—very clever and with hardly any smut. Stayed up there till about 12. It was a pretty wet night and I had capital fun. Afterwards went up to the club where I stayed till about 2 a.m. Otho Williams and I, being the two worst billiard players in the club, have great matches together. I like him very much.

Thursday December 19

Italian Exam, in which I did rather poorly.

Of my college friends so far, perhaps I am most intimate with Minot Weld; almost as much so with Harry Chapin. But I am very fond of Harry Shaw, Dick Trimble, Jack Tebbets, Dick Saltonstall, and also Charley Washburn and Charley Ware.

Have gotten pretty good marks so far this year.

Saturday December 21

Went on to N.Y. It is ever so pleasant to get home again; I enjoy college to the full, and yet I am always only too delighted to get home. Truly these are the golden years of my life. I can not imagine a fellow having a happier time than I have had since I have been in College.

Sunday December 22

Although the family are all so cheerful, yet we can none of us help thinking a good deal of our dear lost one; but now the sweet is overcoming the bitter in our memories of him.

I wonder if I shall ever be very miserable! In spite of the great sorrow—the greatest which could have befallen me—I have yet been very happy these last six months.

Monday December 23

Went to see my old Mission scholars. Poor Cassin is dead. All the Roosevelts are getting engaged. John is crazy with delight, Em confessed to me that he is really deeply in love with Sweet Miss Parish, Doc [West] of course is abjectly devoted to Fanny; Al is carrying on a lethargic love affair with Miss Tuckerman.

Tuesday December 24

Jack Elliott came on from Philadelphia—just the same dear old absentminded fellow as ever. It is a relief to find some one not in love. Am bothered a little by what Doc calls an "ephemeral fever."

Wednesday December 25

Xmas. Had rather a melancholy day. It does seem so very terrible not to have Father with us. He was the perfect life of all our engagements.

Received beautiful presents—chiefly books.

Thursday December 26

Confined to the house by the fever.

As regards my prospects in afterlife it seems to look more & more as if I was going to be a Naturalist. If so I shall have to study three years abroad—it makes me perfectly blue to think of it.

Friday December 27

Still in the house.

Emlen has been very touching about his love for Grace Parish. Dear old fellow! I wish him every success, with all my heart.

Old Nell seems to be doing very well.

What a wonderful set of relations I have got—cousins and all, especially my own family.

Saturday December 28

Went out to Oyster Bay with Jack Elliott. Took a long tramp through the woods and fields. It is cold, although without snow, and there are redpolls and crossbills in the woods; and I shot an Ipswich sparrow.

Passed the evening talking philosophy and playing double dummy whist.

Sunday December 29

Went to Church. In afternoon took a long tramp with Jack. He is the best companion on a trip of this kind I know.

I always enjoy these winter excursions to Oyster Bay so much. The shooting though very poor is great fun, and after the cold and fatigue of the day, one appreciates so a warm supper and rousing wood fires.

Snowed in the night.

Monday December 30

Snowy & windy. Jack & I went out in the rowboat, spending ½ an hour breaking our way through the shore ice. Sailed to Plum Pt., round to Pine Island, where we lunched, & as West Harbour was frozen solid, put out again. There was a heavy surf running & we succeeded in launching our boat through the rollers, getting soaked through & through with the freezing waters. Had the devils own work rowing to Rocky Pt, then hoisted our sail & went like the wind. Plenty of duck, but water was too rough, & they too shy, to come near them. Tired rather.

Tuesday December 31

At 7.30 started through the woods, with Rempson the gunner.[106] As there was 4 inches snow on the ground we took no dog. We tramped about 25 miles across country, not having a mouthful to eat and not sitting down till we reached home at 7.30—having walked 12 hours. So I am tired out, but have never had a more glorious day, the weather was beautiful (clear, cold & still) the sport splendid & I shot very well.

6 quail 8 rabbit 1 squirrel

MEMORANDA

Game Record for 1878

Red Hare	1
Gray Rabbit	8
Squirrel (Gray)	3
Spruce Grouse	1
Ruffed Grouse	16
Quail	6
Woodcock	14
Wild Pigeon	1
Carolina dove	3
Ducks	8
Yellow legs	3
Sandsnipe	9
Heron	4
Loon	1
	~~78~~ 80

(8 ducks=1 old squaw, 2 coots, 2 sheldrakes, 1 buffle head, 1 wood, 1 ruddy)

---

106. "Gunner" refers to a professional hunting guide and handler of the hunting dogs.

Game Record for 1873

2	squirrel
2	Partridge
2	Quail
37	Doves
81	Pigeons
18	Large Plover
36	Little "Shore Birds"
8	Hoopoos[107]
8	Cow Heron[108]
1	Gray Heron
195	

	Game record	1874	'75	'76	'77
1	Deer				1
2	Rabbit	2			
13	Gray Squirrel	3	4	2	4
17	Ducks	2	4	1	10
7	Grouse	2	2		3
1	Quail			1	
1	Snipe	1			
1	Woodcock			1	
11	Plover		2	3	6
24	Beach Birds		6	6	12
2	Loons		2		
27	Herons	7	4	6	10
2	Pigeon		2		
109		17	26	20	46

Cash account 1877

	Received	Paid
Jan	267.00	177.00
Feb		82.50
March	150.00	147.50
Apr	200.00	188.00
May	100.00	122.00

---

107. Hoopoes. Found in Africa and Eurasia. TR likely shot them on his family's trip along the Nile.

108. Cattle egret. Again, with gray heron, likely shot along Nile.

June	300.00	300.00
July	7.00	7.00
Aug	34.00	32.00
Sept	9.00	11.00
Oct	475.00	303.25
Nov		139.75
Dec	200.00	232.00
	1742.00	1742.00

Cash account 1878

	Received	Paid
January	275.00	198.50
February		96.30
March	324.45	304.65
April	735.00	418.00
May		179.40
June		137.50
July	125.00	125.00
August	57.00	57.00
September	33.00	33.00
October	500.00	233.00
November		135.75
December		131.25
	2049.45	2049.45

MEMORANDA 1878

Dress	373.45
Room	220.75
Board	305.50
Education	185.80
Washing	50.00
Charity	147.00
Coal &c	60.60
Travelling	129.25
Science	57.50
Subscriptions	133.75
Sporting	142.10
Athletics	30.00
Presents	80.00
Small Change	19.30
Amusements	32.75
Expressage	15.75
Sundries	65.95
	2049.45

Chestnut Hill

Volume III (1879)

In the back of his diaries, Roosevelt kept an account of the money he spent each year. In 1879 Roosevelt spent more than double what he had in 1878: an astonishing $5200. Of that, only $320 went toward his Harvard education, with another $700 going to room and board. On the one hand, Roosevelt was in a position to spend more money, having inherited from his father an annual income of about $8000 per year. On the other hand, the difference in spending between 1878 and 1879 tells volumes about the way Roosevelt's life continued to evolve as a Harvard undergraduate. He now spent hundreds of dollars on club dues, more than even the cost of his education. At the beginning of his undergraduate career he had kept neither a horse nor a carriage in Cambridge. Now he kept a horse, a sporty two-wheeled "dogcart," and a wintertime sleigh, at the high cost of $650. In 1878 social "amusements" had cost Roosevelt only $32.75. The following year they cost him over $300. His changing habits explained why money spent on "science" had dwindled from over $75 his first year to a mere $15 by 1879. By far, Roosevelt spent more on "presents" than any other expense, nearly $1000. Most of these were given to the young ladies of Chestnut Hill, Rose Saltonstall and Alice and Rosie Lee.

With Dick Saltonstall's return to Harvard in the fall of 1878, he and Roosevelt had become increasingly close. Theodore frequently spent weekends with the Saltonstall family, talking poetry and theology with Mr. Saltonstall until late at night, and playing with Dick's younger siblings. Part of the attraction of Dick Saltonstall's Chestnut Hill home was the fact it was adjacent to the home of his cousins, the Lees. Theodore had been introduced to the young sisters Rosie and Alice in October 1878. By early 1879 he was actively pursuing seventeen-year-old Alice, a pretty, sunny-dispositioned girl with blond curls and striking gray eyes. At the same time, Roosevelt turned his attentions to a wide array of Boston belles including Susie Wheelright, Nana Rotch, and Bessie Whitney. In May Roosevelt called on Julia Bacon, and was uncomfortably surprised to find Alice Lee also there. In June, Bessie Whitney called him a flirt. She and Nana Rotch had "compared notes" and come to the conclusion that Roosevelt was a "gay deceiver." By late June, however, Roosevelt seemed more serious about Alice, escorting her to Harvard's Class Day activities. That summer he found leaving Chestnut Hill harder than leaving Harvard.

The summer of 1879 was spent much like that of 1878. Roosevelt sailed and rowed on Long Island Sound, and took a late summer trip back to the Maine woods. Away from Alice, there seemed to be only one temptation along Oyster Bay: Miss Emily Swan. One morning Roosevelt woke up before dawn to row across the bay to visit Emily, where he was expected at nine a.m. Arriving early, he lay down on a rock and fell asleep, awaking to find that the unsecured boat had floated away. Roosevelt took off his clothes to swim out and retrieve the boat. After securing the boat, Roosevelt lay down to sleep again under the dock—without redonning his clothes. An hour later, he awoke to find that the rising tide had swept away both his boat and clothes, and Miss Swan and a friend were walking on the dock above his head. Roosevelt remained concealed until the girls walked away, and found that the boat with his clothes had drifted into a nearby creek. His sister Corinne claimed that Roosevelt then "conceived an aversion to the lady who so unconsciously had put him in this foolish position," and rowed home without calling on "his fair inamorata."

Summer away from Alice seemed to deepen his feelings for her, and he may have returned to Chestnut Hill that fall determined to win her. The diary entries for October 14–15 are torn out, and quite possibly have to do with Alice and her rejection of a marriage proposal. After that, there are very few mentions of Alice for the rest of the year. And when Roosevelt hosted a lunch party for thirty-four guests, including his sisters visiting from New York, he sat Alice on his left, and Bessie Hooper in the place of honor on his right. When back in New York, Roosevelt even saw Edith several times. By Thanksgiving, Alice and Theodore's relationship seemed uncertain.

To Alice, Roosevelt was probably not her vision of a *beau ideal*.[1] Classmates and other Boston girls remembered Roosevelt as eccentric, if not a bit crazy. Rosie Lee told Roosevelt biographer Carleton Putnam that Roosevelt "danced just as you thought he would dance if you knew him—he hopped." Supercharged and overeager, Roosevelt simply did not have the cool reserve needed to be considered charming or smooth. His naturalist bent did not help matters. Roosevelt stuffed his rooms—and often his pockets—with specimens of birds and reptiles. And Alice Lee was still young, not yet a debutante. Theodore Roosevelt's intense attentions may have been flattering, but they were also off-putting.

---

1. Carleton Putnam, 166.

Christmas seemed to settle things. The day after Christmas a large party of Roosevelt's Boston friends arrived to spend a week with the family in New York City. These included Dick Saltonstall and the Chestnut Hill girls. Perhaps it was one thing to be a guest in the homes of Boston Brahmin families, and another to play host as head of one of New York's top families. "It is perfectly lovely, having the dear, sweet Chestnut Hillers with us," Roosevelt noted, "and so natural." The year ended with a walk with Alice, and much drinking and dancing to welcome the new year. For Roosevelt and Alice, it would be a momentous one.

Volume III
1879 DIARY

Theodore Roosevelt [signature]

Wednesday January 1

Oyster Bay, Long Island

The family came out of town yesterday, with Uncle Jimmie & Aunt Annie to spend New Year's with us. We had a jolly time. They left in the afternoon, then Jack Elliott & I took a brisk tramp through the snow covered woods with our guns.

Thursday January 2

There was quite a heavy snow storm going on, but I went out hunting; but finally the snow completely covered the rabbit tracks so I gave up.

In afternoon went in town. (N.Y.)

3 rabbits

Friday January 3

For some unexplained reason Tom Ludlow has asked me to be usher at his wedding; so has Jack Roosevelt.

Have been made the confidant of West, Em & Al in their love affairs.

Old Nell had two of his friends up to dine with me; I liked one, Russell, very much.

Saturday January 4

It makes me perfectly blue to think of leaving the family; and yet I have a royal time at Cambridge.

Called on pretty Annie Murray.

What an old trump Nell is.

Sunday January 5

Hal Chapin took tea with us. Had such a sweet talk with Muffie.

I wonder if ever a man had two better sisters than I have!

In evening went on to Harvard.

Monday January 6

Arrived early in morning; have begun studying with a will.

Wednesday January 8

Examination in Natural History in which I am afraid I did poorly. (Too true)

Am studying hard; and am also working on an article for the Finance Club (Municipal Taxation) and on a catalogue of the Birds of Oyster Bay.[2]

Saturday January 11

At 10.30 a.m. Harry Shaw's cutter drew up before the Porcellian, and we drove over to the Saltonstalls, where we found Dick and Minot Weld; Also Alice and Rose. The sleighing was splendid; we could not have had a better day—cold, clear and calm. We then drove in town, as I wished to see Mr. Saltonstall about Dick's coming into the Porc. Spent the evening playing whist and billiards with Otho Williams, Van Rensaeler[3] and Charley Morgan.

Sunday January 12

Started my Sunday School class again.

Tuesday January 14

Went on by night boat to New York for Ludlows wedding.

Wednesday January 15

Arrived at N.Y. Went to a rehearsal of the wedding. One of my old flames, pretty Helen White, is a bridesmaid.[4]

Thursday January 16

Bad weather, but Grace church was crowded. I ushered on the middle aisle with Livingstone, Rutherford, and Cruger.[5]

---

2. "Notes on Some of the Birds of Oyster Bay, Long Island," March 1879. A printed list of seventeen birds.

3. William Bayard Van Rensselaer, Harvard 1879.

4. Helen Chanler White, daughter of prominent physician Dr. Octavius A. White.

5. The wedding of Thomas Ludlow to Harriet Carnochan was a large society wedding for which two thousand invitations were issued. As a wedding gift the bride's father gave his daughter a purse of gold coins for the honeymoon trip to Europe. *New York Times*, 17 January 1879.

Took the night train for Harvard; driving down to it in the cutter was upset.

Saturday January 18

Late last night was aroused by a deputation of about half the Porc. who came down to tell me I was elected 5th man of the first nine of the Pudding.[6] I was dressed nolens volens,[7] taken up to the club and all around, and did not get to bed till 6 a.m. The others of the 1st nine are Bob Bacon, Dick Trimble, Billy Hooper, Charley Ware (myself) Harry Jackson, Harry Shaw, Charley Morgan & Jeff Miller.

In the evening we had a Porc. Dinner given by Harry Shaw and Minot Weld; it was a great success and many graduates were out. Late in the evening some of the men, getting awfully drunk, raised particular Cain.

Monday January 20

Began running for the Pudding.

Friday January 24

Was initiated into the Pudding.

Saturday January 25

3 hour examination in the morning. In afternoon went out to Chestnut Hill to pass Sunday. I spent most of the evening with Mr. Saltonstall, looking over his old family papers, comparing our Egyptian and Syrian experiences and talking over things in general. Tom Lee came in and we had a grand theological discussion.

Sunday January 26

Went to church in morning and had a very interesting sermon.

In afternoon we coasted on double runners—a party of about twenty five of us in all. I never had better fun. The more I see of Rose Saltonstall and Alice Lee, the more I like them, especially pretty Alice. The whole family call me "Thee" now. Alice came in to take tea and spend the evening.

Friday January 31

Went to Chestnut Hill to coast on toboggans [sic]; or "resist runners." Besides Alice and Rose, Lulu Lane, Nana Rotch and Bessie Whitney, out there the fel-

---

6. Hasty Pudding Club, a Harvard social club known for its spring theatricals, which include men in drag.

7. Willing or not.

lows were Dick S., Minot W., Jack Tebbets, Ell Whitney, Tom Lee and myself. We had capital fun. Alice, Miss Whitney, Dick & I coasted on the same tobogan.[8]

Saturday February 1

Went out to Worcester to spend Sunday with Charley Washburn. Took him to the Tiffanys; met a pretty Miss Cross. Had a capital sleigh ride behind Charley's trotter.

Sunday February 2

Passed a very pleasant Sunday of the same kind that I always pass at home.

Monday February 3

Began grinding like a trump.

Thursday February 6

Semiannuals began.

Sunday February 9

One year ago today the man, who was not only my father, but was my dearest loved friend, died. O God give me strength to live as he would have wished me! It has been very sad to write to the family. Fortunately I have been studying so hard—and on Sundays almost as hard with my S.S. class &c.—that I have not had much time to think, but there are very sad moments, especially in the evening and at night.

Sunday February 16

Have been working hard all the week.

Friday February 21

Semiannuals ended today. I have been working hard since Christmas, and shall now take a rest.

---

8. A few days later TR wrote his sister Corinne: "I spent most of last week studying, but on Friday afternoon took a holiday and went out to Chestnut Hill for a coasting party. Besides Alice and Rose there were Miss Bess Whitney, Miss Nana Rotch (whose sister Bamie knows) Miss Lulu Lane, Harry Shaw, Jack Tebbets, Minot Weld, Dick Saltonstall and myself. We coasted on 'torborgans'; they are a kind of sled with out runners, going on the crust of the snow; each in fact is a long thin board with the front curled up. They went like the wind, much faster than the double runners we had been on the Saturday before. I rarely passed a pleasanter afternoon." Morison, 3 February 1879, I, 36–37.

Saturday February 22

Our great midyear Porc. supper came off today. Besides the 18 immediates about 40 honoraries attended. All the oldest men had known Father either personally or by reputation, and I had very pleasant talks with them. How I wish I could ever do something to keep up his name!

George Upham came into the club—the other sophomores are Sam Hammond, Dick Sprague & Billy Peters.

Thursday February 27

In the evening started by 7 p.m. train for Island Falls, Maine, where I intend to spend a couple weeks.

Friday February 28

Reached Mattawamkeag about 11 a.m., where I found Will Sewall waiting for me in a sleigh. From there it is 36 miles to Island Falls, where I am now, and it was nearly ten when we arrived here. It was bitterly cold, but still, and we were well wrapped up, so I enjoyed the ride very much. The road was hardly broken out, in places.

Saturday March 1

Tried snowshoing [sic] for the first time. Went about six miles, making the round of Will Dow's "lucivee"[9] traps, which however contained nothing. The woods looked simply perfect, all the evergreens being loaded with snow, I have never seen a grander sight than these northern forests in winter. I got along very well, except in a cedar swamp. We saw many tracks of lucivees, foxes, otters and rabbits; and found a porcupine up in a hemlock. I brought him down quite neatly with the rifle.

Sunday March 2

Read my bible in the morning. In the afternoon took a tramp through the woods; I can not get used to the extreme beauty of the snow covered pine and spruce forest. The cold does not bother me at all in the woods; but if there is any wind it is very disagreeable in the open. I get along very well on snow shoes, but the swamps are very tough work—although perhaps not so bad as in summer. There is very little life in the woods.

Monday March 3

Went off on a tramp through the woods with Will Dow. Walked up to Dyer Brook, then a couple of miles along it, and then struck out in the woods. The

---

9. Canada lynx. The term TR used is derived from the French-Canadian *loup-cervier*.

best walking was on the hard wood grounds; it was fearfully hard work in some of the thick, swampy spruce and cedar thickets, but not as bad as in summer. I saw an arctic woodpecker by a stream and some Hudsonian chickadees in a spruce wood, and two whiskey jacks[10] came round us at lunch time; we saw two or three hare tracks, and once the round footprints of a Canada lynx, and found where a spruce partridge had passed the night: but in an 8 hour tramp, these were the only traces of life.

Tuesday March 4
Spent the day tramping through the woods with Will Sewall. We saw a good many tracks of lucivees, foxes, rabbits, otters, minks, weasels, squirrels, porcupines, but the only living creatures were a couple of chickadees & a woodpecker. Finally we found the footprints of a partridge on some hard wood ground, and following them up roused the bird from under a fallen birch top and I shot it. The snow shoing [sic] is poor, the snow being wet & heavy, and the weather warmish.

1 ruffed grouse

Wednesday March 5
Spent the day snow shoing through the woods as usual—and with my usual ill success as regards game. Otherwise I am enjoying myself to the utmost, but the asthma keeps me up a good deal at night. Lunched at a logging camp. Finally I saw a partridge in the top of a spruce and killed him with the rifle—also a porcupine. By trapping we have caught a lucivee and a fox; but have seen nothing but the tracks of game other than the 2 partridges.

1 Ruffed grouse

Thursday March 6
Seawall [sic], Dow and I started with a pony and a shaggy, lean horse for a logging camp 30 miles distant, reaching it after dusk. When we started the thermometer was 10° below zero, but I was too well wrapped up to heed the cold. The roads were frightful; none but a backwoods horse could stand them. I saw several flocks of snow buntings, a red crossbill, and a small party of grosbeaks which were very tame and confiding. I also saw the tracks of a mouse, probably hesperonys.

---

10. Gray jays. The name TR used is derived from the Cree *Wesakachak*.

Friday March 7

Dow and I started out early in the morning, although there was a heavy snow storm going on, and tramped through the woods till the afternoon without seeing anything, when we roused a caribou in a dense, low spruce wood. I caught a glimpse of him as he vanished not thirty yards distant, but had no chance to fire. We followed his tracks till dusk, where we went into camp. The night was very cold, and we had but little food and no blankets, and so were pretty uncomfortable in spite of our huge fire.

Saturday March 8

Before sunrise we again started on the caribou's trail, the thermometer being below zero. He led a most tortuous course through cedar swamps, hardwood lands, hemlock hedges, &c.; and sometimes would go in a straight course across the great cranberry bogs. Generally he trotted, coming down not only on his hoofs but on his whole lower legs, the snow being over three feet deep, but on bad ground he made great jumps like a huge rabbit. The snow shoing was very bad and after following him till midday without finding where he had stopped to browse or rest, we gave the chase up and reached the logging camp at sunset.

Sunday March 9

I was pretty well fagged out by my two days chase after the caribou and have been lying back and resting all today. I have not been bothered at all by the asthma since I came into camp. I like these lumbermen very much, and get on capitally with them—great, rough, hospitable fellows. I am great friends with one in especial, Charley Brown. It has rained a little and then frozen, improving the snowshoeing greatly, and making the forest look beautifully, each tree covered with glittering icicles.

Monday March 10

Clear and cold. Seawall and I while hunting through the woods found a small deer yard. We approached it from different sides, and I saw the buck first, getting a shot at its head, but I tripped up at the moment and missed it. It then broke out of the yard and ran; after following at full speed about a mile I got another shot and killed it with the rifle. We then dragged it to camp. I spent the afternoon in shooting rabbits, also with the rifle, stalking cautiously through the woods. In the evening we had a royal venison supper—a pleasant change from the ordinary routine of pork & beans.

1 buck 3 white rabbit

Tuesday March 11

Started back for Island Falls. It was warmish, sleeting and raining, and the roads were frightful. Several times when the horse floundered off the track into the deep snow drifts we had to unharness him and drag the sleigh ourselves for a hundred yards or so. It was very fatiguing work, as we walked all the time, and got wet through and cold and hungry. The road was chiefly through the woods, with every now and then clearings, with the shaggy black cattle and sheep crowding around the barns—the pictures of bleakness. Heard some snow buntings singing beautifully. Reached Island Falls in time for tea.

Wednesday March 12

In the morning went the round (7 miles) of the lucivee traps, which contained nothing, but we saw a coon cross the road ahead of us, and following his tracks half a mile I shot him from a dead tree. About 10 a.m. we started through the woods for Mattawamkeag Lake, at the foot of which we camped out for the night. The snowshoeing, for the first time since I have been up here, was capital. On the way down I picked up a couple of spruce partridges in a swamp.

1 raccoon 2 canada grouse

Thursday March 13

We broke camp pretty early and reached Island Falls in time for dinner. The day was clear, calm and cool, and I enjoyed the walk extremely. We came home the entire distance over the lake and river, only needing our snow shoes about half the time. We saw no living thing, but amused ourselves by practising [sic] at long ranges (300–500 yards) with the rifle, and all three of us made very good shots with the "old reliable" (Sharp's business—75).[11]

Friday March 14

Spent the entire morning hunting partridges, without seeing one, and making the round of the lucivee traps, which contained nothing. However I have had good success this trip, and I have never passed a pleasanter two weeks. The skins of the fox, lucivee, coon and buck make quite a set of trophies; and we have shot enough partridges and rabbits to eat—not to mention the venison. I have collected a good many specimens.

---

11. "Old Reliable" was the trademark of the Sharp's Company. In 1876 it added those words to the barrel markings of rifles manufactured in Bridgeport, Connecticut.

Saturday March 15

Started for Mattawomkeag in a sleigh at 5 a.m. It was a very pleasant day. Took the night train for Boston. I am now going to study all the time till Easter, doing double work to make up for my holiday.[12]

Saturday March 22

Sparred for the light weight cup; won against my first man but was beaten by Hanks, the champion.

I have been studying extremely hard the past week and have succeeded in making up pretty much all I lost while I was in Maine.

Wednesday March 26

In the afternoon I went to Chestnut Hill, where I dined and spent the night at the Saltonstalls. They were so cordial and so glad to see me that I felt exactly as if I were at home. I passed the evening at the Lees, with pretty Alice. I am going to send her & Rose the fox and lynx skins, made into rugs.

Thursday March 27

Δ.K.E. theatrical. They were very good; it was rather a "wet" night.[13]

Friday March 28

Pudding Theatricals. They were excellent—I have never seen better. The singing afterwards, both in the room and in the yard, was great fun.

---

12. Upon reaching Harvard the following day, TR penned a long letter to his mother about his trip: "I never have passed a pleasanter two weeks than those just gone by; I enjoyed every moment. The first two or three days I had asthma, but, funnily enough, this left me entirely as soon as I went into camp. The thermometer was below zero pretty often, but I was not bothered by the cold atall [sic], except one night when I camped out on the trail of a caribou (which we followed two days without getting more than a glimpse of the animal). Out in the opens when there was any wind it was very disagreeable but in the woods the wind never blows and as long as we were moving about it made little difference how low the temperature was, but sitting still for lunch we felt it immediately. I learned how to manage snowshoes very quickly, and enjoyed going out in them greatly. I have never seen a grander or more beautiful sight than the northern woods in winter. The evergreens laden with snow make the most beautiful contrast of green and white, and when it freezes after a rain all the trees look as though they were made of crystal. The snow under foot being about three feet deep, and drifting to twice that depth in places, completely changes the aspect of things. I visited two lumber camps, staying at one four days; it was great fun to see such a perfectly unique type of life. I shot a buck, a coon and some rabbits and partridges and trapped a lynx and a fox—so my trip was a success in every way."

13. Full of alcohol.

Saturday March 29

There was a Porc supper but I cut the first part of it to go in to Jack Tebbetts to meet Alice Lee, Rose Saltonstall, the Rotches, Miss Whitney & Miss Lane. I enjoyed myself very much indeed. I came out about 11, in time for the cream of the supper; there were some most absurd scenes; Otho Williams engaged me to act as his second in a duel with Charley Sprague—both being decidedly "mellow."

Sunday March 30

Had a very unusually interesting time at Sunday School, showing the boys a lot of eastern photographs.

Called on Jeannie Hooper & Mrs. Tudor in the evening.

Monday March 31

In the evening drove over to Minot Weld's to see some private theatricals; Miss Bacon and Miss Frothingham both acted, and very well to [sic]. I sat by pretty Alice before and during the performance, and spent most of the remainder of the evening with Nana Rotch; so it is needless to say I enjoyed myself very much. Got back about one oclock and stayed in the Porc, singing and talking, till three.

Tuesday April 1

Otho Williams, Jim Wright, Charley Sprague and myself had a very pleasant game supper in the Porc.

Wednesday April 2

I gave a little lunch party in my rooms. Mrs. Saltonstall matronized; the girls were Alice, Rose, Nana & Emily Rotch, Bessie Whitney & Lula Lane, the fellows Minot, Dick Saltonstall, Jack Tebbetts, Harry Shaw, Gordy Lane & Ell. Whitney. We took them over the Porcellian and Pudding, and passed a lovely day. I gave Alice the lynx skin, made into a rug; and Rose the fox. Alice is making me a pair of slippers. En passant, Nana R. is very sweet & pretty. Took the night boat for New York with Minot & Dick who are going to spend the vacation week with me.

Thursday April 3

Spent the day showing Minot & Dick the sights, both get along beautifully with the family, and the latter is very amusing.

In the evening we went to Aunt Annies; Margy Tuckerman, Fanny Smith & Edith Carow were there, looking very prettily. Edith is just the same sweet little flirt as ever.

Friday April 4

Miss Christine & Miss Lucy Kean lunched with us. I like them very much. Darling little Muffie has gotten sick; and it makes me feel miserable.

Saturday April 5

Nell gave us a dinner at the Jockey Club, with Grove Porter, Ike Iselin, Harold & Smith Haddon. I drove out in Harold Haddon's dog cart, the others coming in drags. We enjoyed ourselves extremely, I like Haddon very much.

Sunday April 6

Poor old Em has been rejected by Grace Parish![14] I had a long talk with him. It is awfully hard on him. Muffie is still not well.

Monday April 7

Emlen gave us a lunch in Down Town Club—a great success. We dined at West's, to go to the theatre.

Tuesday April 8

Went to the dog show. Lizzie Moran lunched with us. Took Annie Murray to the rehearsal of the Fancy Dress Ball. Took the night train for Boston. Both boys have enjoyed the holiday intensely and so have I. Motherling is almost well again.

Wednesday April 9

Started work again.

Friday April 11

Called on Miss Nana Rotch and spent the afternoon there—teaching her the five step waltz.

Friday April 18

Have had 2 examinations this week & so have been studying hard. My horse has arrived; I determined to keep him in Cambridge this Spring. I keep him at Pikes Stable.

Went over to Chestnut Hill in the afternoon, where I intend to pass Saturday & Sunday. We dined at the Lees.

---

14. Over four years later Emlen ended up marrying the same Christine Kean mentioned in the April 4 entry just above.

Saturday April 19

Snowed heavily all day long! But in spite of the weather I took a long walk with pretty Alice. I spent most of the remainder of the day in teaching the girls the five step and a new dance, the knickerbocker. In the evening we played whist and read ghost stories.

Sunday April 20

After church we went to the Francises. In the afternoon Codman & Rose, & Alice and myself went out walking.[15]

Monday April 21

Came back to Cambridge—with much regret after my two days rest.
In the afternoon took my horse out for the first time; he went beautifully, but of course is full of the Old Harry[16]—which adds greatly to the enjoyment.

Tuesday April 22

Took a ride on my horse; it will be the greatest pleasure to me this spring, as I shall ride him every day the weather is even decent. It was the one thing wanting for perfect enjoyment.

In the afternoon I went in to the Jeffries' to look over their collections & dined there. Played whist in the evening.

Wednesday April 23

Now that the beautiful spring weather has fairly set in, I get up in time to study an hour or two before breakfast, and so have my afternoons and evenings pretty much to myself—for I have done my hard studying for this year.

One reason I enjoy riding here so much is that there are so many places—Milton, Jamaica Plains, Forrest Hills, Chestnut Hill &c.—where I can ride over & stay to dinner or lunch. Besides the rides through all the country round Boston are beautiful.

---

15. From Chestnut Hill that same day TR wrote Anna: "I had two examinations last week, and so studied pretty hard till Friday afternoon, when I came over here with Dick. To day we went to Church in the morning. Harry Shaw came over in the afternoon, and Rose and he, and Alice and I took a long walk. I like the two girls more and more every day—especially pretty Alice. All the family are just lovely to me; Dick says he never in his life had such a nice time as he had in New York. I see Edith won a prize for answering the World questions; congratulate her for me."

16. The devil.

Thursday April 24

I rode over early in the morning to Chestnut Hill to spend the day. After lunch I went out driving with Rose, Alice and Endicott. I had to ride back to Cambridge immediately after dinner to go to a "conversazione" at Laughlin's where I met one of the Miss Longfellows—a bright, clever girl.

Friday April 25

I rode up back of Watertown, pretty fast; I am trying to sweat the horses winter coat off him. In the afternoon I went in town with Harry Chapin & dined at Youngs Hotel; afterwards we joined Minot Weld and Dick Saltonstall at the theatre. I went out with Minot to pass the night at Jamaica Plains.

Saturday April 26

Spent the morning looking over Minot's poultry, cattle, &c. In the afternoon we drove over to Chestnut Hill where we found (in addition to Alice, Rose & Rosy Lee) Nana Rotch. I spent the afternoon with the latter and now my conscience reproaches me with having rather flirted with "Nana." I sincerely wish I had not.

In the evening we had a Porc dinner; I sat next to Van Rensaeller whom I have gotten to like very much & who confided to me his devotion to Lulu Lane. In vino veritas.[17]

Sunday April 27

I took my Sunday school for the last time this year, giving each boy a present. They have been very good this year.

Monday April 28

Rode over to Chestnut Hill and afterwards to Jamaica Plains.

Tuesday April 29

1 hour exam.

Spent the evening at the Rotches.

Wednesday April 30

Harry Shaw and I gave a theatre party to Mr. and Mrs. Saltonstall and Rose and Alice. Alice and I sat just behind the others and it is needless to say I passed a very pleasant evening.

---

17. "In wine there is truth."

I had dinner with Harry Shaw previously.

Thursday May 1
Rode over to Jamaica Plains to call on the Welds.

Friday May 2
Had a rifle match, beating Sam Skinner and being beaten by Fred Sharon.

Saturday May 3
In the morning I rode over to Chestnut Hill, lunching at the Lees. After dinner I drove Alice and Rose in town to visit the Rotches. At four oclock George Minot called for me, also on horseback, and after a long ride I went to his house, at Forrest Hills, where I shall spend the night.

Sunday May 4
Went to Church with the Minots in the Morning; afterwards accompanied Miss Julia Bacon[18] home. After lunch drove over to Chestnut Hill where Harry Shaw & Van Rensaler soon appeared in a buggy, and we went out walking with Alice, Rose & Rosy Lee. Alice and I soon separated from the others and we did not return till nearly six. I took tea at the Lees, riding home to Cambridge quite late in the evening.

Wednesday May 7
After lunch I rode over to Chestnut Hill and went out riding with Rose. I dined at the Saltonstalls; in the evening Alice and Frank Lee came in, and we danced, talked &c. Got back to Cambridge a little after 10 in time for the cream of the Δ.K.E. meeting. Woodbury Kane is 1st man of the 1st ten from '82; Charles Dickey 7th.

Thursday May 8
Immediately after breakfast started off on horseback for Stilton. Stopped for a few moments at Chestnut Hill, not reaching the Whitneys till half past ten. Dinner did not come till 3.30, and I spent the whole six hours most pleasantly walking about through the woods and over the farm with Miss Bessie. I rode back about 6.30.

What a royally good time I am having. I can't conceive of a fellow possibly enjoying himself more.

---

18. Bob Bacon's cousin. In a letter to Corinne the next day TR referred to Julia as "rather pretty." Morison, 5 May 1879, 39.

Friday May 9

I rode over and dined at the Bacons where, to my astonishment, I met Rose and Alice. We spent the afternoon playing lawn tennis; I like Miss Julia very much. I rode back to Cambridge in time to go in and take tea at the Tudors.[19]

Saturday May 10

In the morning I went in town to meet Rose and Alice, and we had our photograph taken. I went out with them to Chestnut Hill to pass Sunday. In the afternoon we all went to a bicycle meet of the Suffolk Club; there were a great many people there I knew. Ell Whitney, Minot Weld & Frank Codman had driven over, & also the two Miss Rotches, & we had great fun dancing in the evening. After tea I went out walking with Alice.

Sunday May 11

After Church again went out walking with sweet, pretty Alice. In the afternoon we all went to drive; and in the evening called on the Lowells where there is a large party of fellows and girls.

Monday May 12

I took the longest ride I have yet taken, through the beautiful country back of Waverly.

Went into the O.K. in the evening.

My horse has got his summer coat and is pretty well filled out, so he is looking like a little beauty. It was the best stroke I ever made, getting him on here.

Tuesday May 13

After dinner I rode over to the Lees where I spent the evening. I rode like Jehu,[20] both coming and going, and as it was pitch dark when I returned (about 10.15) we fell while galloping down hill—a misadventure which I thoroughly deserve for being a fool.

---

19. In a letter to his mother about Thursday and Friday, TR wrote: "Last Thursday I spent the day at Milton, with the Whitneys, riding over in the morning and back in the evening. Miss Bessie Whitney is a very sweet girl, and I enjoyed myself very much. Wednesday I went out riding with Rose Saltonstall. Friday afternoon I spent at the Bacons, playing lawn tennis with Miss Julia." No mention of seeing Alice.

20. Common phrase meaning "to ride furiously or recklessly." From the Bible, Second Book of Kings 9:20: "And the watchman told, saying, He came even unto them, and cometh not again: and the driving is like the driving of Jehu the son of Nimshi; for he driveth furiously."

Wednesday May 14

My horse is a little lame from yesterday's exploits; so I could not go to the Saltonstalls to dinner.

Spent the evening in the Δ.K.E. drowning my sorrows; I have been an awful fool to ride the horse so hard.

Saturday May 17

I went in the morning to see the class races, which were exceedingly good; I sat with the Lees. In the afternoon I went out to pass Sunday at Milton with the Whitneys. Whom I like very much, especially jolly Ell and pretty Miss Bessie. We spent the evening singing, dancing, &c.

Sunday May 18

In the morning we drove over to Lake Punkapoag[21] through the Blue Hills; the scenery around here is very beautiful, and the country is now simply perfect. In the afternoon I took a long walk through the woods with Miss Bessie.

Monday May 19

Early in the morning came back to Cambridge. I took tea with the Lanes, and had a very pleasant evening; both of the girls are very sweet, and Miss Lulu very pretty.

Tuesday May 20

After dinner Dick S. and I drove over in a buggy to Chestnut Hill where I passed a very pleasant evening; I brought the girls over some gold and silver charms.

I am afraid I have lamed my horse hopelessly; it is very tough luck; but at least I did have royal sport for the three weeks and a half I had him.

Wednesday May 21

I dined at the Lees in the evening, taking a walk with Alice. Our photographs are a great success. I walked back to Cambridge with John Tebbetts.

Thursday May 22

In the afternoon acted as judge at the Harvard Athletic Ass. In the evening called on the Lanes where I found Alice and Rose; we spent most of the evening in dancing.

---

21. Ponkapoag.

Friday May 23

Glee Club concert in the evening. I sat by Miss Bacon. Afterwards there was dancing in Memorial Hall and I had some lovely waltzes with Alice, Rose, Luly Lane & Miss Francis.

Saturday May 24

In the afternoon Van Ransaeler & I called on the Lanes, taking Miss Luly & Miss Kitty (& Mrs. Lane) round to see Van's room & mine. We then played lawn tennis; and stayed to tea and spent the evening, dancing till I was nearly dead.

My horse is hopelessly lame and I am going to send him back to New York. It is frightfully tough luck; but I deserved it. I miss having him to ride horribly.

I have never passed a pleasanter evening.

Sunday May 25

In the afternoon I drove over in a buggy to Chestnut Hill, and went out walking with the girls.

Tuesday May 27

I drove in a buggy to Chestnut Hill, where I spent the afternoon with the two girls; I then drove over to the Whitneys where I took tea and spent a very pleasant evening with pretty "Bessie" (we are very intimate now). It was pretty dark driving home.

Thursday May 29

I walked over to Chestnut Hill, spending the afternoon with Rose & Alice, and dining at the Saltonstalls. I walked back in the evening.

Friday May 30

In the evening I went in town with Harry Shaw and Dick Saltonstall to a theatre circus party given by Charley Codman. I took Alice there and from it, sitting by her; and the whole thing was a great success.

Saturday May 31

I drove over to the Bacons to take tea and had a very jolly evening. George Minot was there. I like both Miss Nellie and Miss Julia very much. After tea we went to the Frothinghams.

Monday June 2

My first annual examination.

Looking over my diary for the last two weeks it would seem as if I had not studied much; but really I have, getting up every morning at six, and studying till eight; and from half past eight to half past one; and usually (almost half the time) from two till five. So I get in from seven to ten hours a day. During most of the year I rarely work eight hours a day, generally not much more than six. My horse has improved wonderfully, and I exercise him a little every day.

Wednesday June 4

Dick S. and I drove over to the Whitneys, where we took tea and passed a very jolly evening.

Saturday June 7

I passed my third and hardest examination in the morning and so took a holiday in the afternoon. My horse is now perfectly well, and so I rode over to Chestnut Hill; he was in wild spirits, and cut up so that I had hard work to prevent him spraining his leg again. It makes me feel like a new man to have the horse well again; I had a most glorious ride. I spent the afternoon walking with Alice; dined at the Lees; and spent the evening dancing, talking &c., riding back at 10 oclock.

Sunday June 8

Van Rensselaer and I took tea at the Lanes, and spent the evening there, very pleasantly.

Tuesday June 10

Rode over to Chestnut Hill and spent the afternoon at the Saltonstalls.

Friday June 13

Passed my last examination.

In the afternoon I rode over to the Saltonstalls, and spent the afternoon walking with Rose. I took dinner there; afterwards went out walking with Alice.

Saturday June 14

Breakfasted in the Porc at 10, at 11 my horse was before the door and I rode over to the Bacons where I lunched, spending the day very pleasantly with Miss Nellie & Miss Julia. I rode back to Cambridge at about 6 p.m.; at 7.30 had a Porc dinner. Charley Morgan got very drunk, and, not having been sober for a week, nearly had the D.T.s; I slept in his room; walking home next morning in a dress suit nearly walked over a proctor.

Sunday June 15

Van Rensselaer & I drove over to take tea at the Saltonstalls. We went out walking with Rose and Alice in the afternoon, and got drenched in a rain storm. Driving home it was pitch dark, and I came within an ace of smashing up against a wagon.

Monday June 16

I am living a life of most luxurious ease at present; I breakfast in the club about 10; my horse is then before the door, and I ride off—generally lunching at some friends house. It is very pleasant but I do not suppose it would be healthy to continue it too long. When I do not stay out to tea or dinner, I generally have some kind of a spree—a "champagne supper"—up in the club.

Tuesday June 17

It was Rose's birthday; I rode over to Chestnut Hill where I lunched and spent the day, bringing over two fans for Rose & Alice. En passant, these two young ladies have cost me over $150 so far. In the evening I went to the strawberry night of the O.K.

Wednesday June 18

In the afternoon I rode over to call on the Guilds[22] at Forest Hill; I then rode to Chestnut Hill where I dined at the Lees; afterwards taking Alice to a strawberry festival at the Lowells. In the evening I went to the Pudding Strawberry Night.[23]

Thursday June 19

I rode over to Milton and spent the day at the Whitneys. I had great fun teasing pretty Bessie about having called me a flirt; it appears that she and Nana Rotch had compared notes and come to the conclusion I was a "gay deceiver"![24] In the evening went to the Δ.K.E. strawberry night. I got into a row with a mucker[25] and knocked him down; cutting my knuckles pretty badly against his teeth.

---

22. Henry Eliot Guild, Class of 1880.

23. Strawberry festivals are an old New England tradition, celebrating the berry's harvest and the start of the summer's warmest months.

24. A lothario.

25. A person who removes waste from stables, but also a general term for a coarse person.

Friday June 20

Class day; I think I have never passed such a pleasant day. I was one of the Junior Class Ushers; from 11 till 12.30 I ushered in Sanders[26]; then lunched in the Club, then till 4.30 I stayed at Van Rensselears spread in the new gymnasium, dancing with twenty different girls from Boston & New York—especially Maggie Wolf, Helen White, Cornelia Baylies, Susie Wheelright, Paulina Revere, & Rose S. I then ushered at the tree[27]; went to the Pudding Spread where I was with Nana Rotch; I then took Alice to the tea at Morgans, and afterwards to the Lanes; at 8.00 she and I went to the yard, and sat in a window in Hollis till 10. looking at the brilliantly lighted yard and listening to the Glee Club. I never saw her looking sweeter or prettier. We then went and danced at Memorial, and at 11.30 she went home, and I spent a couple of hours in the Club.

Saturday June 21

I rode over to see the Lowells where I passed a very pleasant time. In the evening there was a Porc Supper.

Sunday June 22

In the afternoon Harry Shaw drove me over to the Saltonstalls, where we took tea. Any number of fellows came in to call during the afternoon. Ellerton V. & Rose, Harry & Rosy L, and Alice and myself went out walking.

Monday June 23

Breakfasted, as usual, in the Club, with Harry Shaw. I rode over and spent the day at the Lees, walking with Alice, dancing &c., returning late in the evening. My horse is looking and feeling beautifully, and is in wild spirits. I shall send him home at the end of the week.

Tuesday June 24

In the morning I rode over to call on Susie Wheelright in Jamaica Plains. I then rode to the Saltonstalls, where I shall stay till Thursday. I spent the afternoon talking with Rose, teaching Phil[28] how to shoot and playing with Cotty.[29] In the evening I called on the Lowells.

---

26. Sanders Theater, in Memorial Hall.

27. The Tree of Harvard Yard. It was a Class Day tradition for upperclassmen to link hands in a ring around the tree.

28. Philip Leverett Saltonstall.

29. Endicott Peabody Saltonstall.

Mr. & Mrs. Saltonstall are just too sweet for anything. They have added so much to my happiness this year that I scarcely know how to thank them. So have the Lees. I shall be even more sorry to leave Chestnut Hill than to leave Harvard.

Wednesday June 25

Early in the morning I rode over to Cambridge to usher for Commencement Day. I lunched at the Lanes; they have been very kind to me this year. The four girls—Alice, Rose, Lulu, and Kitty behaved like Samals[30] at lunch. The afternoon I spent in the club and at the ball match with Yale, which we won. I rode back to the Saltonstalls in time for tea.

Thursday June 26

After breakfast I bid goodbye with the most heartfelt regret to Chestnut Hill and rode over to Cambridge. In the afternoon I came out to the Whitneys, where I shall spend a couple of days. Like my other Boston friends they have been exceedingly kind to me.

The two Miss Lanes and Nana Rotch were out there too, and we had an extremely jolly time.

Friday June 27

At 11.10 we started in a special car to see the "Great Harvard-Yale Race" which Harvard won easily. The party consisted of Alice, Rose & Rosie Lee, Bessie W., Nana R., Miss Guild, and the two Miss Lanes, Van R., Jack T, Harry Guild, Dick R., John Sharp, Ell W. & C. I have hardly ever enjoyed myself more. We did not get home till 2 a.m., and I have absolutely no voice left, thanks to the shouting. We sang during most of the return journey. I spent a large proportion of my time with Alice, who never looked prettier.

Saturday June 28

Bade adieu to the Whitneys and came on to New York. So ends my Junior Year; and I can not possibly conceive of any fellow having a pleasanter time than I have had. I doubt if I ever shall enjoy myself so much again. I have done well in my studies and I have had a royally good time with the Club, my horse, and above all the sweet, pretty girls at Chestnut Hill &c.

---

30. An indigenous ethnic group of the Philippines. TR is probably using this as an epithet for "savages."

Sunday June 29

Went out to Oyster Bay; Russell, Haddon, Betts, Maud Elliott & the two Miss Kanes are passing Sunday with us. I was perfectly delighted to see all the family again; Muffie & the two darling girls greeted me so lovingly. I spent the whole day talking with them all. All the "Roosevelt boys" are out here.

Aunt Lucy & Maud Elliott are staying with us.

Monday June 30

Re-commenced the old Oyster Bay life; spent the day putting my rowboat in order, building the boat house, taking a pull to Plum Pt; sailing with Uncle Jimmie (who, with Aunt Annie, is spending the summer here) &c &c. I lead just the same active, out of door life that I always enjoy so much—with my horse, gun and row boat. The swimming is capital. Tiny & Virginia R. are passing the summer with West. Em, poor fellow, is still very much cut up.

Thursday July 3

I have been getting myself into condition with the row boat; rowing to Loyds neck &c. Today I tried my horse jumping; he went fairly, but at one fence we got a regular cropper, the horse rolling right over me. In the evening Em, West, Al & myself sailed down to Matinnicock Pt,[31] where we met Nell who was sailing with the two Haddons, Doug. Robinson and Percy King—all good fellows. Pretty "Little Jane T." has arrived.

Friday July 4

We all spent the day together, sailing, playing lawn tennis, jumping our horses &c.

Saturday July 5

In the morning took a long ride with Emlen, teaching our horses how to jump, then rowed round Hog Island with West. Spent the afternoon with the whole party, playing lawn tennis &c. In the evening we all (about 20 fellows & girls, matrons &c) went out for a moonlight sail; coming home, we danced, sang, told stories &c. I am leading the most delightful life a fellow well could.

---

31. Also spelled Matinecock.

Sunday July 6

Communion Sunday. I like our simple Presbyterian form for the service so much, it always makes me think—and I generally do not do very much thinking on serious subjects.

Monday July 7

Went up to spend the night at the Dodges (I shall return tomorrow night). I like and respect both Earl and Cleave very much.[32] Went out driving, visiting our old places at Mosholu and Riverdale. Saw the two Oyne boys.

Wednesday July 9

Rowed round Loyds neck (16 miles). I am now getting into beautiful condition, and am deep brown from the waist up. In the afternoons after Nell has come up from the city I play lawn tennis, wrestle, and swim with him. I spend the whole time out in the open air; and at night am always tired enough to sleep like a top. Naturally I am in magnificent health and spirits.

Thursday July 10

Alfred stayed up for the day; we rowed around Centre Island, played lawn tennis, rode &c. I am now training my horse to go in harness. Gerty, Tiny & Virginia Roosevelt are staying with West. They are very sweet girls. I spent the evening over there, dancing most of the time.

Friday July 11

Emlen stayed up for the holiday, spending the day with me. We rowed round Centre Island, and led the usual active out of doors life, with at the same time a delightful sense of ease and absence of care that constitutes the chief charm of Oyster Bay to me.

Saturday July 12

Elliott stayed up for a holiday, so I spent the day with him, sailing, playing lawn tennis &c. Am teaching my horse to trot, as I think of putting him in a tilbury next winter.

Monday July 14

Rowed across the sound to Sheffield Island light and back, a distance of 30 miles. Going over there was no wind and the tide was with me, so I took but

---

32. Cleveland H. Dodge, Princeton 1879, was active in New York City business and politics and became an adviser to Woodrow Wilson. His brother William Earl Dodge III died in 1884.

2¾ hours; coming back I took 4½ hours, as there was a heavy head wind and I shipped a good deal of water. In the evening we danced, played charades &c.—there being several fellows and girls staying in the house.

Friday July 18

Alfred, West and I started off for a weeks cruise in the Meteor[33]—a 25 foot jib and mainsail open boat. Our provisions consisted of hard tack, canned meats & coffee.

We started in the afternoon at 2.30 with a light wind on our quarter, which failed us at 7.30 when we anchored off the mouth of the Saugatuck river. This trip we have sailors hammocks, which we sling over the cock pit—a great improvement on our former way of sleeping on the boards.

Saturday July 19

Weighed anchor at 5.30. The winds were not very heavy and dead ahead. During the course of the day I saw a great many terns and gulls and a few coots—also a stormy petrel. In the afternoon the wind died away altogether; and we came to anchor off the Thimble Islands.[34] About nine in the evening however it breezed up so from the southeast that we had to run under the lee of one of the islands for shelter.

Sunday July 20

Under way 5.30. I don't like sailing Sunday but we are short of water & must reach New London. The wind was about north east, so that we had to beat this whole time; it grew heavier and heavier, kicking up a big sea, so that off Bartletts reef we had our hands full to keep the boat going ahead and right side up; we took a great deal of water aboard. Reached New London 7 p.m.

Monday July 21

In the morning we sailed round to the Chapins house where we took dinner; in the afternoon started back, against a strong S.W. wind; at sunset we put in to Saybrook harbour. Saw a shark or two and a good many porpoises—all serving as targets for our revolvers.

---

33. In 1902, the German Prince Henry visited the United States to take possession of the Kaiser's new yacht. In a ceremony at the shipbuilders' on Shooter's Island, New York, attended by Prince Henry and President Theodore Roosevelt, Roosevelt's daughter Alice christened the new yacht *Meteor*.

34. An archipelago of small islands off the Connecticut coast, southeast of Branford.

Tuesday July 22

At 5 a.m. we broke out of Saybrook; we had a great deal of difficulty getting out over the shoals at the mouth of the harbour, and through the tide rips, as there was a strong southwest wind and a big sea. It rained all the morning; at noon the breeze died away leaving a heavy sea running. At 7.30 we came to anchor under the lee of Charles Island.

Wednesday July 23

Under way 5.15; the winds were light and buffering and it was a dead calm from 9 till 6; so, though we worked well at the sweeps,[35] we did not reach Oyster Bay till 11.15.
Al & Doc are not only good friends but extremely pleasant companions. The trip has been a great success.

Saturday July 26

I am leading the most healthful, pleasant, out of doors life—driving, riding, rowing, sailing, swimming, walking & shooting all day long. Two days out of three one of the boys—Nell, Em, Al or West—stays up with me. I wish Johny [sic] Elliott were here. By Jove, these five are friends worth having.

In the evening we read, play whist or dance. A pretty little Miss Hale, a Philadelphian, is staying with Aunt Lizzie; I take her out rowing quite often.

Wednesday July 30

Nellie stayed up from town, and so I spent the day with him; we rowed round Loyds—15 miles, and virtually racing the whole way. As athletes we are about equal; he rows best; I run best; he can beat me sailing or swimming; I can beat him wrestling or boxing. I am best with the rifle, he with the shot gun, &c, &c, &c.

Friday August 1

Went out woodcock shooting with young Pendleton Cruger.[36] We tramped pretty steadily from 7 a.m. till 7 p.m., with pretty good success. He is a pretty good shot—I am not. It was very hot, and the covert[37] was frightful, making

---

35. Single oar, usually with an equal number of rowers on each side.

36. Possibly son of Steven Van Rensselaer Cruger of Bayville, Long Island, a New York lawyer active in Republican politics who ran for lieutenant governor in 1888.

37. Hunting term referring to the thicket that gives cover to game.

it very hard walking; but we were rather cooled by the nature of the ground, which necessitated our keeping wet from the waist down, in the mud holes, swamps, &c.

7 wood cock.

Monday August 4

Went out woodcock shooting with Cruger. We first shot through Fleets swamp, getting half a dozen; then went to Townsend's, where we killed two brace[38]; picked up a couple in the Beckman's; and then went to several little swamps and wet, boggy places, near Locust Valley, picking up two or three more birds. I really shot very well today—rather an unusual incident with me.

10 woodcock

Tuesday August 5

One of the prettiest girls in Oyster Bay, and one of the most charming, is Miss Emily Swan. I have had several very pleasant rows and rides with her.

Thursday August 7

Cruger and I went out in the skiff after snipe; rowing along the beaches, paddling and poling through the broad, shallow lagoons, and narrow, winding creeks of the marshes, and using the little lug sail when ever the wind favoured us. We had to make several portages. We came out of Loyds neck with the tide, which runs very rapidly out of the creek, so that we needed to do nothing but steer & shout.

8 snipe 1 heron

Monday August 11

I row about every day—either to Loyds neck or round Centre Island. If any of the boys stay up I generally play lawn tennis with them. I often take Motherling out walking, or Bysie or Pussie out rowing. I am teaching pretty Miss Emily Swan to play lawn tennis.

Thursday August 14

Went woodcock shooting with Cruger. The birds were moulting, however, and were very much scattered; moreover we shot badly; and so, though we tramped about all day, our bag was small.

---

38. Brace: two foxes, rabbits, or game birds.

Saturday August 16

My marks for last year arrived; my average is over 87%, which is higher than either of my first two years. I am more than satisfied with it. In Zoölogy and Political Economy I lead every body.[39]

In the afternoon, after Nell has arrived, I always play lawn tennis with him—after which we generally get a swim. My horse begins to go quite well in Harness. I shall keep a dogcart & sleigh next winter.

Sunday August 17

Every Sunday we have morning and evening prayers; I wish we could have them everyday.

Motherling is just too sweet and pretty for anything; and I doubt if there ever were too [sic] more lovely and unselfish girls than dear, noble Bysie, and darling Little Pussie. These three, and my best friend, old brother Nell, give me as happy a home as a man could possibly have.

Monday August 18

Tomorrow I leave for the Maine woods; shall stop a day or two at the Saltonstalls on the way. I have had a lovely summer so far—and am brown as a nut, and in capital training. The family, the cousins & everybody are just too sweet to me for anything.

I am thinking pretty seriously as to what I shall do when I leave College; I shall probably either pursue a scientific course, or else study law, preparatory to going into public life.

Tuesday August 19

Went to New York. I wonder if there could be two better guardians than Uncle Jim Roosevelt and Uncle Jimmie Gracie! I can't imagine it.

I dined at the University Club with Robinson, Haddon, Stratton, Sedgwick and Kingsford. We had a very jolly dinner; they are all capital fellows.

Wednesday August 20

Went on to Boston, and came out here to Chestnut Hill, where dear old Dick gave me the most hearty and enthusiastic greeting. Dined with Mrs. Lee. Then we drove over to the Whitneys, who were just so sweet and cordial as they

---

39. Final marks: Zoology (Natural History 3), 97; Political Economy (Philosophy 6), 89.

could be; Bessie looked very pretty, Rose, Rosy and Alice were staying there. Tomorrow is Ell's birthday, and we are going on a picnic, with a whole crowd of fellows and girls—the Guilds, Bacons, Sharps, Greens, Sears, Coolidges, Codmans &c.

Thursday August 21

At nine oclock a.m. Dick and I drove over to the Whitneys, and did not return till after midnight. I had a lovely day, sailing, walking, driving, dancing, playing lawn tennis &c. I really heartily enjoyed seeing dear, honest Rose, pretty little Rosy Lee, sweet Alice, and pretty Bessie again—especially Rose and Alice. The Whitneys are exceedingly hospitable and cordial.

Friday August 22

Drove over to Cambridge in the morning. Went in town to see the girls—Rose, Rosy and Alice—off to the Glades.[40] They wanted me very much to go down to stay a few days with them; and they were all so cordial, and Alice was so bewitchingly pretty that it was frightfully hard to refuse[41]; I took the night train for Mattawomkeag however, as I agreed to meet Emlen. Dined at the Union Club with Frank Lee.

Saturday August 23

Reached Mattawomkeag at 10 a.m. and drove over to Island Falls. With Dave Seawall. Emlen and Mr. Cutler[42] are here, and I shall make a short trip with them to Katahdin.[43]

Sunday August 24

Spent the day chiefly in preparations. I have 2 complete changes of clothes, & plenty of handkerchiefs & woolen socks. I dress in a flannel shirt & light, strong duck trousers & heavy underflannels; carry a heavy jacket & a blanket and have my necessaries in a small bag. I have taken both rifle & shot gun.

---

40. The Glades Club in Plymouth County was a favorite summer retreat of the Boston Brahmin.

41. The same day TR wrote his sister Corinne: "I am going to Maine this evening, which shows the greatest resolution on my part, for it has been awfully hard to resist going down to the Glades for a few days. To tell the truth the only reason I resisted was because it was perfectly impossible to communicate with Seawall, the telegraph not going to Island Falls. Even as it was, Alice was so bewitchingly pretty, and the Saltonstalls were so very cordial that I came near going in spite of everything." Morison, 22 August 1879, I, 40.

42. TR's old tutor who prepared him for Harvard's entrance exams.

43. Mount Katahdin, the highest mountain in Maine.

Monday August 25

Paddled with Emlen down to our old camping ground at the foot of the Lake, and back—about 28 miles. Hunted for partridges, but found none. Picked up a duck in the thoroughfares. Em & Arthur capital fellows for a trip of this kind—unselfish, good natured, and not minding a little fatigue & hardship.

1 wood duck

Tuesday August 26

Emlen, Arthur Cultler, Will Dow, Will Seawall & I started for Mt. Katahdin. Drove 23 miles; and then carried our packs about 10, when we went into camp. I carried about 45 lbs, including my gun & cartridges. Crossing a stream I lost one of my shoes; fortunately I had brought a pair of moccasins tied to my pack.

Wednesday August 27

Walked up to the head of Katahdin Lake where we camped. I get along very well with my pack. Killed 4 ducks in a logan, after a rather neat stable; also picked up a couple of partridges. We caught a few trout. Black flies are pretty bad; but they do not bother us at night; It is very pleasant in the evenings, with the roaring logs of the camp fire.

20 ruffed grouse 7 wood cock 5 black ducks

Thursday August 28

After lunch we started for Katahdin; (before I had tramped about 5 miles after partridges). We caught about 100 trout at Sandy brook; then got lost; and after tramping through frightful ground till after dark camped out by a small water hole; wet, tired and hungry—but happy. There are plenty of fresh tracks of both bear & caribou, but we saw nothing living except the usual woodpeckers, chickadees, jays, &c &c.

Friday August 29

Started before daybreak, walking straight through the woods, & then up Katahdin; it was very difficult walking, & both Emlen & Arthur gave out before reaching the summit, the view from which was beautiful. I find I can endure fatigue & hardship pretty nearly as well as these lumbermen. Coming back we followed a spotted trail[44] which sometimes set at fault even the two skilled backwoodsman [sic]. Reached our camp at Katahdin lake about dark, having caught about 60 trout. It is raining & we are all soaked through but in excellent health and spirits.

---

44. Spotted trail: a path through the woods marked only by ax marks on trees.

Saturday August 30

In the morning walked half way round the lake but saw nothing; there are very few partridges and few ducks round here & larger game is not scarce, but almost impossible to get at. In the afternoon walked some distance down beside Sandy Brook; coming home killed a duck in Moose Pond. Trout of small size are very plentiful.

1 black duck

Sunday August 31

Loafed about camp, cleaning guns, mending clothes, bathing in the lake &c. You get pretty dirty in camp. Black flies have been very numerous this trip, and have been a great annoyance to the others; funnily enough they do not bother me very much. There are plenty of fish round here; game is very scarce; but I am enjoying myself exceedingly.

Monday September 1

Was up before sunrise and took a trip round some barrens and bogs; crippled a duck in a logan, but it crawled off among the rushes. In the afternoon we shouldered our packs, broke camp & started for Island Falls. After crossing the Wissaticook went into camp for the night. Am in beautiful condition & find I can walk, wrestle & shoot with most of the lumbermen.

Tuesday September 2

Started in good season, walking out to the East Branch of the Penobscot, which we crossed, & then drove to Island Falls. I have enjoyed the trip exceedingly; the boys are most pleasant companions.

Wednesday September 3

Spent the afternoon driving about in a buckboard looking for partridges; but saw none.

Thursday September 4

Spent the day preparing for my Munsungun[45] trip; I shall go in a canoe, alone with Seawall. For provisions I took pork and hardtack & some flour; we have a shelter tent, two blankets & some cooking utensils; & one complete change of clothing each. I take 50 cartridges for the rifle and 100 for the shotgun. I shall only use moccasins.

---

45. Munsungan and Little Munsungan Lakes, Maine. The "upper one" TR will refer to is Chase Lake.

Friday September 5

Started at 5 a.m. in a rough wagon to drive to the Oxbow of the Aroostook River—46 miles distant. We reached it 6 p.m. and are staying in a regular backwoods house—fare and sleeping accommodations being both primitive to a degree. I killed a spruce partridge and a red tailed hawk, from the wagon. The rout [sic] all day long was through a sparsely settled, thickly wooded country & for about 3 miles through a dreary waste of burnt land.

1 Canada Grouse

Saturday September 6

Started in fair season in a pirogue or dugout. It stands rough work better than a birch canoe. We went about 20 miles up the Aroostook, paddling sometimes, but poleing [sic] most of the way. The scenery is very beautiful and wild; I saw no trace of man—but also no trace of game. Trout are plenty however. Pitched camp before dark, to cook the bread, trout & partridge. Black flies, mosquitoes & midges pretty plentiful; I don't mind them much.

Sunday September 7

We started as usual, as there was no use of laying up; but I compromised by not shooting or fishing. We poled up the Aroostook till lunch time, when we were near the mouth of the Munsungun; up this we had to wade, dragging our boats—the water now up to our ankles, now to our hips. It was heavy work; moreover it was raining heavily; and towards dusk we pitched camp, drenched through & tired out. Midges bad.

Monday September 8

Rained hard all day. We started early; for several hours it was rapid, shoal water, through which we waded, dragging the heavy dugout over the rocks and shallows; then we got into deeper, dead water, but this was nearly as bad owing to the beaver dams and log jams which we had to cut through or pull round. There were some falls we had to get up, taking everything out of the boat; then we poled up through more dead water; then paddled through the lower Munsungun Lake, & halfway up the middle one, where we camped. Tired out, & wet through, hungry & cold—but am having a lovely time. But no trace of game.

Tuesday September 9

Rained all day; but we paddled up the middle lake and then walked (through most frightful ground) to the head of the upper one.[46] On the way I saw a

---

46. Chase Lake

few partridges; an old moose track; a recent bear track; and a few old signs of deer and caribou. On the lake are a few loons and fish ducks. As game is so scarce I shall go right back to Island Falls, instead of staying up here, as I had intended. Am wet through, as usual, and rather tired, but, although the work is very hard, I am enjoying the trip greatly.

3 ruffed grouse

Wednesday September 10

Rose before daybreak & started before sunrise, down the lake. Paddled through the lake and dead water, running the falls, then waded down through the Munsungun quick water, lunching where we camped Sunday night; then we poled, (making fine time down the swift waters and only occasionally having to get out and wade) until early in the afternoon we reached our Saturday camp where we are now. I am very fond of the evenings round the camp fire, beneath the shelter tent.

Thursday September 11

Started in fair season, paddling down stream in great style; on the way I shot a wood duck. At the Oxbow we disembarked and walked about 15 miles (half of the way across country) to a rough backwoods house, where we are now. Fare pretty rough, but plenty of good milk, and we have shot our own meat—as, besides the duck, I killed a rabbit and a partridge on the way.

1 red rabbit   1 wood duck   1 ruffed grouse

Friday September 12

Walked off through the woods to a pond in a cranberry bog, and back; in all rather over 20 miles. Shot a duck in the pond and picked up 2 partridge and a duck on the way. The walking was pretty good.

1 black duck   2 ruffed grouse

Saturday September 13

Walked down to Island Falls through the woods—about 25 miles. The walking was pretty good, the scenery beautiful—for besides the forests, grand enough in themselves, we passed several waterfalls in deep ravines—and I shot several partridges. Wore one of my moccasins almost out, which made me rather footsore.

5 ruffed grouse

Sunday September 14

Went to "church," read my bible, and spent the day shaving, bathing and getting things ready for a new expedition. I always like these backwoods meeting houses; and I don't know a better or more intelligent race of men than these shrewd, plucky, honest Yankees—all of them hunters, lumbermen or small farmers.

Monday September 15

Rained all day, so did not start.

Tuesday September 16

Started with Bill, in a rough wagon with a rougher horse; the roads were rougher still; and the cabin we are now staying in, after going about 30 miles, is roughest of all.

Wednesday September 17

Walked about 23 miles on through the woods, to a clearing kept by a man named Littlefield—where we were very well treated. Shot one spruce partridge in a low spruce thicket; and another in a tamarack swamp.

2 spruce Grouse

Thursday September 18

Walked back through the woods to where we had left our horse, killing 4 partridges; then drove to Island Falls, shooting a pigeon from the wagon. As usual, it rained; the weather has been awful, for the last two weeks; but I am enjoying myself exceedingly, am in superb health, and as tough as a pine knot.

4 Birch Grouse   1 Pigeon

Friday September 19

Walked down through the woods to the foot of Mattawonkeag Lake where we are now.

Saturday September 20

Walked about 20 miles through the woods; killed 2 partridges on a hemlock ridge or "horseback," and afterwards found a flock of 8 on an "internal," of which I killed 7.

In the afternoon we practiced with our rifles; I shot very well, but not as well as Dow and Seawall.

9 ruffed grouse

Sunday September 21

Paddled up to Island Falls, to stay over night. Packed up for good, as I start tomorrow. A porcupine blundered into camp, and was ignominiously expelled with the tin dipper. What glorious fun I am having this year! No fellow ever had a better time than I have. And my life has such absurd contrasts. At one time I live in the height of luxury; and then for a month will undergo really severe toil and hardship—and I enjoy both extremes almost equally.

Monday September 22

Seawall, Dow & I started in a birch[47] down the Mattawomkeag. We paddled down stream about 10 miles below the Lake, landing several times to look for partridges. Dow and I, by making a circuit through the woods, ambushed a flock of fish ducks, of which I killed several; I had several very long shots at loons and cranes with the rifle, but missed them. I shall be very sorry to end this trip; and yet how I shall enjoy getting back to Harvard.

3 Merganser

Tuesday September 23

Started tolerably late, paddling down to below Wytipitlock, and then camping. We had great fun with ducks in the stream and pigeons along the banks, Dow killing several; but for some reason or other I shot badly, missing most of my birds. However I redeemed this by making some good shots with the rifle at Hawks and owls. Shot a muskrat; both it & the fish ducks were very good eating!

1 merganser   1 Dipper duck   1 pigeon

Wednesday September 24

Paddled down through the dead water, about 12 miles, to Kingman, where I took the train for Boston. I was really sorry to leave both Seawall and Dow; I have had capital fun this trip, and have passed as pleasant a month as a fellow could. Am feeling as strong as a bull.

By Jove, it sometimes seems as if I were having too happy a time, to have it last. I enjoy every moment I live, almost.

Thursday September 25

It is ever so pleasant to get back again among all the fellows, who greeted me with uproarious cordiality. I am keeping my horse and dogcart at Pikes Stable; I have really got a very stylish turnout. I intend to have lovely fun this winter.

---

47. Lightweight birch bark canoe, favored by Native Americans.

Friday September 26

Drove Dick over to Chestnut Hill; they were all so heartily glad to see me that I felt as if I had come home.

Saturday September 27

Drove Harry Chapin over to a lawn tennis party at Minot Welds; Rose, Rosy, Alice, the two Miss Lanes, Miss Bacon &c were there. In the evening went out to Chestnut Hill; to pass Sunday with the Saltonstalls. My cart is the greatest success of the season.

I brought Phil a gun, Cotty some soldiers, a gold pin for Rose and a silver one for Mamie.

Sunday September 28

I am having a lovely time. Dear Mr. And Mrs. Saltonstall are just too sweet for anything, and the girls are as lovely as ever.

In the afternoon took Rose out walking.

Monday September 29

From 8.30 till 10 I study Italian. 10–11; Italian Recitation. 11–2 study Political Economy. 2–3, Pol. Econ. Recitation. 6 hours work. I am going to give an abstract of my studies each day this week—not counting thesis &c. I am perfectly delighted with the horse and cart; it is as swell a turnout as I know.

Tuesday September 30

9–1, work at zoölogy course in the Museum. 2–5, Field work in Geology. 8–9 study Political economy. 8 hours. Called on the Lanes in the evening; they both are just as sweet as they can be, and Miss Lulu is too pretty for anything.

Wednesday October 1

8.30–10 study Italian. 10–11 Recite Italian. 11–12 Study Pol. Econ. 12–1 Geology Lecture. 2–3 Pol. Econ. Recitation. 6 hours work.

About every afternoon I go out in the cart, generally taking some fellow with me; unless I go visiting.

Of all the fellows here, Dick Saltonstall is my most intimate friend, (Harry Shaw coming next?) then Minot Weld and Harry Chapin & John Tebbettss &c. Old Dick I place on a par with the Roosevelts.

Thursday October 2

8½–1, Zoology Course. 1.30–3.00 Study Pol. Econ. 6 hours.

Dick and I drove over in my dog cart to the Whitneys, where we passed a very pleasant evening. The drive home was delightful, there being a most beautiful full moon.

Friday October 3

8.30–10.00, study Italian. 10–11, Recite Italian. 11–1, study Pol. Econ. 12–1, Geology Lecture. 2–3 Pol. Econ, Recitation. 6 hours work.

Drove over to the Saltonstalls where I took dinner; pretty Rosy Lee was there, also Mary Tuckerman and a most charming girl, Harriet Lawrence.

Saturday October 4

9–11 Zoology. 11–1 Review Geology. 4 hours work. In all I work 36 hours a week—generally a little more.

Took Minot out for a long drive in my cart. I shall enjoy this "cart" more than I have anything yet.

In the evening we had a great spree up in the Club—so I did not get to bed till awfully late.

Sunday October 5

In the afternoon walked in town with Harry Chapin to call on the Hoopers.

Recommenced our usual Sunday morning Porcellian breakfast.

Wednesday October 8

I go out in my cart every afternoon; the drives round here are beautiful, and my horse really trots very fast.

Am training for running; go about a mile every day at a fast rate—say 5.15

Thursday October 9

Drove over with Dick to call at Chestnut Hill, but only stayed a very short time, as I had to get back to go to the theatre with Harry Shaw.

Friday October 10

I have my hands altogether too full of society work, being Librarian of the Porcellian, Secretary of the Pudding, Treasurer of the O.K., Vice President of the Nat. Hist. Soc., & President of the A.D.O., Editor of the Advocate.

The evenings I generally spend in the Club, playing whist or billiards, often ending off with a little supper.

Saturday October 11

Had a great Porc. Supper; Dick S. and Jack Tebbets came into the club. The former slept in my room—to the great detriment thereof, Dick being a most obstreperous man when "sprung."

Sunday October 12

Dick being decidedly under the weather from last nights spree, I drove him over to Chestnut Hill, after breakfasting in the Porc. about 11 oclock. I took tea at the Saltonstalls, and went out walking with Rosy Lee; and with Rose afterwards.

Monday October 13

Drove Jack Tebbetts over to call on the Miss Bacons. The horse really trots very well and the cart rides as easily as a cradle.[48]

Thursday October 16

Dick and I took the two Miss Lanes to call on the Chinese Professor and had a most amusing time.

Friday October 17

Drove Minot Weld home, calling on George Minot and stopping at the Saltonstalls for a minute to congratulate Mamie on her birthday.

Saturday October 18

Spent the morning playing tennis with the Miss Lanes. In the afternoon I drove Harry Guild over in my cart to his house, to spend Sunday. I like the Guilds very much.

Sunday October 19

Walked home from Church with the Miss Bacons; in the afternoon drove over to the Whitneys.

Monday October 20

The drive home from the Guilds was just perfection; it was a divine morning and the little horse went like Sancho.

---

48. The same day TR wrote his sister Anna: "My studies this year have been tolerably difficult, but interesting. The other day I found out my average for the three years—82%. I stand 19th in the class, which began with 230 fellows. Only one gentleman stands ahead of me." Morison, 13 October 1879, I, 41–42.

In the afternoon drove Van R. over to the Saltonstalls; we went out walking with the two girls.

Wednesday October 22

Harry Shaw and I gave an opera party to Mr. and Mrs. Saltonstall, Rose and Alice. I drove him over to the Saltonstalls to dinner. We did not get out, after the Opera, till towards 12; the horse was very restive at starting, and finally reared and fell, pitching Harry and me out of the cart. Nothing was hurt however.

Thursday October 23

Took Charley Morgan out driving.

The evenings I generally spend playing whist in the club; unless we make up a theatre party. As I am rather apt to end up with a little supper, I find I do'n't get to bed very early.

Friday October 24

Drove Minot Weld over to his house; the horse goes well except that he plunges and rears when starting, and he sometimes shys [sic].

Took the night boat for New York.

Saturday October 25

Breakfasted and lunched at Aunt Lizzie's; they are just too sweet to me for anything.
Went out to Oyster Bay in the afternoon. Aunt Annie is staying with us. It is perfectly lovely to see all the family again; and they are too lovely for anything.

Sunday October 26

Passed the usual dear old Oyster Bay Sunday; Family Prayers, late breakfast, Church, taking a long walk in the afternoon, and after late tea spending most of the evening in singing hymns.

Monday October 27

My 21st birthday. Uncle Jim, Aunt Lizzie, Aunt Annie, Doc, Em & Al came out to stay with us. In the evening a good many girls including pretty Emily Swan came to tea, and we had great fun dancing, playing charades &c &c. My presents were very valuable, and all are just too lovely to me for anything. I have had so much happiness in my life so far that I feel, no matter what sorrows come, the joys will have overbalanced them. And yet on this I can not help thinking with sadness about Father, my best and most loved and revered friend; may God help me to live as he would have wished.

Tuesday October 28

Spent the day playing tennis, walking and rowing.

Wednesday October 29

Early in the morning started out for a 12 hour tramp with dog and gun. I had pretty good luck in the morning with rabbit and wood cock; in the afternoon I found a large covey of quail in a thick wood & I followed them till after moonrise, but the birds were wild, the covert—a dense cat briar jungle which scratched my hands and arms till my shirt became soaked with blood—was thick, and I shot badly, so I only killed two.

1 gray squirrel   2 gray rabbit   3 wood cock   2 quail

Thursday October 30

Went out sailing in the sound for ducks. There were but few birds, and these were very shy; the wind, moreover, blew so that with the jib bobbed and three reefs in the main sail it was all I could do to keep the clumsy old fish boat going; so I did not get a shot. In the bay I found a stray loon who succumbed after a great deal of powder had been wasted.

1 loon

Friday October 31

Took an old gunner, "Ramson," and drove off to an old farm house about eight miles off; spent six or seven hours walking through the woods and stubble fields. The quail were plenty; but scattered easily and had to be whistled together.

In the evening went to a very pleasant "All Hallow Eve" party at the Swans, where we had great fun, going through the canonical rites and dancing besides.

2 rabbit   3 wood cock   9 quail

Saturday November 1

Went out shooting, spending the whole day tramping about through the woods and fields. Game was plenty but I shot badly.

This week it has been superb, clear, cool autumn weather; I have enjoyed the shooting very much; and the evenings too, spent in the cozy parlor, by the bright wood fire, reading or playing whist with darling mother and the two sweet girls.

Dear old Nell came up this evening, how I wish we could be more together.

2 squirrel   3 rabbit   5 quail

Sunday November 2

In the afternoon I left Oyster Bay with much reluctance and came in to New York to spend the night at Uncle Jim's. In the evening went to call on the Lees, who are staying here; I can do nothing for them myself, but the Roosevelts have come up to time nobly, and they have sprees on hand for every evening next week.

Monday November 3

Went on to Boston.

Tuesday November 4

Started studying with a will; by the end of this week I shall make up all I have lost.

Wednesday November 5

Drove Harry Shaw over to the Lymans, afterwards dined at the Saltonstalls.

Saturday November 8

Drove over to the Saltonstalls in the morning, and thence over to the Whitneys, where I took dinner and had an exceedingly pleasant time; Miss Bessie I like more and more. I then drove over to Harry Minots where I am going to spend the night. Passed the evening playing whist and billiards with the Minot, Whitney and Guild boys.

Sunday November 9

Drove back to Cambridge in time for my Sunday School. Passed the evening very pleasantly with pretty Lulu Lane.

Monday November 10

Drove over in the afternoon to the Lees where I dined and spent a very pleasant evening, not returning till after eleven.

The horse and cart go beautifully.

Wednesday November 12

Drove Minot Weld over to the Saltonstalls; we went out walking with Rosy and Rose.

I spend most of my spare time in Cambridge in the club; and I also go a good deal to the A.D.O, where the fellows are very pleasant and intellectual—a rare thing with college boys. I have been off on a great many sprees this year, and have been studying well and keeping late hours; thanks to the magnificent condition I am in after the summer I seem to stand it pretty well.

Friday November 14

Went on to New York to see our football team play Princeton. Jack Tebbets and Harry Chapin are going to stay with me till Monday when we will all return with Bamie & Conie who are going to spend a week at Chestnut Hill.

Saturday November 15

Our team was beaten. I called on Grace Potter, who is just as sweet as ever and dear pretty little Fanny Smith dined with us. Afterwards we went to the Theatre, then took a supper at Delmonicoes[49] and stayed up till all hours in the Harvard Club where a lot of fellows were singing &c.

Sunday November 16

Spent the usual dear old Sunday. The family are delighted with Jack. Lunched with Aunt Annie. Had a most delightful call on Edith Carow, she is the most cultivated, best read girl I know.

Monday November 17

Came on to Boston with the girls. Class meeting at night.

Tuesday November 18

Rainy; so took buggy with Dick and drove over to the Lees to dinner; a good many fellows came in afterwards and we had the jolliest kind of a time, dancing and talking. It seems very natural to have the girls at Chestnut Hill. Just before starting back Dick took a glass of brandy which rather set him up so that he insisted on galloping the horse, which of course ran way 4 or 5 times; I nearly died laughing.

Wednesday November 19

Drove Jack Tebbetts over to the Lees where we took dinner and spent the evening as usual, dancing and playing games.

---

49. A New York gustatory landmark since 1837, when it was rebuilt at the corner of William and Beaver Street following the great fire of 1835. Delmonico's was the first truly "haute cuisine" French restaurant in New York. For the rest of his life TR was a frequent patron, including as guest of honor for several political dinners.

Thursday November 20
Snowing heavily; Dick & I drove over to the Saltonstalls for dinner.

Friday November 21
Dined at the Lawrences, passing a very pleasant evening.

Saturday November 22
Gave a lunch party of 34 persons up in the Porcellian to Bamie and Corinne. It was the greatest success imaginable.

[seating chart in TR's hand]

<pre>
                       Mr. Whitney
Mrs. Saltonstall ┌─────────────────┐ Mrs. Lee
       Mr. Lane   │   │ Mr. Saltonstall
     Minot Weld   │   │ Bamie Roosevelt
     Nana Rotch   │   │ Otho Williams
  Harcourt Amory │   │ Harriet Lawrence
       Rosy Lee   │   │ George Silsbee
     Jim Parker   │   │ Jenny Hooper
  Rose Saltonstall│   │ Jack Tebbetts
   Dick Trimble   │   │ Dick Saltonstall
     Kitty Lane   │   │ Bessie Whitney
  Charley Morgan │   │ George Griswold
    Julia Bacon   │   │ Nellie Bacon
  Edmund Baylies │   │ Harry Shaw
      Lulu Lane   │   │ Corinne Roosevelt
  Van Rensselaer │   │ Emmons Blaine
      Alice Lee   └─────────────────┘ Bessie Hooper
                        Roosevelt
</pre>

Everything went off to perfection; the dinner was capital, the flowers very pretty and we had great fun with the toasts and speeches. Mr. Whitney and Mr. Saltonstall were especially funny; all the girls looked extremely pretty, the wine was good, and the fellows all gentlemen.

In the evening drove over to the Minots to a little party.

Sunday November 23

Breakfasted in the Club; drove over to Chestnut Hill, and came back to teach Sunday School.

The two girls go back tomorrow. It has been very pleasant to have them on here, and they have enjoyed themselves greatly.

Wednesday November 26

Drove over in the cart to take lunch at the Lees; afterwards drove pretty Rosy to a tennis party at the Lawrences. Had a lovely drive afterwards with her.

I then took up my abode at the Saltonstalls where I intend to stay till Sunday. I am now most thoroughly and happily at home here, and I really love every member of the family. We played whist in the evening.

Thursday November 27

I took dear, honest, funny Rose out for a drive in the dog cart; then I went skating with Phil; at four oclock I went to the Lees to the Thanksgiving dinner. Afterwards we had great fun, playing games, dancing & acting charades.

Friday November 28

I took a long ride in the cart with Alice; got caught in the rain and had to borrow an umbrella from a strange house. In the afternoon went out for a long walk with Alice and Rose, who were just as funny as they could be, making me buy candy &c.

In the evening I stayed up till all hours with dear old Mr. Saltonstall, talking poetry and theology, while sweet Mrs. S at first dozed in a chair and then went to bed.

Saturday November 29

Rainy; so I spent the morning in the house reading, dancing with Mamie & Hattie and telling stories to Phil and Cotty. After lunch went out walking with Ell Whitney, Rose and Alice. Drove over to call on Miss Julia Bacon. Spent the evening at the Lees, dancing and playing whist.

Sunday November 30

After Church I left the Hill with the deepest regret that the lovely five days were over, and drove back to Cambridge. After Sunday School I went in to the Whitneys, where I took tea and spent a most pleasant evening.

Tuesday December 2

Went to a party at the Wares; it was Alice's and Rose's coming out party and I was much amused at seeing all the buds.

Wednesday December 3

Had a little supper up in the Porc.

Thursday December 4

Drove Jack Tebbetts and Minot Weld over to the latter's house, where we stay tonight. After dinner went to a party at the Grays, which was very pleasant.

Friday December 5

Drove back to Cambridge in the morning; in the afternoon drove over to the Lees to dinner. Afterwards drove Frank Lee into Boston.

Saturday December 6

In the morning drove over to Minot Welds where I spent most of the day. Dined in Boston at Harry Shaws, afterwards going to a commerce party at his cousins; where I passed a very pleasant evening with a pretty Miss Silsbee.

I enjoy my horse and cart more and more every day. I am afraid going out will tire me somewhat, as I get up every morning at 7.15 no matter how late I have been up—except Saturday and Sunday.

Sunday December 7

My Sunday School is getting along swimmingly. I took tea with the Miss Lanes and passed a very pleasant evening.

Monday December 8

After, as usual, playing whist in the Club (Jack, Dick, Minot and I do so every night) we all went off on a spree, and had great fun.

Tuesday December 9

Dined with Emmons Blaine at Harry Shaws; later went to a great party at the Amory's.

Wednesday December 10

Dined at the Lanes. They have been very sweet to me, and I like them both very much, especially pretty Miss Lulu.

Thursday December 11

Went in to the first Harvard assembly; I had lovely fun, dancing with Rosy Lee, who looked as pretty as a picture. When we came out to Harvard we had a little "Symposium."

Saturday December 13

Ran 3 miles (slowly, in 21 m) in the morning. After lunch drove Jack and Dick over in the cart to Chestnut Hill. Came back to Cambridge and went in town with Harry Chapin, dining at Youngs and going to the Theatre afterwards.

Sunday December 14

Breakfasted in the Porc as usual. After Sunday School I drove Harry Chapin over to Minot's; where we took tea. Howard Townsend is passing Sunday with him.

Monday December 15

In afternoon drove Jack T. into Boston, where we called on Mrs. Shaw & Mrs. Whitney. In the evening went to the first Papanti Hall party[50] and had a lovely time, dancing with pretty Nan Rotch.

Van Rennsaeler is engaged to Luly Lane! I am very glad of it. They are perfectly radiant. He is a very good fellow, and she an exceedingly sweet girl.

Tuesday December 16

Dined at the Armory's; afterwards went to see a very funny play at the Gaiety,[51] with Harry Chapin and John Tebbetts.

Wednesday December 17

Drove Tom Lee over to the Saltonstalls. Pudding Theatricals in the evening, very good.

Thursday December 18

Took Dick out driving; called on the Lanes and Rotches. In the evening we had a "champagne supper" or rather dinner, and afterwards went up to the Δ.K.E theatricals which were the best I have ever seen; then finished the evening with a punch in the Club. Had an awfully jolly evening.

---

50. Papanti's was a European dance studio in Boston. As author John Phillips Marquand had his character George Apley recount of Papanti's: "Many a romance had its inception in this atmosphere, particularly at the more grown-up series of evening dances we attended later."

51. The comedy "The Tourists in the Pullman Palace Car."

Friday December 19

In the evening took the night boat for New York, with Harry Chapin.

Saturday December 20

It is perfectly delightful to see all the family again.

Sunday December 21

Spent the day, after Church, with the Roosevelts; Doc spends the night with us.

Monday December 22

In the evening Ike Iselin[52] gave me a dinner; there were present (besides Nell) Harold Haddon, Doug Robinson, Bob Sedgwick, Sydney Stratton and Archie Russell—all very good fellows. We had capital fun.

Tuesday December 23

Snowed hard; sleighing excellent. In afternoon Nell and I drove up in a cutter to Jerome Park, where we had a very cosy little dinner; coming home by moonlight towards ten. Then I went to the University Club, to a supper given by the Harvard Glee Club.

Wednesday December 24

Spent the day calling on various friends—among them some very pretty girls, as Annie Murray, Emily Post, the two Miss Kanes the two Miss Potters, Edith Carow, Fanny Smith, Nellie Phelps and Lizzie Moran.

Thursday December 25

Xmas. Lovely time. Received beautiful presents. Nell and I superintended the Newsboys dinner—poor little wretches. The usual Xmas Family dinner was as pleasant as it could be—every Roosevelt present.

Friday December 26

Took lunch with Edith. In the evening Alice, Rosy, Rose, Dick, Harry Shaw & Ell Whitney arrived to spend a week with us.

Saturday December 27

Showed the boys around town in the day. In the afternoon went to a little party at Aunt Annie's.

---

52. Possibly Columbus O'Donnell Iselin, son of the New York banker Adrian Iselin.

Sunday December 28

Spent the afternoon at the Newsboys Lodging house.

It is perfectly lovely, having the dear, sweet Chestnut Hillers with us;—and so natural.

Monday December 29

Jack Kingsford, Ell Whitney & myself showed the three Chestnut Hill girls about town in the morning; we all lunched at West and Hilly's; in the evening Aunt Lizzie gave us a theatre party, and we had an uproariously jolly time.

Tuesday December 30

We all went to an entertainment at the music hall in the afternoon; in the evening went to a very pleasant dinner at Mrs. Haddons; Sat between her and Rosy.

Wednesday December 31

Drove Rose round the park in a buggy; took Alice out walking; Alfred gave the three men & myself a lunch in the down town club; in the evening we had a small party, and danced the old year out and drank the new year in.

GAME BAG
[written across two adjacent pages]

	Total	1874	1875	1876	1877	1878	1879
Raccoon	1						1
Deer	2				1		1
Red Hare	5					1	4
Gray Hare	21	2				8	11
Gray Squirrel	19	3	4	2	4	3	3
Ruffed Grouse	50	2	2		2	16	28
Canada	7				1	1	5
Quail	23			1		6	16
Woodcock	41			1		14	26
Snipe	1	1					
Plover &c.	16		2	3	6	5	
Sandpiper &c.	40		6	6	12	8	8
Wild pigeon	5		2			1	2
Carolina dove	3					3	
Ducks	37	2	4	1	10	8	12
Herons	32	7	4	6	10	4	1
Loons	4		2			1	1
	307	17	26	20	46	79	119

Summary of Cash Account 1879

	Received	Paid
Jan.	550.00	400.65
Feb.		135.00
Mar.		14.35
Apr.	735.00	679.27
May		55.73
June	150.00	148.65
July	109.00	106.00
Aug.	671.15	620.88
Sept.	300.00	290.77
Oct.		40.00
Nov.	383.00	330.50
Dec.	1220.00	1292.00
	4113.80	4113.80

Summary spent in

	1878	1877
Jan.	198.50	177.00
Feb.	96.30	82.50
Mar.	304.65	147.50
Apr.	418.10	188.00
May	179.40	122.00
June	137.50	300.00
July	125.00	7.00
Aug.	57.00	32.00
Sept.	33.00	11.00
Oct.	233.00	303.25
Nov.	135.75	139.75
Dec.	131.25	232.00
	2049.45	1742.00

Bills Payable

	1878	1877	1879
Dress	373.45	320.00	585.80
Room	220.75	307.35	367.50
Board	305.50	296.00	288.00
Education	185.80	220.00	320.80
Washing	50.00	50.00	50.00
Charity	147.00	29.00	224.00
Coal &c	60.60	16.25	21.96
Travelling [sic]	129.25	36.00	93.23

Science	57.50	76.75	15.00
Subscriptions	133.75	106.50	401.00
Sporting	142.10	27.00	65.84
Athletics	30.00	50.50	20.00
Presents	80.00	42.00	960.22
Small Change	19.30	13.00	14.45
Amusements	32.75	64.00	319.50
Expressage	15.75	9.00	18.20
Sundries	65.95	58.65	348.30
	2049.45	1742.00	4113.80
Outside Expenditures (see next page)	252.85	158.00	1092.99
	2302.30	1900.00	5206.59

Expenditures in addition to my regular allowance.

	1877	1878	1879
Travelling	158.00	100.00	250.00
Stable		125.00	652.79
Clothes &c		27.85	
Wedding Presents & clothes			190.00

Married

Volume IV (1880)

The year began with the happiest moment of Roosevelt's life so far: on January 25 eighteen-year-old Alice Lee consented to marry him. Roosevelt traveled to New York to tell his astonished family, and negotiated with Alice's parents to allow a fall wedding. On February 14 he announced his engagement at the Porcellian, an occasion to buy his chums champagne. Now in his final semester at Harvard, Roosevelt spent about five days a week at Chestnut Hill to be close to Alice. He was taking a light course load of only five classes—as opposed to eight or even nine in previous years—including two in his area of expertise, natural history. This allowed him to skip classes and cram when needed. "By way of change spent the day in Cambridge, in the Library," Roosevelt wrote on March 25, "writing up my thesis in political economy." The next day he walked the six miles to spend the night at Dick Saltonstall's, spending the evening with Alice.

At about this time he made the decision to enter law school the following year, abandoning his youthful dream of being a natural scientist. As his accounts indicated, each year he was spending increasingly less time and money on "science." In 1880 he spent a mere forty-five cents, down from almost sixty dollars two years before. The example of his father perhaps spurred Roosevelt to lead a life more engaged with social and political problems, rather than the solitary life of an observer of wildlife. Socializing with the Boston Brahmin elite in their mansions—as well as his own love of luxury—also helped make up his mind. Finally, it was also unlikely that Boston banker George Lee would agree to give his daughter away to a scientist with meager means of support. Roosevelt seemed to understand that. In February when he wrote old friend Hal Minot about his engagement to Alice, he said, "I have been in love with her for nearly two years now; and have made everything subordinate to winning her; so you can perhaps understand a change in my ideas as regards science &c."[1]

Roosevelt graduated from Harvard on June 30. Alice, her sister Rosie, and cousin Rose Saltonstall returned with Roosevelt to Oyster Bay for a short visit. The couple spent their time on walks and drives, but Roosevelt was not yet able to get Alice into the rowboat. When the girls returned to Chestnut Hill, Roosevelt departed for a last trip to the Maine woods. He and brother Elliott followed this trip with a further hunting trip out West, straddling the border between Minnesota and the Dakota Territory. Only later trips were spent much farther west, in the Badlands and the Elkhorn Mountains. Still, there is little evidence that Roosevelt was very enamored of the West during this first visit. True, he was sick during much of it and longed daily for his sweet Alice. Moreover the trip was marred by an almost comical succession of misadventures. He broke both his guns, was bitten by a snake, and was thrown from a wagon, landing on his head. Mostly, Roosevelt loved the hunting and the time spent with his brother. He recorded a "game bag" of 203 kills.

Returning to the East in late September meant enrolling in Columbia Law School and preparing for the October 27 wedding. Roosevelt's marriage meant a windfall for New York jewelers, as the groom spent a hefty $2500 on gifts for Alice, including a ruby bracelet and sapphire ring. Even Roosevelt seemed to understand he was spending too much money: his 1880 expenditures came to $8000, up from $5200 the year before, and three and half times his 1878 spending. After all, Roosevelt planned to be a student for the time being. "I have been spending money like water for these last two years," Roosevelt noted, but promised to himself to economize after the wedding. This was a promise Roosevelt found very difficult to keep.

The couple was married on October 27, Roosevelt's twenty-second birthday. Because of his law classes the newlyweds delayed taking their European honeymoon until the following year, and instead headed to Oyster Bay for a solitary two weeks. In a nice snapshot of Gilded Age life among the wealthy, Roosevelt observed, "We are alone in the house, with two servants and a groom." Alice and Roosevelt spent their time on walks, drives, tennis, and long rows around Center Island. On November 2 Roosevelt cast his first presidential vote for Republican James Garfield. Too soon the honeymoon idyll was over. Alice and Roosevelt returned to the Roosevelt home in Manhattan to live with Roosevelt's mother, Mittie.

After four years of shuttling between Oyster Bay and somnolent Cambridge, Alice and Theodore Roosevelt faced the many challenges of living in America's largest city. While he and Alice may have lived just off fashionable Fifth Avenue, the saloons of Sixth Avenue were only a block away. And although the newlyweds lived on 57th Street, near the southern border of Central

---

1. Morison, to Henry Davis Minot, 13 February 1880, I, 43.

Park, Roosevelt actually spent much of the day walking the length of Manhattan to get down to his law school classes on Great Jones Street. When in later years Roosevelt wrote about the contrast between the rich and poor in Gilded Age New York, he may have been envisioning this very walk. He would likely have started by heading south on Fifth Avenue, passing the grand chateaux still being built for New York's wealthiest. He would have been able to follow the progress on construction of William Vanderbilt's enormous mansion at 52nd Street, before continuing past newly built St. Patrick's Cathedral, Jay Gould's house, and the Waldorf-Astoria. After checking the time on the large clock in front of the Fifth Avenue Hotel at Madison Square, Roosevelt would likely have turned onto Broadway, allowing him to cut southeast toward Union Square. This route would have brought Roosevelt within only a half-block of his old home on Twentieth Street, and past the city's principal dry goods and department stores. In fact his law classes were held just around the corner from his favorite store for men's clothes, Brooks Brothers.

Despite such a fashionable route, Roosevelt still walked past tenements and street vendors, recently arrived immigrants and some of the city's 10,000 homeless children. He walked directly through the 18th Ward, with its 1300 tenements housing over 40,000 residents. He skirted the Bowery, already being transformed into one of the city's seediest neighborhoods. Along Third Avenue, earlier known for the cheap entertainment of nickel museums featuring mermaids and dwarfs, the new elevated line now showered pedestrians with oil and hot coal. Soon there would be little left along the street but saloons and brothels. Roosevelt must have also seen the mountains of garbage that plagued some neighborhoods. Trash barrels overflowed and horse manure remained on the streets so long it became crammed into the cracks between cobblestones. Simply walking the city streets was a chore. No doubt more than once Roosevelt had to pick his way over a pile of trash, a dead horse, or a drunk sleeping it off.

Roosevelt and Alice threw themselves into their New York life. Roosevelt took up many of his father's duties, like the Newsboys' Lodging House. He went to a meeting of the St. Andrew's Society and had a long talk with newspaper publisher and top New York Republican Whitelaw Reid. Alice prepared to join Roosevelt's Presbyterian Church. December marked the beginning of the New York social season, and the newlyweds attended the theater, opera, dinner parties, and the Patriarch's Ball. Roosevelt expressed a fondness for William Waldorf Astor, who was a New York rarity: a young man from one of the city's wealthiest families, also active in New York Republican politics. Astor currently served as a New York state senator in Albany and was preparing to run for Congress. This social connection may have provided an important example for Roosevelt, as 1881 would shape up to be a decidedly political year.

Volume IV
1880 DIARY

Thursday January 1

A beautiful day; a whole party of us went out to Jerome Park[2] to a lunch—a very swell one—which Elliott gave us. Emlen drove Alice Lee in his pair and cutter[3]; Elliott drove Rosy Lee, Harold Haddon drove Conie, Smith Haddon drove Leila Schyler, Annie Murray and myself, and the rest—Bamie, Rose Saltonstall, Dick, Harry Shaw, Ell Whitney, Ike Iselin, Payton, Kingsford, Alfred, Stratton in a great sleigh. We had great fun, dancing waltzes, polka redowas and the Virginia Reel. In the evening Dick and I made a most absurd call on Fanny Smith.

Friday January 2

After breakfast took Alice to drive in the Park. At 11 our guests went back to Boston; we have enjoyed their visit exceedingly. In the evening went to a theatre party and supper with Nell, Julien, Robinson, Russell, Stratton, the two Haddons, and Bob Sedgwick—in fact the whole whist club.

Saturday January 3

Spent the day calling on my various friends, of all sexes & ages.

Sunday January 4

Spent the afternoon at the Newsboys Lodging House. Took night train for Boston.

Monday January 5

Began work again, as usual—up to 5 oclock. Took Jack Tebbetts out to drive in the cart; the horse goes beautifully now though sometimes a little frisky. My cutter has come on; but there is not snow enough yet for sleighing. Spent the evening in the club playing whist and reading.

Wednesday January 7

Drove in town with Jack T. in the evening to go to a great reception at the Homers.

---

2. In the Bronx.

3. A sleigh.

Thursday January 8

Went to the Harvard Assembly; dancing the german with Julia Bacon. Met two very sweet, pretty girls from Albany—the Miss. Rathbones.

Friday January 9

It was rainy, so instead of going out in my cart I hired a buggy, and drove over to the Saltonstalls where I spent the afternoon and evening.

Saturday January 10

In the morning I drove in town to the Brunswick, in my cart, and took Miss Grace Rathbone out for a long drive. I dined at the Whitneys, and went to a very pleasant party at the Amory's afterwards.[4]

Sunday January 11

I was requested to resign my Sunday School Class, as I am a Presbyterian and would not become an Episcopalian! As I have taught there 3 ½ years I thought this rather hard.

Breakfasted in the Club, as usual. In the afternoon I drove over to the Saltonstalls, took Mamie out in the cart; stayed to tea and spent the evening there.

Monday January 12

In the evening I went to the Papanti Party; these parties are the pleasantest of all. I am very fond of dancing; it is my favourite amusement, excepting horseback riding.

Tuesday January 13

Tried my horse in the sleigh for the first time; he went beautifully. In the evening went to the Great Assembly at Horticultural Hall—much the largest ball I have seen in Boston.[5]

Wednesday January 14

Minot W. & I dined in town with Harry S., afterwards going to a very pretty little party at Mrs. Parkman Shaws.

---

4. Boston Brahmin family.

5. Not to be confused with the later Horticultural Hall built in 1901 across from Symphony Hall, this building was built in 1865 and stood at 100-102 Tremont Street at the corner of Bromfield Street until it was demolished in 1901.

Thursday January 15

I drove Jack Tebbets over in my cutter to a very pleasant little dinner at the Saltonstalls. I sat between Mrs. Saltonstall and Kitty Lane.

Saturday January 17

Went to a very pleasant little lunch party given by Van Rennsaeler to the Miss. Rathbones. In the afternoon went to a reception at the Minots; Grace Minot is a marvellously pretty girl. I am exercising pretty regularly in the gymnasium—single stick, vaulting, sparring, and running 3 or 4 miles a day.

Sunday January 18

Spent the evening very pleasantly at the Rotches.

Monday January 19

Went to a very pleasant party at the Dexters.

In the afternoon I had taken Minot W. a long drive in the cart. Now that old Dick is recovering the use of his ankle I do'n't feel that he is the only one I ought to take driving.

Tuesday January 20

It was Rosy's birthday, so I drove over to Chestnut Hill to bring her my present. I spent the afternoon at the Lees, and dined there.

Wednesday January 21

Went to a rather stupid dinner party at the Wales.

Thursday January 22

Went in town to a great A.D.Ø. dinner: over a hundred men present. I left about 11, and went to a party at the Sears, which ended about two oclock.

Friday January 23

Went down to Salem with Mrs. Saltonstall, Mrs. Lee, Rose and Alice. I am staying in a very curious old "House" belonging to Miss Saltonstall. In the evening went to a very jolly party at Hamilton Hall.[6]

---

6. Built in 1805 in the Federalist style, and still in use in Salem.

Saturday January 24

Came back from Salem; dined at Theodore Lyman's; afterwards had a little spree in the Porc.

Sunday January 25

At last everything is settled; but it seems impossible to realize it. I am so happy that I dare not trust in my own happiness. I drove over to the Lees determined to make an end of things at last; it was nearly eight months since I had first proposed to her, and I had been nearly crazy during the past year; and after much pleading my own sweet, pretty darling consented to be my wife. Oh, how bewitchingly pretty she looked! If loving her with my whole heart and soul can make her happy, she shall be happy; a year ago last Thanksgiving I made a vow that win her I would if it were possible; and now that I have done so, the aim of my whole life shall be to make her happy, and to shield her and guard her from every trial; and, oh, how I shall cherish my sweet queen! How she, so pure and sweet and beautiful can think of marrying me I can not understand, but I praise and thank God it is so.

Monday January 26

First examination of the Semi Annuals. Went to the Papanti Hall party in the evening; my little darling looked so pretty; by far the prettiest girl in the room, and the greatest belle; she gave me her favour.

Tuesday January 27

I am only just beginning to realize it; I still feel as if it would turn out, as it so often has before and that Alice will repent.

Wednesday January 28

Went to a small party at the Parkman Shaws; but I hav'n't really cared for a party this winter.

Thursday January 29

Lunched at the Saltonstalls; spent the afternoon with my sweet love; dined at the Union Club with Frank Lee; then went to the Horticultural Assembly; where sweet Alice looked if possible even prettier than usual.

Friday January 30

When I look back at the last four months and realize the tortures I have been through it seems like a dream; I have hardly had one good night rest; and night after night I have not even gone to bed. I have been pretty nearly crazy, over my wayward, willful darling. But I do not think any outsider suspected it; I have not written a word about it in my diary since a year ago last Thanksgiving. It was a real case of love at first sight—and my first love too.

Saturday January 31
Went to tell the Family; who of course were all perfectly delighted and too sweet for anything, though very much surprised.

Sunday February 1
Told the Uncles and Aunts, all of whom were very much pleased. I still feel as if I were in a dream; it is too good to be true.

Monday February 2
Chose a diamond ring for my darling; came on to Boston in the afternoon.

Tuesday February 3
Snowing heavily; but I drove over in my sleigh to Chestnut Hill, the horse plunging to his belly in the great drifts, and the wind cutting my face like a knife. My sweet life was just as loveable and pretty as ever; it seems hardly possible that I can kiss her and hold her in my arms; she is so pure and so innocent, and so very, very pretty. I have never done anything to deserve such good fortune. Coming home I was upset in a great drift, and dragged about 300 yards, holding on to the reins, before I could stop the horse. In evening went to a party at the Rotches.

Wednesday February 4
Superb sleighing; took Dick out for a long drive. The engagement is not to come out till a week from Monday; it is awfully hard to keep away from her.

Thursday February 5
Went to the Harvard Assembly dancing with Lulu Lowell.

Friday February 6
Drove over to the Saltonstalls in my sleigh. Took dinner there, and spent the evening with my pretty darling. I am almost too happy.

Saturday February 7
Drove Minot Weld over to his house and back. Great Porc supper in evening.

Sunday February 8[7]

Started at work at a Mission School over in East Cambridge.

I have certainly got a marvelously hightoned and honorable set of friends; they are not brilliant, but they are plucky, honourable and rigidly virtuous, and with plenty of common sense. First comes Elliott, then Jack Elliott, West, Emlen, Alfred and Dick Saltonstall; then Minot Weld, John Tebbets, Harry Chapin and Harry Shaw. And now that I have won the sweetest and purest of women my happiness is indeed complete.

Took tea and spent the evening most pleasantly at the Whitneys.

Monday February 9

Dined at Jim Parker's; then went to the Papanti party [at] which I danced with Nana Rotch; afterwards drove out with Dick in his cutter to Chestnut Hill. The thermometer was below zero, but we were too heavily wrapped up to heed the cold; and it was a splendid sleigh ride.

Tuesday February 10

Drove on to Cambridge in morning. Went to party at Winthrops in evening. Thank heaven I am absolutely pure. I can tell Alice everything I have ever done.

Wednesday February 11

Went to a small leap year party at the Lowells; seven of us drove there and back in a sleigh. We had great fun, of course my little darling was there, as sweet and pretty as ever.

Thursday February 12

A.D.Ø. dinner of 25 men in town; I presided. It was one of the pleasantest dinners I have ever been to; the songs, stories and speeches were all excellent.

Friday February 13

Raining hard; I drove over in a buggy to the Lees to dinner and, thanks to the storm, spent the night there. In the evening I was all the time with my darling Little Sunshine; she is so marvelously sweet, and pure and loveable and pretty

---

7. Roosevelt penned a letter to his mother this day that indicated her sadness at his engagement: "I am very glad you saw Mr. Saltonstall today and that he cheered you up. Really you mustn't feel melancholy, sweet Motherling; I shall only love you all the more." TR to MBR, 8 February 1880, Morison, I, 43.

that I seem to love her more and more every time I see her, though I love her so much now that I really can not love her more. I do not think ever a man loved a woman more than I love her; for a year and a quarter now I have never (even when hunting) gone to sleep or waked up without thinking of her; and I doubt if an hour has passed that I have not thought of her. And now I can scarcely realize that I can hold her in my arms and kiss her and caress her and love her as much as I choose.

Saturday February 14

Drove back to Cambridge in the morning; announced my engagement to the Club, and "set up" champagne. In the evening went to a leap year party at the Fiskes.

Sunday February 15

After Sunday School drove over in my cart to the Lees. I took Alice out for quite a long drive, although it began snowing; how pretty the little witch looked! I spent the evening with my darling little Sunshine, and stayed all night.

Monday February 16

Drove back to Cambridge in the morning; in the evening went in town to a boxing benefit.

Tuesday February 17

In the evening went in town to meet the family, who came on to see Alice. Took Nell out to pass the night with me.

Wednesday February 18

Drove Nell over to the Saltonstalls to lunch; all my family came out; my own sweet love looked oh so pretty; I spent the afternoon with her; we dined at the Lees, driving home at 10, and spending several hours in the Porc.

Alice has received 42 bouquets.

Thursday February 19

Drove Nell in to Boston in the morning. In the evening dined with the family at the Brunswick,[8] and went to a theatre party given to Bamie and Conie by Frank and Tom Lee. I sat by pretty Miss Sunshine who "matronized."[9]

---

8. A grand Boston hotel built in 1874 at the cost of one million dollars. In 1946 the hotel became a Harvard dorm for student couples.

9. The irony being that Alice herself was only eighteen years old.

Friday February 20

Spent the day with the family; drove to a great family dinner at the Lees. The drive home, in the bright, cold moonlight over the smooth, frozen roads was just perfect. Then I went up to the Pudding, where we had a great fight; staying up till quarter of six, when as it was too late to go to bed I played billiards in the club till breakfast time.

Saturday February 21

Jack Tebbetts and I went in town to see the family off; went calling with my sweet, pretty love; dined with "Uncle" Bill Lee; came out to Cambridge for the great annual Porc. dinner. Got to bed at 12 oclock—after being 44 hours without sleep.

Sunday February 22

After Mission School I drove over to the Lees; I took my little Sunshine out for a drive; to Forrest Hills, and towards Milton; I had a lovely drive, for it was a beautiful day and I had such a sweet, pretty companion.

Monday February 23

Rained or snowed all day, so I was most happy, spending almost all the time with my sweet queen. Oh, how I love my little darling! She is too sweet to me for anything; when we are alone I can hardly stay a moment without holding her in my arms or kissing her; she is such a laughing, pretty little witch; and yet with it all she is so true and so tender. I do'n't think there was ever any one like her.

Tuesday February 24

Drove back to Cambridge in the morning. In the evening went to a surprise party at the Rogers, given to Fanny Peabody.

Wednesday February 25

For a wonder did not go over to Chestnut Hill; but spent the afternoon driving in my dog cart and the evening in the club.

Thursday February 26

Drove over to lunch at Chestnut Hill; took my pretty love out in the cart in the afternoon; in the evening drove in with her and Rose to a dinner at the Bartletts. Sat between Miss Whitney & Miss Sears; and spent the rest of the evening with Miss Perkins.

Friday February 27

Drove back to Cambridge in the morning. In the afternoon we went down to Salem with sweet Alice to pass the night at the Lees. Salem is a quaint old place, and I am enjoying the visit very much; as I could not help doing when I am with my darling.

Saturday February 28

We came up to Boston in the morning; had a cosy tete-a-tete lunch at Parkers.[10] In the evening went to a dinner at the Somerset Club, given by Col. Russel.

Sunday February 29

After Sunday School I as usual drove over to Chestnut Hill, and took my sweet darling out in the cart for a long drive through Forrest Hills and Milton. Spent the night at the Lees.

Monday March 1

At about eleven oclock I drove my pretty love into Boston in the cart to pay calls. We lunched at Ferrar, and drove out in the afternoon in time to get ready to go to a dinner given to us by the Minots.

I enjoy these long drives with my darling Sunshine so much. It is beautiful weather; and the turnout is really very stylish; and my love looks so bewitchingly pretty perched up in the high cart, while plucky Lightfoot bowls us along famously; and I feel so proud of my pretty companion.

Tuesday March 2

Drove back to Cambridge. Delivered lecture before the Nat Hist Society.

Wednesday March 3

Went to the first of a series of very pleasant bowling parties.

Thursday March 4

Drove Dick over in my cart to a very pleasant dinner at the Lees. Sat between Mrs. Jack Peabody and Fanny Peabody.

Friday March 5

Drove over in the afternoon to the Lees; took my pretty, laughing love out for a drive; spent the evening and night there.

---

10. The Parker House was another grand Boston hotel built in 1855.

Saturday March 6

Drove back to Cambridge in the morning.

Dined at the Whitneys.

Sunday March 7

As usual went over in my cart to the Lees, after Sunday School; but my poor little darling had a head ache, and so we could not go driving.

Monday March 8

Drove back to Cambridge in the morning.[11]

Tuesday March 9

Went into a very pleasant dinner given to Alice by Fanny Peabody.

Wednesday March 10

Went to a bowling party in the afternoon, and a stag dinner in the evening.

These bowling parties are great fun. There are to be six in all, given by Alice, Rose, Rosy, Frank & Tom Lee, and myself. Each time six outsiders are invited—Flora Grant, Katy Lowell, Harriet Lawrence, Gus Heminway, Bob Grant, Bob Russell.

The stag dinner was very pleasant; Dick, Ralph Ellis & Peters were awfully funny.

Thursday March 11

Right after breakfast I drove over to Chestnut Hill in the cart. It soon began snowing, and I spent all day with my sweet, pretty, pure queen, my laughing little love. Oh, how bewitchingly pretty she is! I can not help petting and caressing her all the time; and she is such a perfect little Sunshine. I do not believe any man ever loved woman more than I love her.

---

11. TR wrote to sister Corinne this day: "After a long, but very peacable argument with Mr. and Mrs. Lee I finally carried the day, and succeeded in getting their consent to my being married next Fall—either late in October or early in November. It will be very much pleasanter to be settled. I am awfully glad Mother wants us to stay the first winter with her; it is awfully sweet of her; Alice will find it very much pleasanter. Indeed I do'n't think Mr. Lee would have consented to our marriage so soon on other terms." Morison, TR to Corinne, 8 March 1880, I, 44.

Friday March 12

A good deal of snow on the ground; I made a dismal failure of an effort to go sleighing in the Lee's cutter with Rose. Big dinner in the evening.

Saturday March 13

Went over to Cambridge to see the sparring and wrestling. Came back in afternoon, and drove in town with my beloved darling to a dinner at the Amory's.

Sunday March 14

Drove to Cambridge to Sunday School, and back.

Monday March 15

Mrs. Lee took Alice and I to New Bedford to see her parents. Alice and I returned alone. I enjoyed the day very much, with my sweet, pretty love, in the quaint old house, and its still quain[ter] inmates.

Tuesday March 16

Raining, so I did not go back to Cambridge, but spent the day with my sweet Sunshine, my own beloved little Queen. She is too bewitching, and too perfectly lovely with me for anything.

Wednesday March 17

Drove back to Cambridge. Bowling party in afternoon.

Thursday March 18

Dear, old West came in to day. I took him over in the cart to dine at Chestnut Hill, and spent the late evening in the Porc.

The dear old man has been rejected by Fanny. I think she has behaved abominably to him; he means to try again.

Friday March 19

West went back to New York. I went out to Chestnut Hill and drove with Alice, Rosy & Rose to a dinner at the Minots.

Saturday March 20

Came back to Cambridge for the Athletic sports. In the evening went to a very pleasant dinner party at the Shaws.

Sunday March 21

Alice is staying at the Cabots in town, so after Sunday School I went in there to take tea.

Monday March 22

Drove over with Dick to a very pleasant dinner at the Saltonstalls; spent the night there.

Tuesday March 23

Drove back with Dick to Cambridge in the morning. In the afternoon walked over to the Lees to spend the night. Went to a dinner at the Lowells in the evening.

Wednesday March 24

Walked back to Cambridge in the morning. ΔKE theatricals in the evening.

Thursday March 25

By way of change spent the day in Cambridge, in the Library, writing up my thesis in political economy. Since I have been engaged I have studied very little, and cut most of my recitations, and intend so to continue during the balance of my college course. I have always studied well in college, so I can afford to cut now; and it is my last holiday, as I shall study law next year, and must there do my best, and work hard for my own little wife.

Friday March 26

In the afternoon walked over to Chestnut Hill to spend the night. I passed the evening with my sweet little queen. It is perfectly impossible to tell how much I love her; it is not merely thinking of her all the time, it is much more than that; she is always present in my mind. She is so sweet and tender and loving, and so absolutely pure and innocent, and with such a laughing, sunshiney temper; and, oh, so bewitchingly pretty. I can never thank Heaven enough that I am perfectly pure; and can tell her everything I have ever done; and so can she tell me; there is not one thing secret between us. "Whom first we love we seldom wed," but we shall prove exceptions to this rule.

Saturday March 27

Went back to Cambridge to see the sparring and wrestling.

Sunday March 28

Snowing, so after Sunday School I drove over to Chestnut Hill in a buggy, to pass the night.

Monday March 29

Drove back to Cambridge; and in evening returned to Chestnut Hill to pass night.

Tuesday March 30

Drove back to Cambridge. Went to a party at the Bryants.

Wednesday March 31

Bowling party in afternoon. Then went to a dinner at Youngs[12] for "Big Six";—Harry Shaw, Harry Chapin, Minot Weld, Jack Tebbets, Dick Saltonstall and myself. Went to a very funny piece at the Theatre.

Thursday April 1

Started early in the morning with some other students in Adv. Zoology on a collecting tour, to Nahant.

In afternoon drove over in my cart to Chestnut Hill; sweet little Birdie was at the Francises, so I called for her and took her driving. In the evening drove with my darling into Boston, to the Harvard Assembly. In spite of being engaged my own sweet, pretty Queen was certainly the belle.

Friday April 2

Came back to Cambridge for my recitations; returned to Chestnut Hill. Took darling out driving. Spent the evening with her.

I am so absolutely happy, that I sometimes almost feel as if it must be a dream. No mortal ever could be happier than I am.

Saturday April 3

Went back to Cambridge; in afternoon took my sweet Queen a long drive; how bewitchingly pretty she is! And so sweet, and loving and tender; and such a laughing little witch.

In evening we drove in to a dinner given us by the Rotches.

Sunday April 4

Drove to Cambridge to Sunday School—for the last time this year—and returned to Chestnut Hill. Spent the evening, as usual, with my sweet Queen.

Monday April 5

Drove my pretty love in town. I love to have sweet Birdie perched up beside me in the cart; she is so sweet and pretty. Made several calls; one on Fanny Peabody, whom I like more than any Boston girls, except Rose and Rosey.

---

12. Young's Hotel was built in 1860 and designed by William Washburn. In 1881 it became one of the first buildings in Boston to install electric lights. Known for its beautifully appointed billiards room, Young's was a favorite of Harvard students, who often took rooms for poker parties.

Papanti Party in evening; I danced with Rose S.

Tuesday April 6
Drove over to Dick S.'s; then drove him to the Minots; dined at Jack Tebbetts and drove him out to Cambridge afterwards.

Wednesday April 7
Mrs. Lee, Alice and I went on to New York to stay ten days. We were met with open arms; Mother, Bamie, Conie and Elliott are just too sweet to me for anything.

Thursday April 8
I have to spend most of the days working on my thesis.

Family party at night, to introduce Alice—who of course looked as pretty as a picture.

Friday April 9
Aunt Laura Roosevelt gave my pretty darling a great family dinner.

Saturday April 10
Dinner at home; I sat between Miss Moran and Miss Prince.

Sunday April 11
Every body is just too sweet for anything; the cousins, and even more dear old Nell are just as attentive as they can be, sending flowers &c. Mother & the girls are just splendid. All my friends are behaving beautifully.

Monday April 12
Afternoon Tea; in evening took Alice & Bamie to the Harvard Theatricals.

Tuesday April 13
We gave a large party for Alice.

Wednesday April 14
Emlen gave me a stag dinner.

Thursday April 15
Aunt Annie gave a party for Alice.

In the morning I drove her way out beyond Jerome Park.

Friday April 16

Last day of our stay; everyone has done all things possible for Alice.

Saturday April 17

Mrs. Lee, Alice and I took 11 am train for Boston. Went out to Porc. supper to see Charley Dickey initiated.

Sunday April 18

After the Porc Breakfast I drove Dick over in the cart to Chestnut Hill. I took Alice out for a long drive in the afternoon; it was perfectly delicious, the weather being beautiful.

The past three months have been almost a dream of happiness; no man could lead a more ideal life than I do. I have very little work to do, only enough to employ me a few hours a day during three or four days in the week, and I can cut whenever I please; I spend several nights (usually 5) a week at Chestnut Hill, where the whole family are just too sweet to me for anything; the other two evenings I spend in the club; I drive almost every day in my cart; and no man ever loved and was loved by so sweet, tender and pretty a girl.

Monday April 19

Drove Dick back to Cambridge.

Wednesday April 21

Poor old Mrs. Haskill, Alice's grandmother, is dead, and so I went down to New Bedford to the funeral.

Thursday April 22

I drove over in the afternoon to Chestnut Hill, with my bag under my seat, as I intend to stay several days. I took Alice out driving.

Friday April 23

I drove back to Cambridge in the morning; returning to Chestnut Hill in the afternoon. In the evening we play whist, read, or the girls play on the piano, and I generally have an hour or two by myself with my own sweet little queen.

Saturday April 24

Spent the morning with Mamie S. and playing with cunning little Bella. In the afternoon I took my bright, sunny darling out for a long drive, through Milton, Forest Hills and Longwood.

Sunday April 25

Went to the dear little Chestnut Hill church in the morning. Everything out here is perfectly ideal.

I took my darling a long drive in the afternoon, through way beyond the Charles. Words can not tell how I love her; more and more every day.

I doubt if any man was ever more happy than I am; I always enjoyed myself, but I have never been so happy as during these last three months.

Monday April 26

In the morning Alice studied and practised music a couple of hours, while I pumped the water up and studied; then we played tennis, then she sewed while I read Prescotts Conquest of Peru[13] aloud. In the afternoon I took my sweet, sunny faced darling for a three hours ride in my dog cart, all round the country; way up to Dedham and the Blue Hills. After tea, I read aloud to Bella and Georgie, romped with them, and told them stories—the other girls all coming in as auditors. Played whist till nine oclock; then spent an hour alone with my sweet queen. This is a fair sample of my days; and no wonder I am supremely happy.

Tuesday April 27

Drove back to Cambridge in the morning.

Wednesday April 28

In the afternoon played tennis with Harry Chapin. In the morning went to the Pudding Theatricals, which were excellent.

I did not study much the early part of this year, and since my engagement I have hardly studied at all. I never work at all except on three days (usually Tuesday Wednesday and either Thursday or Friday) and do not average more than five hours on these days; but my marks were so good the first three years that I can afford to be idle now.

Friday April 30

Drove over in the afternoon to Chestnut Hill and took pretty Baby out driving.

---

13. William Hickling Prescott, *A History of the Conquest of Peru*, 1847.

Saturday May 1

Spent the morning romping with Georgie and Bella & playing tennis with Rose S; in the afternoon I took darling out for a long drive; it is the most beautiful weather imaginable for driving and tennis.

Sunday May 2

Went to the dear little church in the morning; took Alice out driving in the afternoon. Chestnut Hill is an absolutely ideal place; and the Lee's house is awfully pleasant to stay at; they are all too sweet to me for anything.

Monday May 3

In the morning played tennis with Rose & Rosy; in the afternoon with Alice; and then drove her in to Boston and back. We spent the evening at the Saltonstalls.

Tuesday May 4

Drove back to Cambridge in the morning.

Wednesday May 5

I drove Minot Weld up in the cart to Franklin Codman's farm, at Lincoln, 12 miles away. We spent all day there, and had great fun.

I have certainly lived like a prince for my last two years in college. I have had just as much money as I could spend; belonged to the Porcellian Club; have had some capital hunting trips; my life has been varied; I have kept a good horse and cart; I have had half a dozen good and true friends in college, and several very pleasant families outside; a lovely home; I have had but little work, only enough to give me an occupation; and to crown all—infinitely above anything else put together—I have won the sweetest of girls for my wife. No man ever had so pleasant a college course.

Friday May 7

I drove over to Chestnut Hill in the afternoon. The Miss Rotches are staying at the Lees.

Saturday May 8

The Miss Rotches were at the Lees; Miss Reynolds at the Saltonstalls; Jack Tebbets & Frank Codman & Tom Lee drove over; and we played tennis all day. In the afternoon I drove Jack back to a Porcellian dinner, given by Harry Shaw, Dick and myself especially for some of the older honoraries.

Sunday May 9

After the Porc. breakfast I drove Dick over to Chestnut Hill; in the afternoon took Alice out in the cart.

Monday May 10

The weather was so hot that I took Alice out in the cart after dinner; we had a delightful drive.

Tuesday May 11

Early in the morning I drove back to Cambridge.

Friday May 14

Drove over in the afternoon to Chestnut Hill. Played tennis after tea.

Saturday May 15

Drove my darling little queen in to Boston to the Union Boat Club to see the class races—in which we were beaten. Drove her out to Chestnut Hill afterwards, and very swell I felt, in my stylish turnout, with my bewitchingly pretty companion, driving through Beacon street.

Sunday May 16

Church in the morning; then I took Cotty, Georgie, & Bella out walking in the woods. In the afternoon drove Baby darling way through Waverly & Belmont; a lovely drive.

Monday May 17

Drove Dick back to Cambridge in the morning.

Wednesday May 19

Drove Dick over to make a call on Miss Georgie Heywood, Joe Whitney's fiancée; had an absurd time. Went to a very pleasant O.K. dinner; afterwards to the Δ.K.E.

Thursday May 20

Drove over to the Lees to stay a few days. Played tennis in the afternoon.

Friday May 21

Walked over to and back from Cambridge for my recitations. In the evening, after dinner, took my sweet queen out for a long drive in the beautiful moonlight.

Saturday May 22

Drove Tom Lee over to the Athletic games which were very good; and thence to a garden party at the Dixwells. It was beautiful moonlight, and I drove Alice home.

Sunday May 23

Fanny Peabody & Cotty are staying at the Saltonstalls; after services in the dear little church we all went to walk in the woods. In the afternoon I took pretty Sunshine a long drive through the beautiful country round Auburndale.

Monday May 24

Spent the whole day with my dearly loved darling. In the morning I read aloud while she sewed; though she looked so bewitchingly pretty that I had to stop all the time to pet & caress her. In the afternoon I took her out in the cart, and after making several calls we wound up at the Whitneys, where we took tea and had a very jolly time, driving home in the moonlight about ten oclock.

Tuesday May 25

Drove back to Cambridge.

Friday May 28

Drove over to Chestnut Hill.

Saturday May 29

Spent the morning with my beloved darling; reading Pendennis[14] aloud, while she sewed. In the afternoon I took her the longest drive we have gone yet, through Dedham, Needham, and almost to Wellesly [sic] and back thorough Grantville.

Sunday May 30

Rainy, so after Church spent the day in the house, telling stories to Bella and Georgie, or with my darling.

Monday May 31

In the morning I read Pendennis aloud to darling Baby; in the evening took her out driving.

---

14. *Pendennis* (1848–1850), a novel by William Thackeray. At one point in the story the protagonist, Arthur Pendennis, attends college, but after enjoying an extravagant lifestyle, the young man fails his final examination and is forced to return home. Perhaps a cautionary tale for TR on the eve of his very last Harvard examinations.

Tuesday June 1
Came back to Cambridge early in the morning.

Thursday June 3
Drove over to Chestnut Hill in time for tea; played tennis afterwards.

Friday June 4
Took darling Baby out driving in the cart.

I don't think any man ever could have had such a darling, pretty, little witch of a sweetheart as I have.

Saturday June 5
Spent the day with my darling, reading aloud &c; I took her a long and very beautiful drive in the cart.

Sunday June 6
Rainy, so after church I walked alone; and when it cleared up with my queen.

Monday June 7
Drove back to Cambridge for my first examination. For 10 days now I shall stay in Cambridge, and grind for my final examinations. I have a good deal of work to make up for the time I have loafed; and so shall not go over to Chestnut Hill till the 16th, my last examination. I shall work like a trojan for ten days.

Thursday June 10
Went round to call at the Lanes; very nice girls; Van is a lucky man—and a good fellow.

Sunday June 13
Breakfasted in the club, dined at the Lanes.

Am still up to my ears in work; quite a novel sensation, I have loafed so long. I have been studying nine or ten hours a day; my amusements being an hour's walk or lawn tennis in the afternoon and an hour's whist in the club in the evening. I have missed my darling dreadfully.

Wednesday June 16
Passed my last examination. I have worked well these last ten days; and in fact I had to. In the afternoon I drove or [sic] in my cart to the Lees; it was delightful to get back to the cheerful house, and to see kind, hospitable Mr and Mrs Lee,

the pretty girls and the jolly little children; and far more than anything to be once again with my own, best beloved little Queen; I have missed her so; oh, how sweet and pretty she was.

Thursday June 17

Spent the morning playing with Georgie and Bella; in the afternoon took my darling to drive; then played tennis till dusk.

Friday June 18

In the evening I took sweet Alice for the crowning drive of the season. We started about half past six and came back in the clear moonlight about half past nine. The weather was just sufficiently cool, and the country marvelously beautiful; for we drove through the wild, wooded, hilly region to the north of Wellesly.

Saturday June 19

Drove back to Cambridge; went to a Porc. supper; and went in town to meet Elliott at the 10.45 train; took him up to the club afterwards.

Sunday June 20

Nell and I breakfasted in the club; then loafed about it till 4 o'clock when I drove him over to the Lees (where Mother and the sisters are staying) returning after tea. The families get on beautifully together; and they are all just as lovely as possible.

Monday June 21

Breakfasted in the club with Nell; drove him over to spend the day at the Lees; we played lawn tennis, walked, and had a lovely time.

Tuesday June 22

Drove Nell over to dine at the Lees. Afterwards drove Alice to a garden party at the Winthrops, and back again, in the beautiful moonlight; then drove Nell home.

Wednesday June 23

A whole party of us (all our family, the Lees, Rose & Nannie S., & the Peabodys) went down to lunch at the Lees in Salem, and then drove over to spend the night at the Peabodys. We had a very jolly time, dancing and playing charades and hide and go seek.

Thursday June 24

We came up to Boston in the morning. Ike Iselin came on to spend a few days with me in the afternoon; I took him and Nell up to the ΔKE theatricals, which were very good, ending up at the Club.

Friday June 25

Class Day. Jack Kingsford is also staying with me. At 9.30 our class marched into chapel (all in dress suits & silk hats) at 11.30 into the Theatre. At two our spread in the gymnasium began; I had my hands full superintending &c; then at 5.15 came the exercises round the tree; then we went to the tea at Morgans. At 8.15 I took possession of my darling, and had my reward. I had secured the same room in Hollis that I had had last year, and there we sat for nearly two hours overlooking the beautifully illuminated yard, which looked like fairy land. Alice was in the same dress as last class day, and oh how marvelously pretty! We then went to supper at the Lanes; and thence I went to the club, getting to bed at 4 o'clock.

Saturday June 26

We all breakfasted in the club; then I took Kingsford, Iselin, and Nell over to the Lees, in my cart, to dinner. Afterwards we went to a garden party at the Lowells.

Sunday June 27

Breakfasted in the Club as usual, then drove over to the Hill, in a round about way to show the boys the country. In the afternoon Iselin and Kingsford returned to N.Y. In the evening I took my darling out in the woods, and we had a lovely stroll. She grows sweeter and prettier every day—and yet she could'n't be sweeter or prettier than she is.

Monday June 28

After a late breakfast I drove Nell over to the Lees, where we spent the day. In the evening my darling queen and I went out walking in the beautiful cool summer air.

Tuesday June 29

All the rest went down to Nahant. I stayed to pack up and pay bills. To think of the four years being over I suppose under other circumstances I should feel melancholy; but with Alice to love me life will always seem laughing and loving; who could feel blue with so pure and lovely and fond and beautiful a little bride elect? Only four months before we get married! My cup of happiness is almost too full.

Wednesday June 30

Commencement Day. Received my degree; I actually am an alumnus! I can not imagine any man's having a more happy and satisfactory four years than I have had. Spent most of the day in the club; drove over to a garden party at the Dexters in the evening; from there drove my bewitching Queen to Chestnut Hill; then drove Nell back to Cambridge.

Thursday July 1

Alice, Rosy and Rose went back to Oyster Bay with us; we reached it late in the evening. My cart arrived safely with the horse.

Looking back at my college career it is very pleasant to feel that there is nothing I should care to change in it; my career (both in and out of college) has been more successful than that of any man I have known.

Friday July 2

It is perfectly delightful to have my sweet Queen here. In the morning I drove her with Rose and Ike Iselin on the back seat over to Laurelton and Syosset. In the afternoon we played tennis. The evening I spent with her in the summer house.

Saturday July 3

In the morning I drove Alice through the beautiful country round about here. In the afternoon we all went out sailing. In the evening we went over to Uncle Jim's. The cousins are just too sweet for anything. Douglas Robinson and Romy Colgate are also staying with us, so there is quite a large party in the house.

Sunday July 4

Church in the morning. In the afternoon I took my darling a long and beautiful walk through Fleets woods; in the evening went down to the dock.

How I love her! And I would trust her to the end of the world. Whatever troubles come upon me—losses or griefs or sickness—I know she will only be more true and loving and tender than ever; she is so radiantly pure and good and beautiful that I almost feel like worshipping her. Not one thing is ever hidden between us. No matter how long I live I know my love for her will only grow deeper and tenderer day by day; and she shall always be mistress over all that I have.

Monday July 5

In the morning I drove darling baby over to Cold Spring to get pond lilies. In the evening went to see some clever acting at the Weeks.

Tuesday July 6

Took my Queen out driving in the morning; in the evening went to tea at Aunt Annies.

How intensely happy I am! Most of the day is spent with my love.

Wednesday July 7

In the morning I rowed Alice over to Yellow Banks coming back for Lunch. We played tennis in the afternoon, and went to tea at the Beckman's, where we had a very jolly time.

Thursday July 8

In the morning I rowed; in the afternoon I took my darling a long drive through "Old Kentuck"[15] and back of Glen Cove and Norwich; I spent the evening in the summer house with her.

Friday July 9

In the morning I went out sailing. In the afternoon I took my queen a long drive over the plains, and spent the evening with her in the summer house.

Saturday July 10

The three girls went back to Chestnut Hill; I went in town to see them off. How I hate to part with my bewitching little queen, even for a week! Oh, my own heart's darling, how I love and reverence you!

Wednesday July 14

Am leading the usual Oyster Bay life; tennis, rowing, swimming and sailing—but I miss Alice too much to care so much as I used to for things.

Saturday July 17

Went to Chestnut Hill; how lovely it is to see my darling once more! Oh, how pretty she looked and how lovingly she greeted me!

Sunday July 18

Spent the entire day with my darling. Oh, how blessed I am in her love! And how tenderly I shall love and cherish her. She is the sweetest, prettiest, purest, gentlest and noblest of women.

Monday July 19

As yesterday, I spent most of the day with my Queen; for about three hours I took Georgie, Cottie and Bella on a blackberry picnic.

---

15. The Bellport estate of Colonel William H. Langley.

Tuesday July 20

Rose and Richard and Alice and myself took the night train for Mt Desert[16]; at 11 p.m. got into the boat.

Wednesday July 21

Reached Mt Desert in the afternoon. Alice and Rose are staying with the Welds at Bar Harbour; Dick and I with Jack Tebbets at Schooner Head, 3½ miles off.

Thursday July 22

Rode over to Bar Harbour twice. Played tennis, bowled &c.

Friday July 23

Spent the morning playing tennis; in the afternoon walked round to see the various sights; the scenery is perfectly magnificent.

Saturday July 24

Rather laid up by the cholera morbus; so stayed in the house.[17]

Sunday July 25

In the afternoon Jack drove me over to Otter Creek.

Monday July 26

Dick and I took up our abode at the Welds, where Alice and Rose are staying.

Tuesday July 27

Spent the morning playing tennis; the afternoon and evening with my darling in the woods and on the Rocky shores.

Wednesday July 28

In the afternoon I took darling little Queen out driving in a buggy. Went to a very pleasant party in the even.

Thursday July 29

Alice's nineteenth birthday! Just to think of it! I can even now hardly realize my good fortune in having won her; I can never repay her love, but I shall

---

16. On the Maine coast, now part of Acadia National Park.

17. Of suffering from the cholera morbus, TR wrote Corinne this day: "Very embarrassing for a lover, isn't it? So unromantic, you know; suggestive of too much unripe fruit." Morison, 24 July 1880, I, 45.

do my best to, by unfailing tenderness and care. How I love her! She seems like a star of heaven, she is so far above other girls; my pearl, my pure flower. When I hold her in my arms there is nothing on earth left to wish for; and how infinitely blessed is my lot. If ever a man has been blessed by a merciful Providence, I am he. Oh, my darling, my own best loved little Queen!

Friday July 30

I was pretty sick today; but it's worth while being sick to find out what perfect trumps my friends are. All the rest of "Big Six" (Sammy, Chip, Jack, Dick and Minot) took the best care of me. Above all my own best beloved darling, my purest queen, my sweetest Alice, acted the part of an ideal little wife; she was so sweet and tender and loving and thoughtful; gave up all of her amusements to take care of me; and was such a bright, bewitching little sunbeam that her very presence made me feel well. What a treasure I have won! Was there ever a man as fortunate as I? I can hardly believe it. How I shall try to be worthy of her, and make her happy!

Saturday July 31

Rapidly recovering; Alice took first prize in the ladie's tennis tournament.

Sunday August 1

There was a very good sermon in the morning.

Monday August 2

The Welds are just too sweet to us for anything. In the evening, if we can't go out on the rocks, Alice and I generally retire to the kitchen by ourselves.

Tuesday August 3

In the morning I walked up Newport Mountain.

Wednesday August 4

Rainy, but still I contrived to be most of the day with my darling. Hop in the evening.

Thursday August 5

Drove Darling Queenie over to drive at Schooner Head.

Friday August 6

Shaw, Chapin, Saltonstall, Rose, Alice and myself all left; Alice and I reached Chestnut Hill late at night.

Saturday August 7

It is delightful to be back at Chestnut Hill; I am extremely fond of all the Lees, and love to be with them. I spend all day long with my own sweetest darling.

Sunday August 8

Darling took me out driving. Oh, how happy I am!

Monday August 9

I spend almost all the time with my darling; how bitterly I hate to have to leave her for six weeks day after tomorrow.

Tuesday August 10

As usual I spent the whole day with my darling; she is so bright and bewitching and yet so tender. I read aloud to her (from Hawthorne or Thackeray) a good deal; and we are both very fond of poetry—Longfellow, and parts of Shelly [sic] and Swinburne.

Wednesday August 11

Spent a lovely day with my sweetest Queen, and at last, with a heavy heart in spite of the shortness of the proposed separation, bade her farewell for seven weeks; and took the night train for New York.

Thursday August 12

Spent the day shopping; came out to ol [sic] O.B. in the evening; where were darling Mother; Aunt Susie and Uncle Hill, and the two Lockes.

Friday August 13

Played tennis with Frank; paddled with Emlen in his canoe.

Saturday August 14

Spent the day packing for my western trip, and walking in the woods and driving mother in the light wagon.

Sunday August 15

Elliott arrived while we were at lunch. I am frightfully homesick all the time for Alice; I miss her more than I can tell; she is never absent from my thoughts.

Monday August 16

Nell and I took the night train for Chicago.

Tuesday August 17

Travelled all day through the wooded hills of Pennsylvania and the rolling praries [sic] of Ohio. It is great fun to be off with old Nell; he and I can do about anything together; we never lose our temper and always accomplish what we set about.

Wednesday August 18

Reached Chicago in morning. Thanks to a great free-mason meeting could hardly get rooms. Boiling hot; do'n't know where to go; in a general stew.

Later in the evening got hold of a man named Wilcox, and will go to his farm till Sept.

Thursday August 19

Went to Wilcox's farm, at Huntly,[18] 60 miles from Chicago. In the afternoon Nell and I took a preliminary tramp through the great rolling fields after prarie chicken; we found a small flock late in the evening; he missed his bird, I killed mine.

It is great fun to try the open plains shooting, to which I am entirely unaccustomed—among such vast, almost level fields, with so few trees. The farm home fare is pretty rough.

1 prarie chicken.

Friday August 20

In the morning took a four hour tramp after chickens; each of us got several shots; Nell killed two brace, I but one bird.

1 Grouse

Elliott 4 grouse

Saturday August 21

E. & I started off in a wagon, and shot all day. When we came to a good looking place we would tie the horses to a fence, and spend an hour or two hunting through the stubble fields and pastures for chicken, or by the slews and ponds

---

18. Huntley, Illinois.

for ducks, snipe and plover. The roads are excellent and almost level and the country beautiful; and I have rarely passed a pleasanter day.

2 grouse 2 doves 4 plover 6 snipe

Elliott shot 4 grouse 1 duck 3 plover

Both of us also shot hawks, gophers &c.

Sunday August 22
Both fare and accomodations [sic] here are of the roughest; pork & potatoes being the invariable meal, except for what we shoot. But I like the men a great deal; and Nell and I are the greatest companions. Elliott is a good shot; I am not. But I am improving steadily.

In spite of enjoying my hunting so much, I miss Alice dreadfully; I would give up everything just to see her sweet face again. In the evening we got all hands (male & female) together & sang hymns.

Monday August 23
Went on an all days hunting trip in the wagon; I never shot worse, while Elliott hit about everything he fired at.

1 grouse 1 rabbit 2 plover 6 sand snipe

Elliott 9 grouse 4 snipe 2 plover

Tuesday August 24
Before the sun was up we started off, tramping in sullen silence through the wet prarie grass; but we found few birds and shot very badly.

2 dove 2 plover 2 sandsnipe

E 2 grouse

Wednesday August 25
Rained all day; we stayed in the house. Two of the men, a Texan desperado and a jovial stalwart irish boy got fighting drunk; I expected a row but it did not occur. The other two men (a canny scot and a goodnatured german) were on the side of peace. Anyhow, Nell and I are travelling on our muscle, and do'n't give a hang for any man.

Thursday August 26
Spent the day shooting but with very poor luck.

Alice is always the first thing I think about in the morning, and the last at night, and I doubt if she is ever absent five minutes from my thoughts—or even from my dreams.

1 Bittern 2 sandsnipe

E. 1 grouse

Friday August 27
We tramped through the morning after game, but saw nothing. The country is shot out, and we shall leave it tomorrow.

Saturday August 28
Came into Chicago; stayed at Sherman House,[19] where the accomodations seemed regal compared to what we have had at the farm house.

Sunday August 29
In the morning went to Methodist Church; I liked the earnest though rather startling preacher and the congregation; of the latter the large majority were men—generally they are women.

Monday August 30
Waiting for Wilcox with whom we start out West; so have been seeing the city.

Tuesday August 31
Still waiting for Wilcox. Drove round Chicago, read, played whist, went to Theatre, took a long walk, a Turkish bath &c; so passed the time very pleasantly. Dear old Nell and I always enjoy ourselves when together; but I keep getting more and more homesick for Alice; I think of her all the time, and nothing can compensate me for being away from her.

Wednesday September 1
At last Wilcox made his appearance and we shall leave in a day or two.

---

19. Over the years the Sherman House Hotel was built and rebuilt five times, including after the Great Chicago Fire of 1871. The last version was demolished in 1973.

Friday September 3

Finally we started; Nell, myself, an engineer, and an ex confederate soldier.

Saturday September 4

Reached Caroll[20] at 4 in the morning; started as soon as possible in a two horse wagon out on the beautiful, rolling, fenceless prarie, and did not reach home till nine o'c p.m. There were more birds than we have before seen, and I shot better than I yet have, though I missed several easy shots. Troubled both by colic and asthma.

6 grouse 2 quail

E 6 grouse

Sunday September 5

After breakfast we again left in the wagon and drove about 2.5 miles south where we put up for the night at a farm house, where of course the accommodations are pretty rough. The country is broken up into numerous rolling hills of slight elevation, absolutely treeless and sparsely scattered over with settlers houses. Birds are not very plentiful and are wild; but I shot pretty well, fully as well as or better than Elliott.

6 grouse 2 quail

[Elliott] 8 grouse

Monday September 6

Early in the morning started back over the rolling prarie; our horses work beautifully and go anywhere, except through the slews, or where the sluggish streams flow in their deep narrow beds with steep banks. Three of our setters work well; the other two are simple nuisances. Not only the hunting itself is great fun; but I enjoy greatly riding across country in the wagon. We did not get in till after dark, one horse dead lame, and having nearly upset in a mud hole. I shot well; rather better than Elliott.

8 grouse 1 quail 1 bittern

E. 6 grouse

---

20. Carroll, Iowa.

Tuesday September 7
After breakfast started in the wagon for Wall Lake[21]; passing through much flatter and less settled prairie than yesterday; we stopped before lunch to kill some chickens in a patch of long grass; after lunch I stalked and killed some snipe by a bayou, getting up to recover them, and getting bitten by a snake when I came out. Then we hunted through the stubble fields till dusk and put up for the night at a remarkably neat, comfortable little farm house. Shot fairly; about as well as Elliott.

8 grouse 8 yellow legs 1 quail

E 6 grouse

Wednesday September 8
Early in the morning I shot round the shores of the lake after yellowlegs and saw a most beautiful sunrise over the misty waters. There was a large flock of yellowheaded blackbirds along shore. After breakfast we went off in the wagon after chickens; I shot wretchedly while Elliott did splendidly. Am having a lovely time but am a good deal bothered by the asthma. Am in splendid walking trim, and can tramp all day easily.

4 grouse 6 yellowlegs 1 grebe

E. 14 grouse 2 ducks

Thursday September 9
In the morning we started off after chickens getting a couple of dozen before dinner; it is glorious autumn weather, cool and clear and driving around in the wagon over the prairie is great fun. In the afternoon Nell and I paddled round the lake in an old flatbottom after ducks and snipe; he shot well and I didn't. Finally my second and last gun also broke! which knocks me up for the present. We have had very hard luck this trip; a constant succession of unavoidable accidents.

6 grouse 21 yellowlegs &c

E 8 grouse 3 ducks 1 grebe

---

21. Wall Lake, Iowa.

Friday September 10

Drove back to Caroll in the wagon; on the way we nearly upset over a big rock, both the driver and I being sent flying out of the wagon on our heads, but we were very little hurt. Took the night train for Chicago.

Saturday September 11

Reached Chicago safely.

Sunday September 12

Took communion at Methodist Church; the services were simple and impressive.

Much though I have enjoyed the trip it has not made up to me for being away from my darling; nothing ever could. But it has done my health a world of good.

Monday September 13

Left in the night train for St. Pauls. Both Elliott and I had to buy new guns; and we parted with the other two men, whom we dislike.

Tuesday September 14

Left St Pauls in the evening, with two new guns and a stub-tailed old pointer for Moorehead,[22] Minnesota, on the Dacotah boundary, to see old Jack Elliott.

Wednesday September 15

Reached Moorhead in the morning. In the afternoon Nell and I took a buggy and drove off to some huge stubble fields, which we hunted through with great success till dark, or rather till old stub-tail found and attacked a cursed skunk. It was great fun to be off entirely alone and among a new kind of grouse, too. When we went back to the miserable old hotel we were overjoyed to find dear old Jack, who is entirely unchanged, except that he is more of a man and really good looking. We stayed up till all hours talking things over.

2 Sharptail grouse 2 golden plover

E 5 "   "   3 pinnated grouse

Thursday September 16

Spent the day with old Jack, whom we have not seen for nearly two years; it is lovely to see the old man again. I am now feeling in superb health and strength.

---

22. Moorhead, Minnesota, adjacent to Fargo on the other side of the state line. The Dakota Territory became the states of North and South Dakota simultaneously in 1889.
23. Buffalo River, a tributary of the Red River.

Friday September 17

Nell and I started out in a wagon and pair driven by a solemn old german; driving north beyond the buffaloe river.[23] We hunted grouse in the stubble fields and ducks in the slews; the grouse were wild, and we only saw the "white bellies"—no chickens. I shoot well, better than Elliott. We saw jack rabbits for the first time; we stopped shooting after sunset and drove five miles in the light of the full moon to the rough but comfortable house of a settler.

4 sharptail grouse 3 dipper ducks 1 hooded drake

1 grebe 1 coot 1 jack rabbit

E. 5 sharptails 1 jack rabbit

Saturday September 18

We had very much the best days sport we have had; there were innumerable grouse, though they were ["very" crossed out] wild. But I had to sit up most of last night with the asthma, I was so troubled with continual attacks of colic that I could hardly walk, and it rained most of the day, so I shot badly; Elliott however did splendidly. We have had pretty good fare and accomadations up here, so far, and great fun; but I shall be perfectly overjoyed to get back to Alice.

12 sharptail grouse 7 pinnated grouse

E 27 "   " 15   "   "

Sunday September 19

Started early in the morning and drove over thirty miles in a cold, driving rain storm; but I feel much better than yesterday. We lost our way several times driving across the prairie, and finally had to put up for the night at the house of a settler. A little before sunset it partially cleared, and we sallied out with our guns, returning with several ducks and grouse. Our new drover is a stocky little barkeeper; a nice little fellow.

2 sharptails 2 pinnated 2 ducks

E 2 "   4   "   4   "

Monday September 20

Had a lovely night; I had to sleep on the floor under a buffalo robe, the wind howling round the neat but frail little house. We started off before sunrise, lying in the cornfield for ducks, and during the day tramping a long distance over the fields after chickens; we both shot well. All day long there was a furious

---

23. Buffalo River, a tributary of the Red River.

cold northwesterly gale blowing with continual rain showers. We have had very good food (principally what we have shot ourselves lately) and accommodations lately, and are having the best time we have yet had on this trip; now I am feeling in superb health.

8 prairie chicken 4 duck

E 10 "   "   5 "

Tuesday September 21

Cold but quite clear. We started off in good season, driving straight across country and nearly getting mired in a slew. We shot some grouse in the stubble fields, the old pointer working well; we also killed several ducks from the wagon, and finally hid behind some wheat sheafs and shot two geese out of a flock which flew overhead. When night overtook us we went into camp among the timber on a bend of the buffalo river. We feasted on roast duck & chicken, and then lay down under our blankets before the roaring wood fire.

1 goose 4 ducks 2 sharptail 3 prairie chicken

E 1 " 4 "   2 "   5   "

Wednesday September 22

Started in tolerably good season, hunting through the stubble fields after chicken and whitebellies; we both of us shot pretty well. At dusk we again camped in the woods in a bend of the river; we have no tent or regular outfit, and sleep on the ground; we haven't even a frying pan.

4 sharptails 3 chicken 2 plover 2 dove

E 3 "   7   "   2   "

Thursday September 23

Got off pretty early; it was cloudy all day, raining sometimes. We had only fair success in the stubble fields, but I had capital fun in a big slew, wading about after ducks, until I went head over heels in a mudhole, gun & all. Reached Moorehead in the evening, which we spent with dear old John Elliott. We have had great fun this trip; I have never had a better hunt; but I am awfully homesick for Alice, and shall be too delighted to see her again.

3 chicken 4 duck 2 dove 4 plover 2 grebe

7 "   6 "   2   "

Friday September 24

Spent the day with old Jack. Our bag is as follows.

	T	E	Total
Sharp tail grouse	26	44	70
Pinnated grouse	69	119	188
Quail	5		5
Dove	8		8
Snipe		1	1
Plover	16	9	25
Shore Snipe	51		51
Rail	1		1
Coot	1		1
Goose	1	1	2
Duck	17	25	42
Grebe	4	1	5
Bittern	2		2
Hare	1	1	2
Rabbit	1		1
	203	201	404

17 duck=4 mallard 1 wood duck 1 green teal 2 blue teal 2 bluebill 2 dipper 1 widgeon 1 sprigtail 2 redhead 1 hooded merganser

16 plover=3 upland 5 golden 2 blackbreast 6 others

51 shoresnipe=33 winter yellowlegs 12 summer yellowlegs 6 sandpiper

Saturday September 25

Left for St Pauls. The trip has been great fun; but how glad I am it is over and I am to see Alice!

Sunday September 26

Reached Chicago.

Monday September 27

Left Chicago.

Tuesday September 28

Stopped at Niagara Falls.

Wednesday September 29

Reached New York and in the evening Chestnut Hill.

Thursday September 30

I am so happy that I hardly know what to do. My own beautiful queen is the same as ever and yet with a certain added charm that I do not know how to describe; I can not take my eyes off her; she is so pure and holy that it seems almost profanation to touch her, no matter how gently and tenderly; and yet when we are alone I can not bear her to be a minute out of my arms. I have been gradually getting frightfully homesick for her; my happiness now is almost too great.

Friday October 1

Spent the day with my own heart's darling, my sweetest mistress.

Saturday October 2

I am living in a dream of delight with my darling, my true love.

Sunday October 3

In the evening I with intense regret had to go back to New York; but it will be the last separation from my darling, for three weeks from Wednesday we are married—it makes me so happy I am almost afraid.

Monday October 4

I am staying with dear Aunt Annie & Uncle Jimmie; in their cosy little house. I am busy with wedding presents and getting all ready—and am dreadfully homesick for Alice.

Wednesday October 6

Entered the Columbia Law School; I shall be there every day about six hours, from nine till half-past three. Am having a lovely time at Aunt Annie's but miss Alice dreadfully. I am going to give her a diamond crescent a ruby bracelet and a saphire [sic] ring—in all about 2500 dollars! I have been spending money like water for these last two years, but shall economise after I am married. Three weeks from today we are married! I hardly dare believe it; it is too good. Oh my darling, my darling!

Friday October 8

Went out to Oyster Bay. Everything looked very cosy and homelike and it was lovely to see the dear quartette—Elliott, Pussie, Bysie & Mother. We have very much to talk over about the wedding.

Saturday October 9

Spent the day in the open air, chiefly playing tennis with Nell and Fred Weeks, both of whom I beat. Emlen, Alfred and Griswold came up to pass Sunday.

Monday October 11

Went back to New York. I like the law school very well so far.[24] The cousins have all acted like trumps, and have sent Alice beautiful presents; Emlen a pearl ring, West a bracelet &c &c.

Wednesday October 13

Only two weeks from today; my happiness is so great that it makes me almost afraid.

Dined at Edith's with Fanny and Grace, who are all going to the wedding. So are all my relatives and most of my friends.

Friday October 15

Came out to Oyster Bay.

Saturday October 16

Spent the day walking through the woods and playing tennis with Johnny and Freddy Weeks.

Sunday October 17

This is the last Sunday I shall spend here before I am married; when next I come to Oyster Bay it will be with my darling bride. I do so hope and pray I can make her happy; I shall try very hard to be as unselfish and sunny tempered as she is. It almost frightens me, in spite of my own happiness, to think that perhaps I may not make her happy; but I shall try so hard; and if ever man loved woman I love her.

Monday October 18

Went in to New York; shall leave for Boston on Friday. Until then I shall have my hands full attending to various affairs. Alice's bridesmaids are Corinne, Rosy, Rose and Fanny Peabody. My ushers are Emlen, West, Dick, Frank Lee, Tom Lee, Cottie Peabody,[25] Frank Peabody, Jack Tebbets, Minot Weld, & Walter Trimble.

---

24. Columbia University opened its law school in 1858.

25. Endicott Peabody (founded Groton School, was headmaster there when FDR attended, and officiated at FDR and Eleanor Roosevelt's marriage).

Friday October 22

Took night train for Boston.

Saturday October 23

Early in morning went out to Chestnut Hill, and, oh! how delighted I was to clasp my beloved darling again in my arms! She has received about 250 presents. In the afternoon I went out with dear old Cottie Peabody (whom I am very fond of) to the Peabodys house at Kernwood, Salem. It is a superb place, both grounds and house being strikingly handsome.[26] Besides, I like the whole household very much; they are all so well read and intelligent—and the boys such stalwart, manly fellows.

Sunday October 24

Cottie and I walked into Salem to church; then I went into see sweet, old "Grandma Lee." We took tea at Fanny Peabodys; she was just as pretty and cunning as ever.

Frank's fiancée is also visiting here; she is Miss Rosamund Lawrence, a strikingly handsome and exceedingly well cultivated girl.

Monday October 25

Spent the day making the final arrangements for the wedding; in the evening Cottie & I chopped down some trees and had larks generally.

Tuesday October 26

Went in to Boston; lunched with all of both families out at the Lees; dined & spent the night at the Brunswick; Elliott, of course, is best man.

Wednesday October 27

At 12 o'clock, on my 22d birthday, Alice and I were married. She made an ideally beautiful bride; and it was a lovely wedding. We came on for the night to Springfield, where I had taken a suite of rooms for the night.

Our intense happiness is too sacred to be written about.

Thursday October 28

Came on to Oyster Bay where we are to spend a fortnight; we are alone in the house, with two servants and a groom.

---

26. Now site of the Kernwood Golf Club.

Friday October 29

Alice has been resting from the journey.

Saturday October 30

My horse is in magnificent condition and we have the most beautiful drives. The tennis is laid out; and my rowboat is in the water. We breakfast at 10; dine at 2; and take tea at 7.

Sunday October 31

Instead of going to Church I read my bible aloud, and we took a beautiful walk; the weather is lovely and cool, and the wooded hills are red and yellow gold. I read aloud to her, from Quentin Durward,[27] Pickwick Papers[28] and The Newcomes.[29]

Monday November 1 [Entry continues into November 3.]

We are all alone in the comfortable country house, with its roaring wood fires and warm rooms, and it is beautiful autumn weather. Mary Ann & Kate are model servants; and the old Negro Davis (who always alludes to Alice as "the good lady") takes excellent care of the horse. The horse, by the way, and a dear, clumsy, handsome colly dog, Dare by name, are really friends, as much as if they were human; and besides them we have an idiotic small calf and a melancholy cat, both of which Baby can never resist teasing. It is impossible to describe the lovely, little teasing ways of my bright, bewitching darling; I can imagine no picture so pretty as her sweet self seated behind the tea things in the daintiest little pink and gray morning dress, while, in my silk jacket and slippers, I sit at the other end of the table. She seems in beautiful health; and she looks even prettier than she ever has before; the little laughing, blushing darling, with her sweet, winsome ways; and oh, she is such a tender and devoted little wife. We have the loveliest drives and walks together; we play a great deal of tennis, being about equally matched, and wander about the woods and shores. In the evenings I read aloud while she sews; or she plays on the piano; or we play cards together.

On Tuesday I drove over to Norwich to deposit my first vote for president—for Garfield.

---

27. The 1823 historical novel by Walter Scott.

28. The 1836 *The Posthumous Papers of the Pickwick Club* by Charles Dickens, under the pseudonym "Boz."

29. The 1855 novel by William Thackeray.

Thursday November 4

There is hardly an hour of the twenty-four that we are not together; I am living in dreamland; how I wish it could last for ever.

Friday November 5

Spent the usual healthy, happy day.

Saturday November 6

Rainy, so we stayed in the house. I love to talk over everything with Baby, from Politics to Poetry, and to read aloud to her, either from a History or standard novel or from the daily newspaper that forms our only intercourse with the outside world.

Sunday November 7

In the morning I read aloud from the bible; in the afternoon we took a long walk through the woods and fields, in the beautiful, clear, cool Autumn weather. Alice is a beautiful walker, with her long, firm step, and clambers over fences about as easily as I do.

My old hunter keeps us pretty well supplied with woodcock & partridge.

Monday November 8

We took a very long drive, going way out beyond Syosset on the brush plains beyond Syosset, coming back through the beautiful valley of Coldspring, and through Laurel Hollow and Oak Openings. In the afternoon we played lawn tennis.

Tuesday November 9

A beautiful Indian Summer day; in the morning we played tennis and sat on the piazza while I read aloud from "The Betrothed"[30]; in the afternoon I rowed my sweet Baby round Centre Island, and we saw a beautiful sunset on the water.

Wednesday November 10

We took a lovely long drive towards Desauraus Island,[31] Locust Valley and Glen Cove.

I doubt if there was ever a happier honeymoon than ours has been.

---

30. The 1825 novel by Sir Walter Scott, first of two *Tales of the Crusaders*.
31. Dosoris Island.

Thursday November 11

Rainy, so we stayed in the house in the morning, but went to drive in the afternoon.

Friday November 12

We took a long walk "across country" almost to Syosset; Alice is a fast walker, but our progress is not very rapid, as she stops to pet or to teaze [sic] every blessed calf, sow or horse we meet, and runs away if she sees a bull or a turkey cock—the latter—or still more, a guinea hen—being an object of intense interest to her. Dear old Dare, the colley, accompanies us on all our walks, and in fact every where, and is a great companion; lying by the log fire in the cosy little parlor at night.

This is the last day of our honeymoon; how sorry I am! We have had an ideal time; but what a happy life we look forward to!

Saturday November 13

With great regret we left Oyster Bay and drove in to New York, where we found, however, a perfect ovation awaiting us.

Sunday November 14

Alice is going to join the Presbyterian Church. I went to the Newsboys Home in the evening. Our rooms are too lovely for anything; we are going to live this winter with mother.[32]

Monday November 15

In the afternoon I took Alice out in the park in my cart, which looks as swell as possible. In the evening we went to the opera; Hilborne gave Alice his box.

Tuesday November 16

Alice received in the afternoon.

Wednesday November 17

I go to the law school at 8.30 (walking down & up) & get back at 4.00; then I drive Alice in the cart.

---

32. At the house on W. 57th St.

Thursday November 18

Went to a very jolly meeting of the St. Andrews Society[33]; had a long talk with Whitelaw Reid.[34]

Friday November 19

Drove Alice up the Riverside Park; Opera in evening.

Tuesday November 23

In the evening we are very apt to have a great many visitors, even if we do'n't go out; but we always have some lovely home time. The little Queen is just too lovely for anything; I always, if possible, drive her out in the afternoon, or, if she can't go, mother or one of the sisters.

Wednesday November 24

A good deal of snow, so Alice and I had a lovely sleigh ride. The law work is very interesting.

Thursday November 25[35]

Emlen and I gave the newsboys a big dinner; about a hundred came.
We had a great family dinner in the evening; Alice looked like a little Queen.

Friday November 26

Went to a dinner given to us by Aunt Annie. I sat by Annie Murray; met a bright fellow, Archie Alexander.

Saturday November 27

Dear Mr. & Mrs. Lee and Kitty have come on. I was perfectly delighted to see them. They dined with us.

Sunday November 28

The Lees and several other people took tea with us.

My darling little wife has decided to join the church.

Spoke to the newsboys, as usual.

---

33. Founded in 1756, the St. Andrew's Society of the State of New York was one of the nation's oldest benevolent societies. Its objects were "the promotion of social and friendly intercourse among the natives of Scotland and their connections and descendants in the city and vicinity, and the relief of such as may be indigent." *King's Handbook of New York City*, 411.

34. Longtime owner and editor of the *New York Tribune,* and influential Republican.

35. Thanksgiving.

Monday November 29

Ilanof, one of the Russian legation, dined here; an exceedingly clever man. I took Kitty out driving.

Tuesday November 30

John & Nannie dined with us.

Wednesday December 1

Went on a long drive with Baby; in the evening went to the Theatre with the Lees.

Friday December 3

We had a very large dinner party; I sat between Mrs. Newbold & Mrs. Astor; & also talked a good deal to Mrs. Cutting & Mrs. Potter. Enjoyed it very much; I like Astor[36] & Cutting.

Saturday December 4

Drove Mother up the Riverside Park.

I like the law school very much.

Tuesday December 7

Went to a rather stupid dinner at the Millers. Sat by a Miss Duncan.

Wednesday December 8

Great ball at our house for Alice & Conie; every living individual I know came.

Friday December 10

Preparatory service before Alice joins the church.

Saturday December 11

There was a grand reception at our house; I enjoyed it very much, as I could move round and talk to whomever I wanted to. I like some of the New York girls (more especially the married women, as Mrs. Astor, Mrs. Cutting & Mrs. Newbold) very much, but I am not very fond of going out. However, Alice is universally and greatly admired; and she seems to grow more beautiful day by day. She couldn't grow any sweeter, or lovelier. She seems very happy; and oh, how happy she has made me!

---

36. William Waldorf Astor, ten years TR's senior and at the time a New York State senator.

Sunday December 12

I love Sunday; we breakfast late in our morning dresses and jackets. We then go to church; come home to dinner; in the afternoon I walk with Alice, or if it is bad weather stay in the house with her; at tea West, Hilbourne, Uncle Jimmie and Aunt Annie appear; then I go down to the News Boys; and when I return to the house, spend the rest of the evening with the dear family.

My purest, saintliest little darling has joined the church. Now we are one in everything. My cup of happiness is almost running over.

Monday December 13

Went to a very jolly little dinner at the Iselins.

Tuesday December 14

Went to the Mendelsohn [sic] Concert, which was very fine.

Wednesday December 15

The horse is in superb spirits, and the weather is beautiful; I enjoy my drives with Alice most intensely; especially when we go up the Riverside Park by the beautiful Hudson. When my sweetest little wife can't go I always take the dear little mother. It is lovely to live as we are now: it would be hard to imagine a pleasanter home. The little wife is just the sunniest, brightest, prettiest little queen imaginable; and I perfectly worship her. How I marvel at my good luck!

Friday December 17

Went to a great afternoon reception at the Iselins; and to another at the Morans. I like these "teas"; I never stay more than two minutes with any girl and so don't get talked out.

Saturday December 18

In the evening I gave a whist club (at Alice's instigation—she is too sweet to me in everything); Doug Robinson, Harry Haddon, Archie Russell, Ike Iselin, Bob Sedgwick, Gasper Griswold, Willys Betts, West, Em, and myself. We had great fun. I like all the fellows (especially Doug—who may become a connection[37]) very much.

I also like young Bigelow, Trimble, and the Dodges.

---

37. Corinne Roosevelt married Douglas Robinson on April 29, 1882.

Monday December 20

Went to the Patriarch Ball[38] which was great fun; Corinne was a great belle, and my own sweet little mistress had a great deal of attention. I had some superb waltzes with Lucy Tuckerman, Emily Post, & Miss Livingstone.

Wednesday December 22

When the ground is very slippery I use the buggy instead of the cart. I love to take my sweet little wife up by the Riverside Park; it is a beautiful drive now, with the snowy palisades showing in fine relief against the gray winter skies, with the dark waters of the Hudson, covered with ice, at their feet.

Friday December 24

Alice and I went on to spend Xmas at Chestnut Hill; it was perfectly lovely to see all the dear people again, and just as sweet as ever.

Saturday December 25

Xmas. In the morning I saw all the little Lees receive their presents; then we went coasting; all the Saltonstalls came over to dinner.

Sunday December 26

Went to the dear little Church in the morning; coasted in the afternoon.

Monday December 27

Had great fun coasting; finally smashed up against a tree. In the afternoon I took Rosy out for a long sleigh ride; the sleighing is superb.

Tuesday December 28

Went in to Boston for some things; when we came out, found that Rosy had the measles so moved directly over to the Saltonstalls who at once took us in most kindly.

Wednesday December 29

It is perfect shame about the measles; I am almost afraid to go home; it is very hard on Mrs. Lee; the Saltonstalls are just as kind as possible.

Friday December 31

Darling Wifie and I decided to go home to-morrow.

---

38. The Patriarchs' Ball, the annual round of balls for the cream of New York society, presided over by Caroline Astor. TR's Uncle James was considered one of the "patriarchs" of New York.

Thus ends by far the happiest year I have ever spent, for in this year I have won the fairest and purest and sweetest of women for my wife. I never conceived it possible that there could be such a bright, sunny, unselfish girl. I can never express how I love her; and if I should love twice as much and as tenderly it would not be nearly as much as she deserves; I never can understand how I won her!

CASH ACCOUNT—SUMMARY SPENT

	1879	*1880*
January	400.65	282.87
February	225.00	172.96
March	214.35	39.02
April	679.27	460.15
May	205.73	481.47
June	148.65	904.57
July	106.00	989.16
August	770.88	101.00
September	290.77	660.40
October	542.79	3300.90
November	330.50	195.00
December	1292.00	405.00
	5206.59	7992.50

SUMMARY OF EXPENDITURES

	1878	*1879*	*1880*
Dress	401.30	685.80	761.59
Room	220.75	367.50	293.15
Board	305.50	288.00	171.50
Stable	125.00	930.79	449.78
Education	185.80	320.80	350.48
Washing	50.00	50.00	60.00
Presents	80.00	1050.22	3889.80
Charity	147.00	224.00	235.55
Coal &c	60.60	21.96	19.38
Travelling	229.25	343.23	558.07
Science	57.50	15.00	.45
Club Dues & Subscriptions	133.75	401.00	545.92
Sporting	172.10	85.84	231.00
Amusements	32.75	319.50	293.20
Sundries	101.00	102.95	132.73
	2302.30	5206.59	7992.50

GAME BAG

	Total	'73	'74	'75	'76	'77	'78	'79	'80
Lynx	1						1		
Fox	1						1		
Raccoon	1						1		
Deer	2					1	1		
Jack Rabbit	1								1
White "	5						1	4	
Wood "	22		2				8	11	1
Gray Squirrel	19		3	4	2	4	3	3	
Syrian "	2	2							
Canada Grouse	7					1	1	5	[grouse total] 152
Ruffed "	50		2	2		2	16	28	
Prarie "	69								69
Sharptail "	26								26
American Quail	28				1		6	16	5
Gray Partridge	1	1							
Redlegged "	1	1							
Syrian Quail	2	2							
Wild Pigeon	5			2			1	2	[pigeon total] 134
Carolina Dove	11						3		8
Egyptian "	37	37							
Rock Pigeon	81	81							
Hoopoo	8	8							
Woodcock	41				1		14	26	
Snipe	1		1						
Upland Plover	4						1		3
Golden "	9					2	2		5
Blackbreast "	6					2	2		2
Ringneck &c "	13			2	3	2			6
Whitetailed "	3	3							[plover total] 50
Spinning "	2	2							
Crocodile &c "	6	6							
Pecweet &c "	7	7							
Winter Yellowlegs	38						2	3	33
Summer "	16						2	2	12
Sandsnipe (Beach birds)	73	36		6	6	8	5	6	[beach birds] 127
Rail	1								1

	Total	'73	'74	'75	'76	'77	'78	'79	'80
Coot	1								1
Gray Heron	1	1							
White "	8	8							
Blue "	1					1			
Green "	10		1		2	4	2	1	
Night "	19		6	4	4	3	2		
Bittern	3					1			2
Least Bittern &c	1					1			[heron total] 43
Goose	1								1
Mallard	4								4
Black duck	6					1		5	
Widgeon	1								1
Sprigtail Duck	1								1
Green Wing Teal	1								1
Blue " "	2								2
Wood Duck	6					2	1	2	1
Redhead	2								2
Blue Bill	2								2
Dipper	4						1	1	2
Old squaw	6		2		1	2	1		
Ruddy Duck	1						1		
Surf Duck	5			1		4			
Whitewing Scoter	6			3		1	2		
Sheldrake	6						2	4	
Hooded Merganser	1								[duck total] 54
Loon	4			2			1	1	
Grebe	4								4
	707	195	17	26	20	46	79	121	203

SUMMARY OF GAME BAG

	Total	'73	'74	'75	'76	'77	'78	'79	'80
Lynx	1							1	
Fox	1							1	
Coon	1							1	
Deer	2					1		1	
Rabbit	28		2				9	15	2
Squirrel	21	2	3	4	2	4	3	3	
Grouse	152		2	2	3		17	33	95
Quail &c	32	4			1		6	16	5
Pigeon	134	118		2			4	2	8
Woodcock	41			1			14	26	
Snipe	128	36	1	6	6	12	8	8	51
Plover	50	18		2	3	6	5		16
Rail, Coot &c &c	10	8							2
Heron	43	9	7	4	6	10	4	1	2
Goose	1								1
Duck	54		2	4	1	10	8	12	17
Loon &c	8			2			1	1	4
	707	195	17	26	20	46	79	121	203

[Notes made later.]

In 1881, made but one shooting day, when I got 5 scoter ducks on Long Island Sound.

In 1882, at Sayville in August shot

    2 marlin
    1 jack
    2 willet
    3 yelper
    7 yellow legs
    5 dowitcher
   15 ringneck
   <u>25</u> "peep," "oseye" &c.
   60

at Oyster Bay

   <u>7</u> clapper rail
   7

at Oyster Bay

3	broadbill duck
4	old squaw
17	coots
24	
91	

[notes on inside back cover]

E owes me 60.40
Spent in Aug 100 dollars
Shot in Aug 35 birds

	Spent in Sep		319.00
	Janion's bill		15.40
	Grenning bill		126.00
	Law School		100.00
	Presents		100.00
			341.40
			660.40
	-sporting		100.00
	-Travelling		159.00
	-Present		35.00
	-Church		25.00
Aug	13th	Spectacles	10.00
	15th	Loan to Elliott	16.75
		[crossed out]	
	"	Church	5.00
	"	To Chicago	35.00
	18th	Hotel &c	10.00
	28th	Books &c	10.00
	"	Board bill	20.00
	31st	Carriage hire	5.00
	"	Photos	6.00
			101.00
Sept	3	Hotel	28.00
	"	Cars &c	10.00
	8	Board &c	10.00
	11th	Dogs	15.00
	"	Board &c	25.00
	"	Wagon	14.00

13th	Books	5.00
"	Wilcox	15.00
"	Ticket &c	20.00
25th	Hunting	50.00
"	Travelling	67.00
"	Presents	35.00
"	Church	25.00
		319.00

FIGURE 1. Theodore Roosevelt in 1877. Courtesy of the Theodore Roosevelt Collection, Harvard College Library.

FIGURE 2. Martha Bulloch Roosevelt. Courtesy of the Theodore Roosevelt Collection, Harvard College Library.

FIGURE 3. Theodore Roosevelt Sr. Courtesy of the Theodore Roosevelt Collection, Harvard College Library.

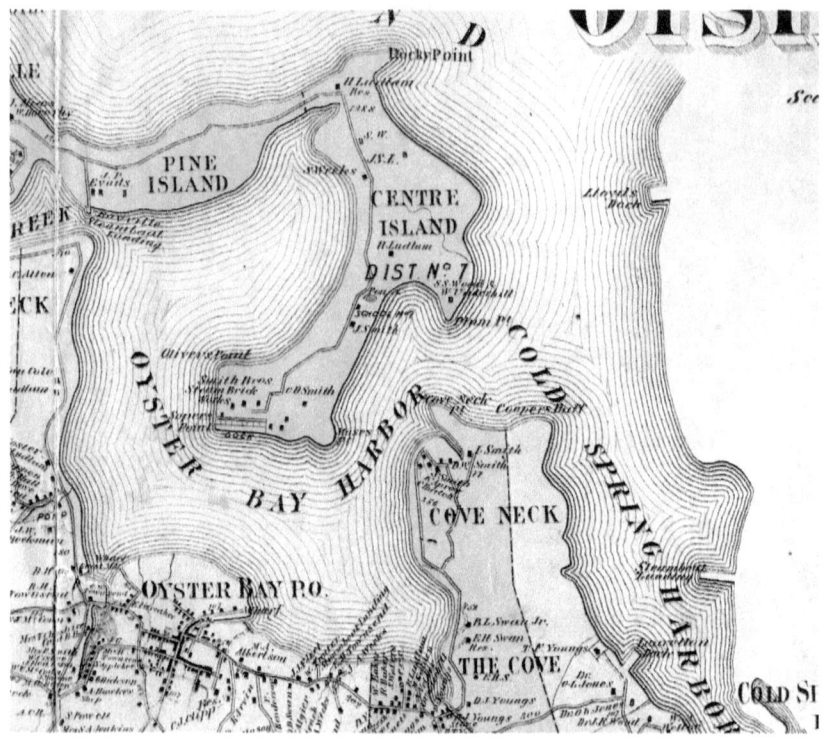

FIGURE 4. Map of Oyster Bay and Centre Island, 1873. Courtesy of the Oyster Bay Historical Society.

FIGURE 5. Theodore Roosevelt's room while at Harvard. Courtesy of the Theodore Roosevelt Collection, Harvard College Library.

FIGURE 6. Theodore Roosevelt in the Maine woods, 1879. Courtesy of the Theodore Roosevelt Collection, Harvard College Library.

FIGURE 7. Alice Hathaway Lee, Rose Saltonstall, and Theodore Roosevelt, 1879. Courtesy of the Theodore Roosevelt Collection, Harvard College Library.

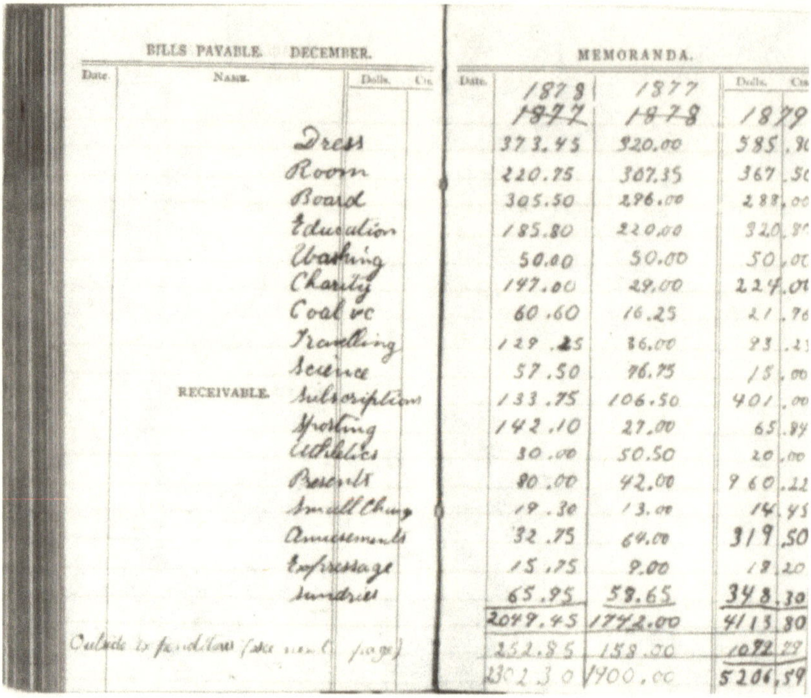

FIGURE 8. Summary of Roosevelt's annual expenditures, from 1879 diary. Theodore Roosevelt Papers at the Library of Congress. http://www.theodorerooseveltcenter.org/Research/Digital-Library/Record/ImageViewer.aspx?libID=o288505&imageNo=154. Theodore Roosevelt Digital Library. Dickinson State University.

FIGURE 9. The Porcellian Club, 1880. Roosevelt is seated in middle row, third from left. Courtesy of the Theodore Roosevelt Collection, Harvard College Library.

FIGURE 10. Roosevelt's Harvard chums, 1880. From left to right, front row: John Tebbets, Harry Chapin, and Harry Shaw; back row: Richard Saltonstall, Christopher Minot Weld, and Roosevelt. Courtesy of the Theodore Roosevelt Collection, Harvard College Library.

FIGURE 11. Theodore Roosevelt and brother Elliott en route to Roosevelt's first western hunting trip, 1880. Courtesy of the Theodore Roosevelt Collection, Harvard College Library.

FIGURE 12. Alice Lee Roosevelt, ca. 1883. Courtesy of the Theodore Roosevelt Collection, Harvard College Library.

FIGURE 13. Library of Roosevelt home at W. 57th Street, New York City. Courtesy of the Theodore Roosevelt Collection, Harvard College Library.

FIGURE 14. From left to right, Alice Roosevelt with Roosevelt sisters Corinne and Anna, ca. 1883. Courtesy of the Theodore Roosevelt Collection, Harvard College Library.

FIGURE 15. Theodore Roosevelt in his first year in the New York State Assembly, 1882. Courtesy of the Theodore Roosevelt Collection, Harvard College Library.

FIGURE 16. Roosevelt's Cities Committee, 1882. Roosevelt is bottom row, third from right. Courtesy of the Theodore Roosevelt Collection, Harvard College Library.

FIGURE 17. Roosevelt's closest friends in the Assembly, 1884. From left to right, back row: William O'Neil and Roosevelt; front row: Isaac Hunt, George F. Spinney, and Walter Howe. Spinney was the Albany correspondent for the *New York Times*. Courtesy of the Theodore Roosevelt Collection, Harvard College Library.

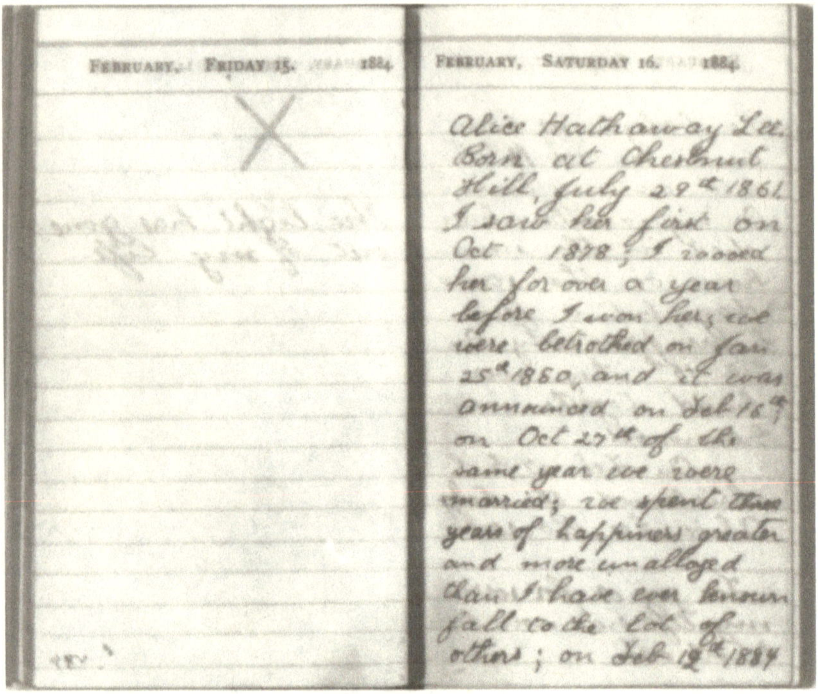

FIGURE 18. Diary page from February 16, 1884, the day of the double funeral for Roosevelt's wife Alice and mother Martha. Theodore Roosevelt Papers at the Library of Congress. http://www.theodorerooseveltcenter.org/Research/Digital-Library/Record/ImageViewer.aspx?libID=0284449&imageNo=12. Theodore Roosevelt Digital Library. Dickinson State University.

FIGURE 19. Alice Roosevelt, 1885. Courtesy of the Theodore Roosevelt Collection, Harvard College Library.

FIGURE 20. Theodore Roosevelt in the Dakota cattle round-up, 1885. Courtesy of the Theodore Roosevelt Collection, Harvard College Library.

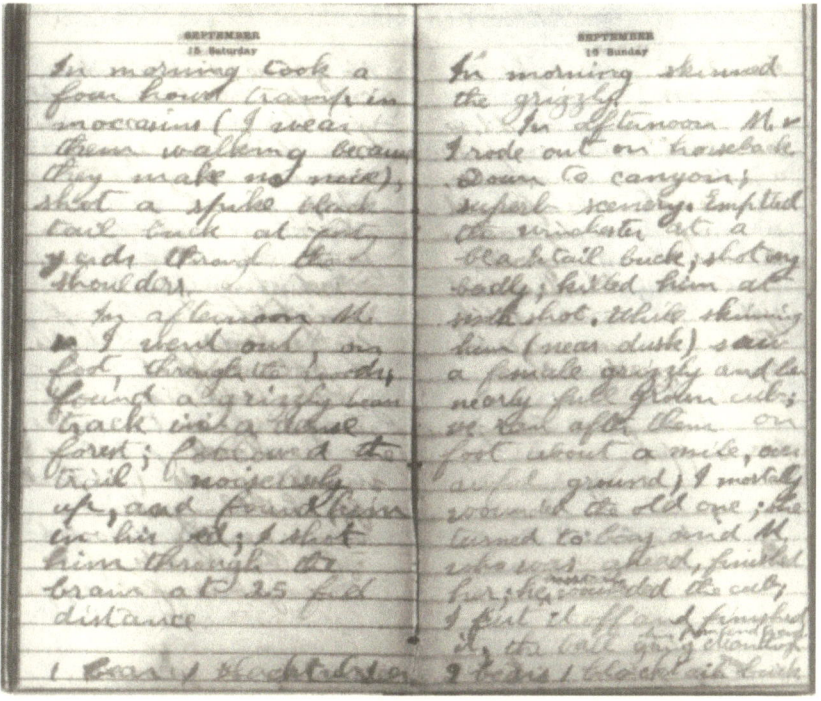

FIGURE 21. Diary pages from September 1883 describing Roosevelt's bear hunt. Theodore Roosevelt Papers at the Library of Congress. http://www.theodorerooseveltcenter.org/Research/Digital-Library/Record/ImageViewer.aspx?libID=0288501&imageNo=25. Theodore Roosevelt Digital Library. Dickinson State University.

FIGURE 22. Roosevelt's Elkhorn Ranch house in Dakota, ca. 1886. Courtesy of the Theodore Roosevelt Collection, Harvard College Library.

FIGURE 23. Roosevelt guarding the captured boat thieves, 1886. Courtesy of the Theodore Roosevelt Collection, Harvard College Library.

FIGURE 24. Long Island's Meadowbrook Hunt at Roosevelt's Sagamore Hill estate, 1885. Courtesy of the Theodore Roosevelt Collection, Harvard College Library.

Figure 25. Edith Kermit Carow, 1885. Courtesy of the Theodore Roosevelt Collection, Harvard College Library.

Politics

Volume V (1881)

The year began as it had ended, with Alice and Theodore kept busy by a social season consisting of balls and dinner parties. Perhaps spurred by conversations with Whitelaw Reid and William Waldorf Astor, Roosevelt began attending meetings of his Twenty-First Assembly District in the barnlike room of Morton Hall. It helped that Morton Hall was virtually around the corner from the Roosevelt home. Despite the strange sight of Roosevelt attending the meetings in formal wear en route to the opera or Patriarchs' Ball, the twenty-two year old was no dilettante. He attended the meetings regularly, and a month after attending his first meeting addressed those assembled on the proposed new city charter. What brought Theodore Roosevelt into politics was one of the most basic facts of living in New York City: it was filthy.

In 1881 there was no separate street-cleaning department in New York City. Instead, responsibility for street cleaning lay with the Board of Police Commissioners, a four-man body split evenly—and often deadlocked—between Democrats and Republicans. The result, as Justice Patrick Daly said to a Cooper Institute meeting only days after Roosevelt addressed his district association, was that New York was "the dirtiest city in the universe." Reformers called for a separate, nonpartisan department to clean New York's streets. In an age of political patronage, not everyone agreed. When the sitting Assembly member for the Twenty-First District voted against a bill that would have established a separate department of street cleaning in the city, Roosevelt set out to secure the man's defeat. "Am going to try to kill our last years legislator," he noted in his diary. Roosevelt had taken the first step in his political career.

By the spring of 1881, Roosevelt was juggling a full slate of responsibilities. He was married, studying law, attending political meetings, escorting Alice to the opera, balls, and dinner parties, acting as trustee for the Orthopedic Dispensary and the New York Infant Asylum, and working on his naval history. For a twenty-two year old not long out of college, Roosevelt had quickly acquired all the trappings of full adulthood. Not surprisingly there was still something of the adolescent about him. As Roosevelt made plans for their European honeymoon, Alice left to visit her family in Chestnut Hill for two weeks. Roosevelt was primed to make full use of the absence of "Darling Wifie." With Alice away, Roosevelt stepped up his own social activities. Within a week of her departure Roosevelt gave a whist party to some of his male friends, invited old Harvard chum George Minot to stay with him in the city, and took a couple of women out for drives—including his old flame Edith Carow. Very quickly this second bachelorhood came to an end. Roosevelt retrieved Alice from Chestnut Hill, and the following month the couple departed for Europe.

This was Roosevelt's first trip to Europe since he was a boy. The couple followed much of the same path Roosevelt and his family had taken years before. Theodore and Alice went to London, Paris, Venice, Milan, and Lake Como, spending some time up near the border between Italy and Switzerland. During their stay there, Roosevelt heard the news that President James Garfield had been shot on July 2. In every city they visited the couple ran into friends from New York and Boston: the Chapmans, Gardiners, and Kennedys; and Charley Alexander, Nicholas Fish, Minot Weld, Harry Chapin, and Harry Shaw. For Roosevelt the climax of the trip may have been his August 4 ascent of the Matterhorn. The following day he wrote his sister Anna that "after seeing a most glorious sunrise which crowned the countless snow peaks and billowy, white clouds with a strange crimson irradescence [sic], reached the summit at seven." After that Alice and Theodore retraced their path back to London and Liverpool, where they spent time with uncles Irvine and Jimmie Bulloch, Mittie's brothers who had lived abroad in exile after their service for the Confederacy during the Civil War.

After a long summer abroad the couple returned home in early October. By the end of the month the Republican Party for Roosevelt's district had nominated him for the New York Assembly. Roosevelt himself had spoken in favor of censuring the current legislator, William Trimble, after Trimble had voted against the street-cleaning bill back in April. That October, Independent Republicans of the district had sent out a circular announcing a meeting to nominate an anti-machine candidate for the Assembly. There was also a fight brewing between the current boss of the district, Jake Hess, and another local leader, Joe Murray. As Roosevelt himself recounted years later, Murray thought the best way "to make a drive at Jake Hess" was in the fight over the Assembly nomination. Murray asked Roosevelt to stand for the nomination, and they beat Jake Hess and Trimble by a vote of sixteen to nine. Roosevelt made sure all knew of his independence. When the district committee visited Roosevelt at his home to officially offer the nomination, Roosevelt said he would not be subservient to local bosses. He also said he would vote with the Republican

Party in national politics, but in local affairs he would keep his own counsel. Thus Roosevelt began the difficult balancing act between his independence and his loyalty to the Republican Party that would mark the next thirty years of his political career.

On November 8, the voters of the Twenty-First District elected Theodore Roosevelt to the New York Assembly by a healthy majority of over 1500 votes. In this first campaign Roosevelt was aided by several factors. The Twenty-First was a relatively safe Republican district. In the press Roosevelt was always described as the son of Theodore Roosevelt Sr., a name above reproach in New York and associated with honesty and philanthropy. Roosevelt was also aided by family friends and prominent city Republicans such as lawyers Elihu Root and Joseph Choate. Finally, Roosevelt was aided by an astoundingly poor Democratic opponent, William Strew. Two years before Dr. Strew had been removed from his position as medical superintendent of the New York City Lunatic Asylum on Blackwell's Island for gross mismanagement. Although Roosevelt would not take his seat until after the New Year, he got right to work researching a bill to build a new aqueduct to ensure the city an adequate supply of water. Like the street-cleaning issue, the aqueduct bill reflected Roosevelt's endeavors to make city living healthier and safer. A dedicated supply of clean water would prevent the outbreak of both disease and a devastating fire. It was a good start for the man who would one day become the leading figure of the Progressive Era.

Volume V
1881 DIARY

[cover]
Theodore Roosevelt
6 West 57th St.
New York
Alice H. Roosevelt
6 West 57th St.
New York
United States

Saturday January 1

Alice and I came on to New York.

Sunday January 2

Went to Newsboys Home in evening as usual. West and the other cousins at tea as usual.

Monday January 3

Holiday. Took Alice a 30 mile sleigh ride. Sleighing beautiful. We dined with Hill & Frank & went to theatre.

Tuesday January 4

Began work at Law School. Took mother on sleigh ride. Whist Club at Robinsons. Always walk up and down to & from Law School.

Wednesday January 5

Took Alice a long sleigh ride. Went to dinner at James Roosevelts, then ball at Delmonicos—Mrs. Kings.

Thursday January 6

Dinner at Astors. Organizing free trade club. Every moment of my time occupied.

Friday January 7

Two Miss Rathbones arrived.

Very pleasant little party at Aunt Annies.

Saturday January 8

Took Alice Rathbone out sleighriding.

Monday January 10

Took Mother out sleighriding. Dinner at our house; sat between Grace Rathbone & Lucy Tuckerman.

Tuesday January 11

Took Fanny Smith out sleighriding. Dinner at Delanoes; sat between Mrs. Astor & Mrs. Drayton.

Wednesday January 12

Sleighing superb. Drove Alice beyond Harlem. Very jolly theatre party & supper at Tuckermans.

Thursday January 13

Great ball at Astors.

Friday January 14

15 of us started in special car for Niagara; Robinson, Betts, Beekman, Whitmore, Emlen, Colgate, Weir & myself; Alice, Corinne, Bamie, The Miss Parishes, Turnbull & Robinson. Greatest kind of fun.

Saturday January 15

Ideal day; perpetual spree. Saw falls, rapids, & whirlpool; took long sleighrides; ended up with every kind of dance in evening. Took hotel by storm. Everybody so jolly & congenial.

Sunday January 16

Sleighed to Church. Went under Falls; grand sight. Took night train for N.Y. Ghost Stories, & songs. Trip is the success of the season.

Monday January 17

Went to Patriarchs Ball.

Tuesday January 18

John Elliott came to visit us.

Took Flora Grant out sleighing.

Wednesday January 19

Took mother out sleighing. Went down to oversee newsboys night school.

Thursday January 20

Took Alice out sleighing.

Friday January 21

Argued case in moot court; successful.

Saturday January 22

Took Harriet Lawrence out sleighing.

Monday January 24

Dinner at our house for Lowell, Miss Grant & Miss Lawrence.

Tuesday January 25

Very jolly dinner at Rosy Roosevelts.

Wednesday January 26

The sleighing is better this year than I have ever seen it; I take my darling wifie out every day.

Thursday January 27

Took Rosamina Peabody out in my sleigh. Party at Oothoudts.

Friday January 28

Dinner at the Morans.

Saturday January 29

Evening party with juggling feats at Hilbornes.

Sunday January 30

A good many people at the tea, as usual.

Monday January 31

Took Fanny Peabody out sleighing.

F.C.D.C.[1] in evening.

Tuesday February 1

Dinner at Keans; went down to oversee coffee-house with John Firman.

---

1. Family Circle Dancing Class. Ball given at Delmonico's.

Wednesday February 2

Rosy, and Rose S., arrived for a visit.

Thursday February 3

Took Rosy out sleighing. Theatre party in evening.

Friday February 4

Took Rose S. out sleighing; dinner in evening.

Saturday February 5

Took mother out sleighing; small "party" in evening.

Sunday February 6

At last, after very much vacillation & unhappiness, darling little Corinne has accepted Douglass.[2] Am very glad. He is a splendid fellow.

Monday February 7

Took Aunt Annie a sleigh ride.

Dinner at the Leavitts.

Tuesday February 8

Dinner at Aunt Laura's.

Wednesday February 9

Took Rosy a sleigh ride.

Party at the Robinsons; great spree.

Thursday February 10

"Tea" at Julian Weir's. Dinner at Griswolds. Both of them great fun.

Friday February 11

Preparatory communion lecture at Dr. Halls. Sleighed with Mother.

---

2. Douglas Robinson. Corinne had her coming out party in December 1880, after which her family pressured her to marry Robinson, the wealthy manager of the Astor properties. Roosevelt liked the manly Robinson and ignored Corinne's great unhappiness in being forced to marry the quick-tempered Scotsman. It was not a happy marriage, and Corinne spent much time at the 57th Street house being consoled by Mittie and Alice.

Saturday February 12
Dinner at Weekes.

Monday February 14
Took Rose S. out driving. Political meeting[3]; then Patriarchs Ball.

Tuesday February 15
Mendelsohn Concert.

Wednesday February 16
"Tea" at Percy Kings. Little party at Aunt Annies.

Thursday February 17
Went to primary of Republican Association. Drove Alice in buggy; snow all gone. Rosy and Rose went back to Chestnut Hill.

Friday February 18
Musical at the Betts. Drove Corinne.

Monday February 21
Very pleasant little "Niagara Party" at the Betts; tableaux, wax works, Virginia Reel, Polka Redowa, Highland Schottische.

Tuesday February 22
Alice (& I!) matronized a little party out to Keans place to spend the night.

Wednesday February 23
Came back to N.Y. Took Missy Robinson out driving.

Thursday February 24
Went round to the Primary Political Club. Then to Bachelors Ball which was very swell.

---

3. This appears to be TR's first visit to Morton Hall, the Republican headquarters for the Twenty-First District, on East 59th Street, very close to the Roosevelt home. The hall was a great, barnlike room over a store, decorated with little more than regularly spaced spittoons. As TR was heading afterwards to the ball, it seems likely he wore his silk top hat and tails to the meeting, something he made a habit of doing during the social season.

Friday February 25
Took Alice a long drive. Mr. and Mrs. Meusing at dinner.

Saturday February 26
Took mother out driving. Dinner at Stuyvesant Fishes.[4]

Sunday February 27
News Boys, as usual.

Monday February 28
F.C.D.C. in evening.

Tuesday March 1
Johnson's party in evening.

Have been studying law pretty hard.

Wednesday March 2
Took Alice a long drive.

Thursday March 3
The Thayers came to dinner, I went to a primary (Republican) after.

Friday March 4
Theatre party with John & Nannie Roosevelt, & Walter Suydam & his wife.

Monday March 7
Took Alice out in the cart, for Spring seems to have set in at last.

Wednesday March 9
Took Alice a lovely drive up the Riverside park.

Thursday March 10
Small dinner.

---

4. Son of Hamilton Fish, former New York governor, US senator, and Grant's secretary of state. Stuyvesant Fish was an executive with the Illinois Central Railroad (later its president) and active in the Republican Party.

Friday March 11

Republican Primary (& Opera) in evening.

Monday March 14

Dinner at Free Trade Club. Addressed Republican Association on new charter.[5]

Tuesday March 15

Took Corinne a long drive.

Wednesday March 16

Took Alice a long drive up Riverside Park.

Thursday March 17

Went to see Newsboy's home and afterwards to reception at the Tuckermans.

Friday March 18

Am elected a trustee of the Orthopedic Dispensary & the New York Infant Asylum. Kudos[6]; but work.

Monday March 21

Took Alice a long drive. Am now working very hard at my law; have been rather loafing lately. Opera in evening, at Hilly's Box, & dined with him.

Tuesday March 22

Took Fanny Smith out driving—as Alice always receives on Tuesday.

Wednesday March 23

Drove Bamie in the Park. Walk up and down town everyday—about 6 miles. That (& driving in the park) is my only exercise.

Thursday March 24

Take Alicy [sic] a long drive every day. Am still working hard at law school; & at one or two unsuccessful literary projects.[7]

---

5. In Albany, a special committee had been convened to draw up a bill to revise the city's charter. The week before TR addressed the district meeting, the committee had debated a number of the sections of the bill, especially the one relating to street cleaning. At the time, street cleaning was under the authority of the four-man police commission. TR and others advocated establishing a separate city department for street cleaning.

6. Honor.

7. Roosevelt was working on a naval history of the War of 1812.

Friday March 25
Lunched at the Kennedys to meet Lord & Lady George Campbell.

Dear Uncle Jimmie arrived in the evening.

Sunday March 27
Darling Wifie and I went to church in the morning to Doctor Halls as usual; Newsboys in the evening of course. The Regular family Sunday tea, cousins, aunts & all.

Monday March 28
Darling Wifie went on to spend a fortnight at Chestnut Hill; I miss my sweetest queen more than I can tell.

Took Uncle Jimmie out driving.

Wednesday March 30
Am studying very hard at the Law School.

Tad & Bigelow dined with me.

Friday April 1
Took Edith to drive.

Saturday April 2
Dinner Party; sat between Maria Potter & Christine Kean; afterwards talked to Lulu McAllister. Pleasantest one I have been to this winter.

Monday April 4
Took Bamie to drive.

Tuesday April 5
Took Aunt Annie to drive.

Gave a whist party in the evening to Beckman, Sedgwick, Iselin, Colgate &c &c.

Wednesday April 6
Took Conie to drive.

Thursday April 7
George Minot is staying with us. Dinner party in the evening.

I took Lizzie Moran to drive in the dog cart.

Friday April 8

Took mother to drive. Went to Republican Primary; grand row; very hopeless.[8] Afterwards to the John Taylor Johnstons.

Saturday April 9

Went on to Chestnut Hill. Perfectly delightful to see my darling wife, and all the dear family again.

Sunday April 10

Church as usual in the dear little chapel. Tea at the Saltonstalls.

Took Georgie & Bella to walk.

Monday April 11

Went to the Porcellian Club, and to see Cotty Peabody. The country and everything is lovely.

Tuesday April 12

Played with the children, and loafed round all day.

Wednesday April 13

Came back to N.Y. Succeeded in arresting a swindler, had quite a struggle with him.

Thursday April 14

Took Alice a long drive. Dinner party in the evening.

Monday April 18

Meeting of executive committee of Young Mens Republican Ass.

Tuesday April 19

Had the swindler indicted by the Grand Jury.

The weather is superb for driving.

---

8. The assemblyman from the Twenty-First District, William J. Trimble, voted against the measure to establish a separate department of street cleaning. At Morton Hall that night reformers introduced a resolution of censure, of which Roosevelt spoke in favor. The resolution was defeated by a large majority, and was replaced by a resolution endorsing Trimble.

Friday April 22

Corinne acted Private Theatricals with Paul Tuckerman. Excellent. Dancing afterwards.

Saturday April 23

Mamie Saltonstall & Hattie Lee arrived for a few days visit. I am working tolerably hard at my law.

Sunday April 24

Went to the Newsboys lodging house, for the last time till October.

Douglass Robinson is a perfect old trump.

Wednesday April 27

Went down to the "Newsboys dinner" which of course was great fun.

Friday April 29

The driving is perfectly delightful, and my horse never went better.

Saturday April 30

I had the swindler put in the penitentiary for six months.

Sunday May 1

Rosy Lee is staying with us.

Monday May 2

Besides working pretty well at the law, I spend most of my spare time in the Astor Library,[9] on my "Naval History."

Wednesday May 4

Every afternoon I take the little wife out driving; generally up Riverside, by the beautiful Hudson.

Thursday May 5

Went round to the "Primary meeting"; as usual, rather a free fight.

---

9. Astor Library, founded in 1854, one of the precursors of the New York Public Library. Today the building houses the Public Theatre on Lafayette Street.

Friday May 6

Dear, funny old Dick Saltonstall has come to stay with us.

Saturday May 7

Little theatre party for Rosy, Dick & Fanny Smith & Romy Colgate.

Sunday May 8

Excellent sermon at Dr. Halls.

We have had no end of bother packing up.

Monday May 9

Went to a meeting of the Directors of the Orthopedic Dispensary.

Tuesday May 10

The weather is perfectly beautiful and the drives lovely.

Wednesday May 11

My law school work is over; my will drawn up; and my horse going to the country.

Thursday May 12

At 3 oclock sailed on the "Celtic" for England. Lots of people down to see us off. Hurrah! for a summer abroad with the darling little wife.

Friday May 13

I am perfectly well but poor little Alice is sicker than the devil.

Saturday May 14

Alice gets worse.

Sunday May 15

Alice sicker than ever; I am still in beautiful health.

Wednesday May 18

Confound a European trip, say I! Alice wretchedly sick; I have'n't been at all sick but tired out by taking care of her.

Saturday May 21

Landed at Queenstown. Alice revived at once, very much. Steamed up the River to Cork; most beautiful sail. At Imperial Hotel; good.

Sunday May 22

Dear little English Church in morning. In afternoon heard bells of Shandon,[10] then drove to Castle Blarney; crumbling, ivy covered ruin. Flowers all out; birds singing; everything lovely.

Monday May 23

Took R.R. for Killarney. Excellent hotel, by beautiful lake. Jaunting car to ivy-covered Mulcross Abbey & Ross Castle; & Torc Cascade. Boat home. Scenery lovely. Hurrah!

Tuesday May 24

We drove to Dunloe's Gap[11]; Alice on pony, I walked through it; very wild and grand; then took boat down through beautiful upper lake. Most lovely day. Poor devil fainting from hunger. Had him fed & sent to Cork.

Wednesday May 25

Took train to Dublin. Alice is best traveling companion I have ever known. By Jove, what luck I have had! This is the lovliest [sic] trip I ever was on.

Thursday May 26

Went out to Bray, then to Powerscourt, and through the beautiful glen called Dargles. Lovely scenery. Are leading most luxurious life!

Friday May 27

Boat to Holyhead; cars to Liverpool. Are staying Aunt Hattie Bullochs.[12] They are all too kind for anything.

Sunday May 29

Spent the afternoon with Uncle Irvine & Aunt Ella; they have a most lovely little house.

Tuesday May 31

Came on to London, at Queens Hotel. Harry Shaw, Minot Weld & Harry Chapin came round to see me.

---

10. The bells of the Church of St. Anne, in the Shandon District of Cork.
11. Dunloe Gap: a narrow mountain pass.
12. Martha Roosevelt's brothers, James and Irvine Bulloch, had served in the Confederate Navy during the U.S. Civil War. Denied amnesty following the war, they moved to Liverpool, England. James married Harriot "Hattie" Cross Foster in 1857.

Wednesday June 1

Went to national gallery. Rembrandt, Rubens, (Reynolds, Gainsborough), Murillo, Velasquez; I am very fond of Rembrandt & Murillo. Turner—idiotic.[13] Zoölogical Gardens.

Thursday June 2

Took Miss Jenny Tuckerman to the Tower. Crown jewels & armour, very interesting. Opera in evening; Haymarket, Nilson.[14]

Friday June 3

We drove out on a coach to the Epsom races, with Shaw, Weld, Chapin & the Lawrences. Great Fun. Theatre in evening.

Saturday June 4

South Kensington Museum[15]; very interesting; Gilbert & Sullivans's new Comic Opera in evening.[16]

Sunday June 5

St. Pauls in morning; lovely music. Westminster Abbey in afternoon; excellent sermon from Dean Stanley.[17]

Monday June 6

Lunch with some of Douglasses [sic] relations; British Museum (beautiful sculptures); dinner at Kingsfords.

Tuesday June 7

We went out on coach to Windsor castle; rainy but great fun. Dined with Chapin, Weld & Shaw.

Wednesday June 8

Grosvenor Gallery; shopping; Shaw & Chapin to dinner.

---

13. J.M.W. Turner, the Romantic landscape artist. A precursor of the Impressionists, Turner painted with intense displays of light and color that drew harsh reviews from conservative critics.

14. Haymarket Street, center of the West End theater district; Birgit Nilsson, Swedish soprano.

15. Early name of the Victoria and Albert Museum.

16. *Patience*, a satire of the aesthetic movement.

17. Arthur Stanley, dean of Westminster and author of many works on the history of the Anglican Church, died the following month.

Thursday June 9
Dorée Gallery; very fine. Bought presents. Tried on clothes.

Friday June 10
Shopping; British museum.

Saturday June 11
Came on to Paris. Hotel Bellevue; very good.

Channel very smooth.

Sunday June 12
Church. Walked to place de la concorde & champs Elysees.

Monday June 13
Shopping. Bois de Boulogne, Column Vendôme, Magnificent Arc de Triumphe.

Tuesday June 14
Louvre. Venus de Milo. Rubens and Murillo. Superb.

Friday June 17
Left in morning train for Venice.

Saturday June 18
After some slight misadventures arrived at Venice, very dirty & rather tired. But Venice is lovliest place we have been to yet; fairy [sic—likely means "ferry"].

Sunday June 19
Hotel Danielli[18]; old Palace; lovely rooms facing San Georgio Majiore[19] & Liddo. In evening rowed through the water-streets. Beautiful.

Monday June 20
In the morning to see Titian's masterpiece[20], then through palace of doge. In evening in gondola to the Liddo. Then to Piazza San Marco to hear Music.

---

18. Hotel Danieli. The central building is a fourteenth-century palazzo that belonged to the Dandolo family.
19. San Giorgio Maggiore.
20. "Assumption of the Virgin," 1516–18, Basilica di Santa Maria Gloriosa dei Frari.

Tuesday June 21

San Marco; in evening again rowed through Venice.

Wednesday June 22

Came on to Milan.

Thursday June 23

Saw the beautiful Milan Cathedral. Came on to Lake Como. Are staying at the Villa d'Este.

Saturday June 25

The Lake is too beautiful for anything. Nicholas Fish & his wife are here; Alice and I drove to Como, to see the cathedral. Excellent hotel.

Monday June 27

We went by steamer up to Colico; then took our carriage & three horses, driven by Lombardino (good driver & nice fellow) & came on to Chiavenna. Are going in same carraige [sic] for a fortnight.

Tuesday June 28

Went over Slugen Pass. Took lunch in a vile inn at Campo Dolcina. The pass was very grand. Are spending night in Splugen; good german-swiss inn.

Wednesday June 29

In morning drove through the wildly magnificent Via Mala; Lunched at Thusis & walked up to Rhaetian[21] Castle. Then through beautiful gorge to Tiefenleasten. Torrent roaring under our windows.

Thursday June 30

Crossed the barren Julier Pass into Upper Engadine, and came on to Samaden.[22]

Friday July 1

Took Alice out donkey riding.

---

21. Ancient Roman province that encompassed today's eastern Switzerland and western Austria.

22. Samedan.

Saturday July 2

Alice on horseback & I on foot climbed the Muottas Mountain; lovely view; excellent exercise.

Monday July 4

Again took to our carraige & crossed the Bernina; lunched at the Hospice, the snow drifts some feet deep. Then to Le Prese on the lovely Lago di Poschiavo.

Tuesday July 5

Came up through the Vatellina[23] to the Baths of Bormio. Very good accommodations.

Just heard of Garfields assassination; frightful calamity for America.

Wednesday July 6

Later news say Garfield is not dead. This means work in the future for all men who wish their country well.

Thursday July 7

Crossed the snow-covered Stelvia; very grand. After we had crossed summit heavy rains washed away road, hemming us in, and we turned back & spent night at Trafoi.

Friday July 8

Into the Adige valley. Lunched by the Heiden See; most amusing inquisitive german hostess. Are staying at Hoch-Tinstermunz, by superb gorge. Lombardino knows no german; so I have to translate for him.

Saturday July 9

Drove down through the beautiful Inn-Thal, with alternate rain and sunshine. Are staying at Imst, at a regular old Tyrollese Gasthaus.

Sunday July 10

Came on through the beautiful valley of the Inn to Innsbruck.

Monday July 11

Came on to Munich, after having seen the sights of Innsbruck.

---

23. Valtellina.

Tuesday July 12

Went through the Picture Gallery &c.

Wednesday July 13

Came on to Lucerne.

Friday July 15

Walked up to Mount Pilatus from Alpnacht[24] and came down it to Hergeswly.[25] Excellent walk; rather tired.

Saturday July 16

Somehow or other we got it into our heads that it was Sunday and only found our mistake in the afternoon.

Sunday July 17

Poor sermon at the English Church.

Monday July 18

Ascended the Rigi Kulm and saw most glorious sunset.

Tuesday July 19

Arose at three to see a beautiful sunrise and then came down to Lucerne.

Wednesday July 20

We drove over the Brünig Pass to Interlaken.

Friday July 22

Drove to Grindelwald in the rain; are staying at the Schwartzer Adler.[26]

Saturday July 23

Alice on horseback and I on foot went to the Rigi-Grindelwald and back.

Sunday July 24

At 8.15 a.m. left for the Jungfrau, with the guides Peter Egger and Hans Baumann—both excellent. Reached the Bergli Hütte at 4.45, and there spent the night.

---

24. Alpnach, Switzerland.

25. Hergiswil.

26. Schwarzer Adler.

Monday July 25

Started off at 3.15; very windy and somewhat cloudy. Over the Mönchjoch, Jungfraufirn and Roththalsabtel to the top at 8.55. Great fun coming down. Grindelwald at 6 p.m. Rather tired.

Wednesday July 27

Alice in chaise-a-porter and I on foot went to upper Glacier. In afternoon we drove to Interlaken.

Thursday July 28

Took carraige and drove to Kandersteg.

Friday July 29

Over the magnificent Gemmi Pass to Leuk, and on to Visp, where to our astonishment we met Charley Alexander.

Saturday July 30

Alice on horse back and I on foot came out to Zermatt, in company with Alexander, who is very good company.

Sunday July 31

Sermon poor, as usual. Took a walk with Alexander to the Glacier. Have met several friends. Gave them a little dinner.

Monday August 1

We went up to the Gorner Grat,[27] still with Alexander, and spent the night at the Riffel.[28]

Tuesday August 2

Came down to Zermatt. Alexander left us, to our regret. The Gardiners & Baylies & Kennedys are here.

Wednesday August 3

At 9 a.m. started for the Matterhorn with two guides, Tangwalder & Zum Tangwald. Club hut at seven.

---

27. Gorner Ridge, Swiss Alps.
28. Riffel Lake.

Thursday August 4

Started from hut at 3.45; summit at 7.00; back at Zermatt at 3.30, very llaborious and rather dangerous, but I am not very tired. Am in excellent training.

Friday August 5

Started in afternoon, Alice and baggage on two mules, and went to Stalden.

Saturday August 6

Left at 4.30, Alice on a mule, to Visp; then by train to Martigny; then by Rickety wagon to Chamounix,[29] coming in by the beautiful moonlight.

Sunday August 7

The Chapmans are staying here. Church poor.

Monday August 8

We drove on in the diligence[30] to Geneva.

Wednesday August 10

Went through to Basle.[31]

Thursday August 11

Very much interested in the Munster,[32] especially in the medieval collection. Went on to Strasburg.

Friday August 12

Cathedral very beautiful and imposing, especially the outside. Bought some very handsome old silver.

Saturday August 13

Came on to Margence.[33]

---

29. Chamonix, France.
30. *Diligence*: French coach.
31. Basel, Switzerland.
32. Old Protestant church in Basel, originally a Catholic cathedral.
33. Margency, France.

Sunday August 14
Turn-verein in full force.³⁴

Monday August 15
Took the boat to Cologne.

Tuesday August 16
Saw Cathedral; liked it better than any except that at Milan.

Wednesday August 17
General and Mrs. Cullum³⁵ are here; very pleasant.

Went down to Amsterdam.

Thursday August 18
Went all round Amsterdam to the picture galleries &c. In the afternoon drove out to clean little Brock.³⁶

Friday August 19
Came on to the Hague.

Saturday August 20
Went to the Picture Gallery, and Dutch Museum, and walked all round the town.

Monday August 22
Went to Antwerp. Saw the Cathedral.

Tuesday August 23
Came on to Brussels.

Wednesday August 24
Picture Gallery in the morning.

---

34. TR is referring to anti-French German nationalism, especially in the Alsace region around Strasburg, which had been annexed to Germany in 1871.
35. George Washington Cullum, a Civil War general who retired to New York City.
36. Broek in Waterlands, about five miles from Amsterdam. Guidebooks mentioned the cleanliness of the small, picturesque village.

Thursday August 25
Came on to Paris.

Monday August 29
Went to Notre Dame.

Wednesday August 31
Hotel Cluny.[37]

Thursday September 1
Tomb of Napoleon.[38]

Friday September 2
To London. Bath Hotel.

Tuesday September 6
Shopping, Dorée Gallery.

Wednesday September 7
Capt A. Thompson gave us a dinner and a box at the Theatre.

Thursday September 8
National Gallery.

Friday September 9
Went to see Colonel Gawler at the Tower.

Saturday September 10
Came on to Liverpool to stay with Uncle Irvine.

Wednesday September 14
Have enjoyed the time so much. Spent most of the day with the dear old sea captain, Uncle Jimmie Bulloch.[39]

---

37. Hôtel de Cluny. Dating back to 1334 and built as the town house of the abbots of Cluny, in 1843 it was made into a museum dedicated to the Middle Ages.

38. The newlyweds apparently did not see too much of Paris as their stay was, according to TR, "mainly devoted to the intricacies of dress buying." He was very impressed with Napoleon's tomb. TR to Anna, 5 September 1881, Morison 51–2.

39. James Bulloch arranged for construction of the notorious Confederate raider *Alabama* during the Civil War.

Thursday September 22

Sailed in the Britannic.

Bob Grant aboard, very pleasant.

Tuesday September 27

Alicey really enjoys the voyage.

Sunday October 2

Arrived. All of both families met us.

Thursday October 6

Began at the Law, and also started work at the Primaries. Am going to try to kill our last years legislator.

Saturday October 8

Out to Oyster Bay to pass Sunday.

Friday October 14

Alice is on in Boston. Am living entirely alone in the house, with old Dora to take care of me.

Monday October 17

Am working fairly at my law, hard at politics, and hardest of all at my book ("Naval History") which I expect to publish this winter.

Friday October 21 [Crossed out. Rewritten on October 28 and November 4.]

Much to my surprise was nominated to the Assembly from the 21st district. My platform is; strong Republican on State matters, but Independent on local and municipal affairs.

Saturday October 22

Uncle Jim, Em & Al bitterly opposed to my candidacy, of course.

Wednesday October 26 [Crossed out. Rewritten on November 1.]

Most of my friends are standing by me like trumps.

Have a good chance of being elected if I am not sold out.

Friday October 28

Much to my surprise was nominated to the Assembly from district.

Tuesday November 1

All my friends stand by me like trumps, except Al, Em & Uncle Jim.

Friday November 4

My platform is Republican, but Independent on Municipal matters.

Tuesday November 8

Was elected to the Legislature from the 21st Assembly District by a majority of 1501 over William Strew, the Democratic candidate.

Wednesday November 16

All the family are in town.

I take Alice out driving in the dogcart almost every day.

Sunday November 20

News Boys lodging house as usual. Also taking care of Orthopedic.

Thursday November 24

Alice and I are spending Thanksgiving with her Mother at Boston.

Saturday December 3

Book is in the hands of the publishers—Putnams.[40]

Tuesday December 6

The going out has fairly begun; all are it, from dinners to balls.

Thursday December 15

Am trying to work on an Aqueduct Bill.[41]

---

40. Roosevelt later bought a share of the publisher.

41. A dedicated supply of clean water would prevent the outbreak of both disease and a devastating fire. During the summer of 1881, some city districts had received an insufficient supply of water, and the legislature had passed a bill authorizing the city to construct a new aqueduct. Republican Governor Alonzo Cornell vetoed the bill. There followed a terribly dry summer and autumn, reducing the city's daily supply of water to one-tenth its usual level. Everyone was discussing the current water shortage, and the *Times* even had an editorial on the matter just days before the election. The paper noted that while the city needed a new aqueduct, the governor had been justified in objecting to the vast expense required and the

Wednesday December 21

I think we shall live with Mother another winter.

Monday December 26

Celebrated Xmas as usual.

MEMORANDA

[crossed out, May 10th]
May 10th 1881
Due to Alice $445.00
Total Amt I started abroad with £1000
$445.00
May 15th; I hold of Alices money
On hand $470.00

Trip abroad

Return Ticket $320.00
Trunks &c   180.00
Started May 12th with 1045 pounds

TRIP ABROAD

			£	s	d
May	20th	Doctor & Fees	8		
"	22d	Hotel (2 days)	4	8	8
"	"	Parasol &c & Fees	2	11	4
"	23d	Fares &c	1	5	0
"	24th	Hotel Bill	7	1	10
"	"	Charity, Fees &c	3	13	2
"	25th	Fares &c	4	0	0
"	26th	Excursion	2	0	0
"	"	Bill	4	0	0
"	28th		9		
			45		

---

vast power given to the city's commissioner of Public Works, Hubert O. Thompson. In his veto, Cornell noted that the legislature's bill would have given Thompson sole authority to require the city to issue bonds to build the aqueduct, thus adding to the city's debt burden. Cornell objected to such "immense and arbitrary powers" for an unelected city official.

June 1st—10th	Presents	20
" "	Amusements	30
" "	Travelling	50
June 10th		

CASH ACCOUNT

	1880	*1881*
Dress	761.59	
House expenses &c	544.03	
Stable	449.78	
Education & Business	350.48	
Presents	3889.80	
Charity & Subscriptions	235.55	
Travelling	558.07	
Amusements	1070.12	
Alice		
Sundries	133.18	
	7992.50	

CASH ACCOUNT

	1880	*1881*
January	282.87	482.60
February	172.96	200.40
March	39.02	203.00
April	460.15	114.00
May	481.47	
June	904.57	
July	989.16	
August	101.00	
September	660.40	
October	3300.90	
November	195.00	
December	405.00	
	7992.50	

[inside back cover]
Joseph E. Murray[42]
109 E. 85th St.

---

42. Member of TR's Twenty-First district, who tried to use TR's assembly candidacy to "make a run" at the leadership of district boss Jake Hess.

Albany

Volume VI (1882)

Roosevelt kept two diaries this year: a personal diary and a legislative diary about his first session in the Assembly. The legislative diary contains detailed descriptions of the makeup of the Assembly, the factional fights, and observations about his fellow members. This diary resembles others Roosevelt kept during earlier birding expeditions and later hunting trips, which eventually became the material for books. In 1885 and 1886 Roosevelt published two articles about his time in the Assembly: "Phases of State Legislation" and "Machine Politics in New York City." Both articles drew on material found in the diary.

The legislative year began with the Republican caucus in Albany, through which Roosevelt became acquainted with the factions within his party. While Roosevelt and others considered themselves "independent," most Republicans nationwide divided themselves into two groups, the "Stalwarts" and "Half-Breeds." The factions were the result of recent conflicts within the Republican Party. Ever since 1872 the party had experienced internecine conflict that threatened to rend it asunder. This was paralleled by a resurgent Democratic party in urban Northern states after the Depression of 1873, and in the South with the end of Reconstruction. As a result, Democrat Samuel J. Tilden nearly won the presidency in 1876 after securing the majority of the popular vote. Rutherford B. Hayes became president only because Republicans still controlled the electoral process in three Southern states.

At the 1876 national convention Republican reformers from New York and New England had succeeded in throwing the nomination to Hayes, an advocate of civil service reform. New York reformers such as Roosevelt's father, Theodore Roosevelt Sr., had stood shoulder to shoulder with Massachusetts reformers, such as Roosevelt's future best friend, Henry Cabot Lodge. By

1880, however, party bosses revolted against Hayes's distributing patronage to Democrats and slight moves toward civil service reform. One of these moves had included the unsuccessful nomination of Roosevelt Sr. to one of the most coveted and historically corrupted of federal appointments, the collector of import duties at the New York Custom House. New York Republican leaders had torpedoed the nomination. Especially in states like New York where the Democrats were gaining strength, bosses could not allow changes that diluted party strength and threatened party cohesion. By 1880 they looked to former president Ulysses S. Grant to restore the old ways of party patronage, adamantly backing the former president for a third term. These so-called Stalwarts were led by the Republican boss of New York State, U.S. Senator Roscoe Conkling.

The Stalwarts were opposed by an anti-Grant alliance derisively called Half-Breeds, a slur that indicated they were not pure Republicans. The most prominent contender for the Half-Breed nomination in 1880 and again in 1884 was U.S. Senator James G. Blaine of Maine, a very popular former speaker of the House. But Blaine was dogged by accusations that while speaker he had backed legislation favorable to a railroad company in return for a hefty bribe. When letters surfaced purporting to prove the accusations, Blaine came into possession of them and refused to turn them over to a Congressional investigating committee. For reformers, Blaine was an unacceptable alternative. In 1880 these reformers, led by the Massachusetts men like Lodge, succeeded in throwing the nomination to dark-horse candidate James Garfield. Conkling lieutenant and Stalwart Chester Arthur was picked as his running mate.

By the time Roosevelt went to Albany, these factional divides had solidified at even the state level, as indicated by the fight over nomination for the speaker—an honorific, since the Democrats controlled the Assembly. The Democrats, too, were divided between upstate Democrats and Tammany Hall Democrats from New York City. With Tammany holding the balance of power in the Assembly, its members forced the legislature into a deadlock that lasted weeks. This gave Roosevelt ample opportunity to sit and observe his fellow members.

He did not like what he saw. Roosevelt took special aim at those he called the "City Irish": "vicious, stupid looking scoundrels." He noted one absurd exchange between the Assembly clerk and a "celtic liquor seller" named Bogan. When Bogan stood to object to the rules, the clerk pointed out there were no rules. "Indade! That's quare, now," Roosevelt wrote, with an ear for Bogan's accent. "Viry will! Thin I move that they be amended till there ar-r-r!" His anti-Irish sentiments aside, Roosevelt certainly had a knack for description, whether it was a cowbird in the Adirondacks or a Celt in the Assembly. And his mimicry of the Irish brogue foreshadowed the farcical writings of Chicago journalist Finley Peter Dunne and his character Mr. Dooley. Years later, when "Mr. Dooley" wrote a mocking review of Roosevelt's *The Rough Riders,* he concluded, "If I was him I'd call th' book, 'Alone in Cubia.'" Roosevelt loved it, and Dunne became a frequent guest at the White House.

When fellow Republicans tired of the deadlock and suggested they throw in their lot with regular Democrats, Roosevelt rose to give his first speech. He understood that a quarrel among the Democrats could only serve Republican interests. When Republicans suggested that they needed to get on with the business of passing legislation, Roosevelt made a joke of it. He had spoken to a number of people in the city, Roosevelt said, and came away quite convinced that "they could get along quite nicely on their present allowance of legislation." The remarks drew laughter from the Assembly, and left Roosevelt pleased that his speech had been "very well received."

Roosevelt also rapidly became acquainted with the bosses and wirepullers in Albany. He noted few assemblymen made up their own minds on legislation, most receiving their orders from men representing the machine bosses. He noticed Hubert O. Thompson, the powerful commissioner of Public Works of New York City, who spent all his time in Albany. Roosevelt observed that Thompson kept a number of hotel parlors stocked with food and alcohol to host political figures. Thompson also sported expensive clothing and jewelry. With New York's infrastructure rapidly expanding, Thompson oversaw one of the richest city departments, with an annual budget in the millions of dollars, and growing every year. At some point Roosevelt must have wondered where Thompson got his money. Within only a couple of years Roosevelt would be investigating Thompson and corruption in the Public Works Department.

With the parties so evenly represented in the Assembly, not only Tammany Democrats had the power to obstruct and delay. Roosevelt quickly allied himself with other Independent Republicans who could wield the same power. When Tammany Democrats and many Republicans hatched a scheme to deprive the speaker of his power to make appointments to the various committees, Roosevelt rallied Independent Republicans and readied to "bolt"—to act independent of Republican leaders and the party. "I hate to bolt if I can help it," Roosevelt wrote, and in the end he did not have to. From that moment on, throughout Roosevelt's career he would be faced with situations when he disagreed with his party leaders and claimed his right to act independently. Yet despite some very public quarrels with his party—such as at the 1884 Republican National Convention—until 1912 Roosevelt always stayed true to the party.

As he wished, Roosevelt was assigned to the Cities Committee, the organ for writing legislation concerning New York State's largest cities, including New York. He introduced two pieces of legislation that indicated his dedication to making New York City more livable, and the government more effective. With New York facing chronic water shortages, especially in summers, Roosevelt introduced a bill to build a new aqueduct for the city. With constant conflict between the mayor of New York and the Board of Aldermen, who were appointed rather than elected and had vast power to obstruct mayoral decisions, Roosevelt introduced legislation to have aldermen elected by their districts rather than appointed. Both bills failed, but the aldermanic bill represented a key element in Roosevelt's progressive agenda for the city: to enhance the executive power of the mayor, while undermining the aldermen and the machine politicians who pulled their strings. Roosevelt would attempt this again in 1884, leading to one of his greatest Assembly fights, and one of his greatest victories.

Volume VI
1882 DIARY

Sunday January 1

New York. Alice is at Montreal with the girls on their great party; so I am keeping house with Mother while Wifie is absent. Aunt Annie and Uncle Jimmie, Aunt Ella and Uncle Irvine, Aunt Susie & Uncle Hill,[1] took tea with us.

Monday January 2

Went up to Albany to begin my duties in the legislature. Attended the Republican Caucus, at which "Old Salt" Alvord[2] was nominated for speaker; I voted against him.

Tuesday January 3

The Assembly opened. We were all sworn in; and then adjourned.

Wednesday January 4

Ballotted for speaker. There are 61 Republicans in the house, there are 67 democrats, but of these 7 are Tammany Hall men, who are "striking" for their own candidate, and so a deadlock has come about. Adjourned till Monday.

Thursday January 5

Went down to New York. Katie Lowell, and dear little Rosy are passing a few days with us. My book seems to be getting on rather slowly.

---

1. Hilborne West, Mittie's brother-in-law, a Philadelphia doctor.

2. For speaker of the Assembly, Stalwarts preferred George H. Sharpe of Ulster County, while the Half-Breeds backed Thomas G. Alvord of Onondaga County. Alvord, known as "Old Salt," was over seventy and had a political career reaching back before the Civil War. He had served as speaker several times, the first time being in 1858, and had even been lieutenant governor. Sharpe's career seemed to have crossed paths with that of every prominent American since the Civil War. During the war he had served on the staffs of generals Joseph Hooker, George Meade, and Ulysses S. Grant. As assistant provost marshal at the end of the war, Sharpe was responsible for paroling 28,000 Confederate soldiers, including Robert E. Lee. In 1867 Sharpe traveled to Europe at the request of Secretary of State William Seward to find and return to the U.S. John Surratt, son of Mary Surratt, hanged as one of the conspirators in Lincoln's assassination. By 1877 Sharpe was serving under Chester Arthur in the New York Customhouse. As surveyor, Sharpe was one of the officials President Hayes tried to remove as he took on Conkling and the Republican machine.

Monday January 9

Back to the legislature again.

Tuesday January 10

I very much like my fellow members as a whole, especially those from the country; the city members are of a much poorer stamp, especially the democrats, who are mainly Irishmen. The wrangling goes on with great bitterness between the Tammany and anti-Tammany factions, while we Republicans can look on with indifference.

Thursday January 12

Again adjourned and [I went down to New York—crossed out].

Friday January 13

I went on to Boston.

Monday January 16

Came back to Albany.

Tuesday January 17

Attended the funeral of Senator Wagner.[3]

Friday January 20

Adjourned and Alice and I went down to New York.

Monday January 23

Returned to Albany.

Tuesday January 24

Made my first speech (which was very well received) advising a policy of strict neutrality between the warring democratic factions.[4]

---

3. Webster Wagner, founder of the Wagner Palace Car Company, a Pullman competitor, who served in the New York State Senate from 1872 until his death in a rail accident while riding in one of his own sleeping cars.

4. The Assembly was entering its fourth week of, as the *Times* said, "its unorganized existence" as the Tammany men continued to deprive the regular Democrats' nominee for speaker a majority. Roosevelt said in his speech that while this might be a hindrance to legislation, "he has talked with a number of representative manufacturers and business men, and he was satisfied that they could get along quite nicely on their present allowance of legislation."

Friday January 27

Adjourned; but as Alice and I are all settled here, with our books and everything, as comfortable as possible, we decided to spend Sunday here in Albany.

Monday January 30

Legislature reopened. Deadlock still in force.

Thursday February 2

Deadlock broken at last; the Tammany men made some sort of bargain, and the Regular Democratic candidate for speaker was elected and installed.[5]

Friday February 3

Legislature met and adjourned over till next Wednesday at 12; Alice and I shall stay in Albany.

Wednesday February 8

The Tilden and Tammany Democrats combined to elect Speaker Patterson (apparently a good man), but the deadlock seems to be as complete as ever as regards the rest of the slate.

Friday February 10

Adjourned, without doing anything. Alice and I went to New York.

Monday February 13

Bamie came up to Albany with Alice and myself; she will stay at the Knickerbocker.

Tuesday February 14

Speaker announced his committees; I am just where I wished to be, on the committee on cities.

Introduced bill regarding the election of aldermen in New York.

Alice and I went to a most amusing commerce party at the Knickerbockers in the evening.

---

5. Charles E. Patterson, of Rensselaer. The press speculated that the regular Democrats promised Tammany places on two committees, Cities and Railroads. "The Tammany tail has succeeded in wagging the body of the Democratic dog," the *Times* observed. *NYT* 3 February 1882.

Wednesday February 15

Tammany so dissatisfied that it again broke and elected the Republican clerk. Introduced bill to provide for water supply of New York.

Pleasant party at Lansings in evening.

1882 Legislative Diary

Diary of Five Months in the New York Legislature

Jan 2nd 1882
The Legislature has assembled in full force; 128 Assemblymen, containing 61 Republicans in their ranks, and 8 Tammany men among the 67 Democrats. Tammany thus holds the balance of power, and as the split between her and the Regular Democracy is very bitter, a long deadlock is promised us.

In the evening the Republicans held a caucus to nominate our candidate. The contest lay between Sharpe and Alvord; the former a "stalwart," a man of ability and shrewd enough to recognize the advantage of being considered respectable, but unless I am mistaken decidedly tricky and unquestionably a machine man pure and simple; the latter a rugged, white headed old countryman, a "half breed" or independent, but a bad old fellow. As a choice of evils I voted for Sharpe—but Alvord was chosen.

Jan 7th
Work both stupid and monotonous. Every day we meet and cast a couple of ballots; we voting for Alvord, the regular Democrats for Patterson of Troy, and the Tammany men for a tall, thin Irishman named J.J. Costello, a thorough faced scoundrel, and therefore a fitting candidate for the lowest branch of the low New York Democracy.

Certainly there can be no comparison between the personnel of the two parties, as shown by their representatives in this Assembly chamber. A number of republicans, including most of their leaders, are bad enough; but over half the democrats, including almost all of the City Irish, are vicious, stupid looking scoundrels with apparently not a redeeming trait, beyond the capacity for making exceeding ludicrous bills. One of the Tammany men, a little celtic liquor seller, about five feet high, with an enormous stomach, and a face like a bull frog today perpetrated rather a good one. The house has so far adopted no rules, and the Clerk presides. The following dialogue occurred.

Bogan. "Mr. Clur-rk!"

Clerk. "The gentleman from New York, Mr. Bogan."

Bogan. "I rise to a pint of ardther (order) under the rules!"

Clerk. "There are no rules."

Bogan. "Thin I objict to thim!"

Clerk. "There are no rules to object to."

Bogan (meditatively) "Indade! That's quare now; (brightening up, as he sees a way out of the difficulty) Viry will! Thin I move that they be amended till there ar-r-r!" (smiles complacently on the applauding audience, proudly conscious that he has at last solved an abstruse point of parliamentary practice)

Jan 12th
There are some twenty five Irish Democrats in the house, all either immigrants or sons of emigrants, and coming almost entirely from the great cities—New York, Brooklyn Albany, Buffaloe. They are a stupid, sodden vicious lot, most of them being equally deficient in brains and virtue. Three or four however (Obrien, Walsh, Haggarty and M.J. Costello) seem to be pretty good men, and among the best members of the house are two Republican farmers named O'neil and Sheehy, the grandsons of Irish emigrants.

But the average catholic Irishman of the first generation as represented in this Assembly, is a low, venal, corrupt and unintelligent brute. The average democrat here seems much below the average Republican. Among the professions represented in the two parties the contrast is striking. There are six liquor sellers, two bricklayers, a butcher, a tobacconist, a pawn broker, a compositor and a type setter in the house—all democratic; but of the farmers and lawyers, the majority are Republican. Of course there are some democrats—such as Hampden Robb of New York—as good as the best Republicans; and some of the latter are bad enough, in all conscience's sake. But even if the worst elements of all, the twenty low Irishmen, were subtracted, the Republican average would still be higher than Democratic.

Jan 24th
The deadlock continues, growing more and more tedious. There is a good deal of growling, and some calls among our members of interfering to help

the regular democracy; this I utterly disapprove of, as I consider it no part of ours to interfere in a family quarrel, it being a very pretty fight as it stands. The public as far as I can find out rather approves of the absence of legislation. Today Hickman, the Independent Republican from Erie, and an honest little fellow, made a speech threatening to interfere and help the regular democrats; so I made one in response advocating a policy of strict non intervention. This of course is just what the Tammany men desire, and, to my intense amusement, they all thanked me very warmly afterwards.

Haggerty is not here at present, and their seven remaining members are totally unable to speak with even an approximation to good grammar; not one of them can string three intelligible sentences together to save his neck (their argument being all of the "ad hominem"[6] character—"you lie") and they are proportionately grateful to any outsider who comes to their aid; which I hate to do, with such scoundrels. The members of the country Democracy from New York are only a little better; and two of our six City Republicans are pretty bad.

Of course such a hopelessly ignorant set of men as these Tammany members are can not do their own thinking; they are managed entirely by the commands of some of John Kelly's lieutenants who are always in the Assembly chamber; among these outside leaders the chief seems to be General Spinola, born in Ireland,[7] fought in the civil war, profane, obscene, corrupt, and withal possessing plenty of pluck and rough good humor.

The County democrats are all (bar Robb) whipped into line by the Commissioner of Public Works, Hubert O. Thompson, who spends most of his time up here, instead of in his place at New York. He is a gross, enormously fleshy man, with a full face and thick, sensual lips; wears a diamond short pin and an enormous seal ring on his little finger. He has several handsome parlors in the Delavan house, where there is always champagne and free lunch; they are crowded from morning to night with members of assembly, lobbyists, hangers on, office holders, office seekers and "bosses" of greater or less degree.

Feb 14th
Thank Heaven, at last the two wings of the democracy have come together and elected Paterson of Troy as speaker.

Today he announced the Committees. The only important one that I am on is that of Cities. I do not much fancy my companions on it. The Chairman is an Irishman named Murphy, Colonel in the Civil War, a Fenian; he is a tall, stout man, with a swollen red face, a black moustache, and a ludicrously

---

6. Ad hominem: an argument made personally against ones opponent rather than against his/her argument.

7. Francis B. Spinola was Portuguese-American, born in Suffolk County, New York.

dignified manner; always wears a frock coat (very shiney[8]) and has had a long experience in politics—so that, to undoubted pluck and a certain knowledge of parliamentary forms, he adds a great deal of stupidity and a decided looseness of ideas as regards the 8th commandment.[9] Next comes John Shanley of Brooklyn, an Irishman, but born in America, much shrewder than Murphy and easier to get along with, being more Americanized but fully as dishonest; then comes MacDonough, an American-Born Irishman from Albany; Higgins, a vicious little, Celtic nonentity from Buffaloe; Gideon, a Jew from New York, who has been a bailiff and is now a liquor seller; Dimonn, a country Democrat, who is either dumb or an idiot—probably both; and, as the last of the Democrats, a Tammany Hall gentleman named MacManus, a huge, fleshy, unutterably coarse and low brute, who was formerly a prize fighter, at present keeps a low drinking and dancing saloon, and is more than suspected of having begun his life as a pick pocket.

The four Republicans are myself, Monk, a well-meaning but very weak man from Brooklyn; Goddard, an old North Country farmer, Colonel of the 61st during the war, who led the charge up Lookout Mountain at Chattanooga, but though a good man, yet apt to waver; and finally Carley, the very essence of negation. Altogether the Committee is about as bad as it could possibly be; most of the members are positively corrupt, and the others are really singularly incompetent.

Feb 21st

The Tammany members have been savagely angry with the regular democrats ever since the committees were announced, having received but small attention by the Speaker; they have now hatched up a deal with some of the Republican leaders (chiefly stalwarts but with a few half breeds) to take away the Speaker's power of appointment. The parties are so evenly matched in the house that a few men one way or the other can control the balance of power. And I knew that enough Independent Republicans would act with me to ensure the defeat of the scheme by "bolting" if necessary; but I hate to bolt if I can help it, and luckily there was no need for it, as we beat them in the caucus.

In the morning Raines,[10] a stalwart Republican from Ontario, rose and offered the motion to take away the Speakers power of appointment; it lay over

---

8. Shiny, i.e. a bit old and worn.

9. "Thou shalt not steal."

10. John Raines. In 1896, when Theodore Roosevelt was police commissioner in New York, State Senator Raines championed a bill prohibiting liquor being served on Sundays in establishments other than hotels. The result was "Raines Law Hotels": saloonkeepers rented out the rooms above their establishments to make them "hotels," which increased the incidence of prostitution and gambling.

under the rules for one day. I had risen to debate it, and it was at once known that I was bound to fight it as hard as I could; so during the eight hours that elapsed before the Republican caucus was called I received all kinds of telegrams and deputations promising me political advancement ad libitum[11] if I would only consent to be called off—which I politely but firmly and sweetly declined.

When the caucus met, Raines rose and urged the adoption of his resolution in a rather elaborate speech. He is a tall, strongly built, finelooking man, with a long brown moustache and gray-blue eyes, speaking easily and loudly and evidently experienced in it; but entirely unprincipled, and with the same idea of Public Life and the Civil Service that a vulture has of a dead sheep. The one and the other are alike desirous of getting all they can out of the carcass, with small regard to how they befoul themselves doing it. As no one seemed much disposed to take up the cudgels I responded, and pitched into him mercilessly and we had a fiery dialogue. He was supported by many, if not most, of the stalwarts and such half breeds as corrupt "Old Salt," smooth, oily, plausible and tricky C.S. Baker of Munro. I was supported by Hunt of Jefferson, a tall, thin, melancholy country lawyer from Jefferson, thoroughly upright as honest and uncompromising as some great mastiff dog; Noyes, an equally good man from Cayuga; Erwin, a very shrewd, able lawyer from St. Lawrence, with more intellect than any of the former, but by no means of such unbending integrity; Fletcher, a quiet, firm, independent young gentleman farmer from Long Island, fond of horses and shooting, and caring nothing for the wiles or commands of politicians; Paige of Wyoming, an upright, strait forward old farmer; and Greenwood, a crabbed old countryman, shrewd and honest, but narrow and wild on the subjects of temperance. We beat them by a narrow vote.

Mar 1st

I have introduced several bills, the most important being one to build a new aqueduct which has no chance of passing. I also have one to make aldermen elected by assembly districts, which I expect to have pass in spite of the opposition of some of my New York republican colleagues, such as Brodsky the German stalwart, a good natured little fellow but the lowest kind of spoils politician, and Crane, whose intellectual capacity about equals that of an average balloon. The bill may do away with some of the dickering that now goes on in the city.

---

11. Ad libitum: "at one's pleasure," most commonly shortened to "ad lib."

Albany and "Dakotah"

Volume VII (1883)

The shortest of the diaries, the 1883 volume is mostly filled with notes about Roosevelt's 1884 summer hunting trip. For chronological consistency, these have been transcribed for the diary for that year.

After Roosevelt won re-election in 1882, he found himself nominated for the speakership. With Republicans in a minority again that year, the nomination was merely honorary. Still, Republican Party leader Senator Warner Miller set out to defeat Roosevelt. Miller had just become head of the New York Republican Party, and Roosevelt's becoming speaker would have undermined Miller's new authority. Moreover, as leader of the Blaine forces on the eve of the presidential election, Miller could not allow an independent assemblyman hostile to both Blaine and Chester Arthur to hold such a prominent Republican position. Had Republican assemblymen been allowed to vote freely, Roosevelt likely would have been chosen. But Miller brought to bear pressure by the state party machine and city bosses to defeat him. This defeat at the hands of his own party leaders engendered in Roosevelt strong animosity toward Miller he recalled years later. Writing in his 1913 memoirs, Roosevelt remembered being beaten for the speakership by "the bosses," both Stalwart and Half-Breed: "Neither side cared for me."

In the Assembly Roosevelt sat with other members who supported his efforts at reform. These included Walter Howe, Isaac Hunt, and William O'Neil. That same year Roosevelt and these three colleagues, joined by Albany correspondent for the *New York Times* George Spinney, posed together for a picture. O'Neil Roosevelt described as his closest friend in the Assembly for the three years he served. Howe was one of the few fellow Republicans from New York City, and Isaac Hunt later gave a series of interviews to Roosevelt biographer

Hermann Hagedorn describing Roosevelt's Albany career. Roosevelt's friendship with journalist Spinney began a lifetime spent courting public opinion through a sympathetic press. At about this time, in March 1883, Spinney wrote of Roosevelt in the *Times*: "The rugged independence of Assemblyman Theodore Roosevelt and his disposition to deal with all the public measures in a liberal spirit have given him a controlling force on the floor superior to that of any other member of his party. Whatever boldness the minority has exhibited in the Assembly is due to his influence, and whatever weakness and cowardice it has displayed is attributable to its unwillingness to follow where he led." At only age twenty-four, Roosevelt was making a name for himself.

The diary ends with Roosevelt's game bag for the two-week hunting trip he took in September. Although he and brother Elliott had spent a little time in the Dakota Territory on their pre-wedding hunting trip in 1881, this was Roosevelt's first real experience of the American West, ranging all the way to the Little Missouri River and the border of Montana. Roosevelt had gone west to hunt buffalo, knowing it might be his last chance: the great herds had been slaughtered to near extinction in the 1870s and early 1880s. Roosevelt described the hunt in his 1885 book, *Hunting Trips of a Ranchman*, in a chapter called "The Lordly Buffalo." On horseback, Roosevelt and his guide stalked a few scattered buffalo, with the nearsighted and bespectacled Roosevelt missing a number of shots. Finally, Roosevelt was able to shoot one in the shoulder, bringing the bull down with two more shots to the flank. Roosevelt and his companion cut the head off for a trophy and sat down to a meal of fresh buffalo meat.

During the buffalo hunt Roosevelt had used a cattle ranch as a base. By the early 1880s, books, articles, and even government reports were calling Montana and Dakota ready for a cattle boom, with beef barons claiming returns in excess of fifty percent. Roosevelt had already invested $10,000 in the Teschmaker and Debillier Cattle Company, which ran a herd north of Cheyenne. In his 1883 diary Roosevelt indicated in his accounts an income of $500 from that investment, a return of five percent. At the same time, Roosevelt had made large investments back East. He put $20,000 in the publisher G.P. Putnam's Sons, and had bought ninety-five acres of land on Oyster Bay where he would soon start constructing a home for himself, Alice, and their expected brood of children. He had even contemplated buying a farm in the Adirondacks, scene of his youthful birding trips. By the fall of 1883, Roosevelt was on the lookout for several things: an investment that would provide him with a healthy and regular annual return; a nice piece of working agricultural land that would also afford him the enjoyment of outdoors life and opportunities for hunting; and an active, healthy, part-time occupation that would balance his more sedentary pursuits of politics and writing. No wonder that on that first trip to western Dakota Roosevelt was primed to make a snap decision, one that would have large personal and financial ramifications for him. With a handshake and a personal check, Roosevelt returned to New York and his seat in the Assembly having invested one-third of his net worth in two cattle ranches.

VOLUME VII
1883 DIARY

Theodore Roosevelt [signature]

Monday January 1

Albany. I received the complimentary Republican nomination for Speaker of the Assembly. The Stalwarts made a strong fight against me; but the Independents stood firm; and we beat them two to one. My strength lay among the country Republicans, all of them native Americans, and for the most part farmers or storekeepers or small lawyers; they are all shrewd, kindly, honest men, with whom I get on admirably. Hunt,[1] a lean, melancholy, humorous yankee and O'Neil,[2] a bright, straightforward backwoodsman, were my two main backers. All of the 43 Republicans are native Americans with the exception of two who were born in Germany. Howe, my colleague from New York, is a very good man; a gentleman of broad culture.

Tuesday January 2

The Legislature organized, and the Democratic majority elected as Speaker Chapin[3] of Brooklyn, by all odds the ablest man on either side of the House, a scholar and a gentleman, but a thoroughly cold and selfish man. The Democrats seem to have good material in their ranks, though most of the city members are corrupt and ignorant Irish Catholics. Chapin appointed a committee on privileges and elections, of which I am one, to hear the case of the contestants for seats. The committee went down to New York.

Wednesday January 3

Back again in my own lovely little home, with the sweetest and prettiest of all little wives—my own sunny, darling. I can imagine nothing more happy in life than an evening spent in my cosy little sitting room, before a bright fire of soft coal, my books all around me, and playing backgammon with my own dainty mistress.

---

1. Isaac Hunt.

2. William Thomas O'Neil, a storekeeper from the Adirondacks, whom TR described as "my closest friend" for his three years in the Assembly. *Autobiography* 65.

3. Alfred C. Chapin of Kings County. A graduate of Williams College and Harvard Law School, he was injured in the same rail accident that killed Senator Wagner. Later Chapin was elected mayor of Brooklyn, then to Congress.

Thursday January 4

Today we heard the evidence in the case of the contested election between Sprague and Bliss. The former was counted out beyond a shadow of a doubt.

Friday January 5

Went to drill my company (B, of the 8th Regiment) as usual.[4]

Saturday January 6

All through today, as also yesterday, the committee has been wading through the mass of perjury involved in the Brooklyn contested election cases.

Sunday January 7

Church in the morning at Dr. Halls. The family dinner was at our house; in the evening we took tea with Motherling.

Monday January 8

Committee sat all day. In evening passed my examination for Captain in the 8th.

Tuesday January 9

Went back to Albany. Chapin announced his committees, which seem to be very good.

Crane,[5] of my New York colleagues, is honest but light weight; House[6] is marvellously conceited and noisy. I think he will prove a nuisance. Old Cleavland[7] is a very fine fellow, with a grand head, his hair and beard both snow white.

Hunt, Oneil, Howe and myself sit together—a pleasant quartette.

Wednesday January 10

Had another fight with the stalwarts in the caucus to nominate a regent, and beat them again, my nominee, Matthew Hale, receiving the somewhat empty honor. On the floor of the house I opened session by a brush with Murphy & "Tim" Campbell, and got the better of those "renowned leaders."

---

4. Roosevelt had joined the New York State militia, in which he served as captain.

5. Leroy B. Crane.

6. Fred B. House.

7. Stafford C. Cleveland, Yates County.

MISCELLANEOUS

Sporting trip on Little Missouri, Dakotah, Sept 10th–26th, 1883

1	buffalo bull	1
2	blacktail bucks	2
4	Jack rabbits	
6	cottontail "	6
7	sage cock	7
21	sharptail grouse	21
2	geese	2
4	mallard	4
7	teal	

Shot with Sharp's rifle, 45 calibre, 100 grain of powder (ball weighing nearly two ounces) and with no. 10 double barrel choke bore, given me by Elliott—the last by all odds the best gun in my battery.

17th 1 buf
18 6 grouse, 1 jack rabbit
19 1 blacktail
20 10 grouse, 4 teal
21st 5 grouse 3 teal
22nd 1 blacktail
23nd 6 cotton tail

Date	Income Ac't		Income Ac't	
Jan	1st 1883	carried over	In Gallatin Bank	689.44
"	3rd	Income for December	Roosevelt & Son	1250.00
"	5th	Dubuque & Dakota	J.K. Gracie	150.00
"	"		Dubuque & Dakota	700.00
"	12th		Union Trust Co.	44.00
"	15th		Wilmington & Weldon	162.00
Feb	3rd	(Rock & Pittsburg)	Union Trust Co.	150.00
"	8th		Mobile & Ohio	50.00
"	"	From Book	G. P. Putnam's Sons	114.75
Mar	3rd	Past income for Dec	Roosevelt & Son	1618.02
"	"		Iowa Falls & Sioux City	105.00
April	5th		Dunhill & Dubuque Bridge Co.	100.00
"	"	By J. K. G.	Rock. & Pitts.; Can. Trust	210.00
"	"		S. & Allegheny R.R.	140.00
"	"		J. K. Gracie	4.20

"	22d		Roosevelt & Son	1500.00
May	4th	(350 was stolen)	Legislature	1200.00
"	"		St. Paul, Minn. & Manitoba	300.00
June	2d		Iowa Falls & Sioux City	105.00
				7992.41

[Next page]

Date				Amt.
			Carried Over	7992.41
July	15th		Union Trust & Co.	88.00
"	"		Dubuque & Dakota R.R.	150.00
"	"		Dunhill & Dubuque Bridge Co.	75.00
Aug	1st		Roosevelt & Son	2,000.00
"	3d		Mobile & Ohio	75.00
"	"		Rock & Pittsburg Bonds	150.00
Sept	5th		Iowa Falls & Sioux City	105.00
"	25th		Teschmaker & Debrillier	500.00
Oct	4th		Dubuque & Dunhill Bridge Co.	75.00
"	6th		Rock & Pitts, Can. Trust	210.00
"	10th		Union Trust Co.	55.00
Nov	1st		Shenango & Allegany [sic]	144.20
"	"		St. Paul Minn. & Manitoba	300.00
"	"		Roosevelt & Son	2000.00
				13919.61

"The light has gone out of my life"

Volume VIII (1884)

Roosevelt's final year in the New York Assembly promised to be his greatest. With Republicans back in the majority, Roosevelt became chair of his Cities Committee. He quickly introduced three bills, including one to give the mayor of New York complete power to name his department heads, without reference to the Board of Aldermen. Like the bill he had introduced his first year in the Assembly, Roosevelt sought to enhance the mayor's executive power at the expense of the unelected aldermen, who owed their positions to the party bosses. Roosevelt and other reformers' model was Brooklyn, where a similar law had invested Mayor Seth Low with sole appointing power. The result seemed to be better department heads and more public interest in municipal politics with a visible and more powerful mayor. In Brooklyn more people voted for mayor than voted for governor. The Aldermanic Bill, dubbed the "Roosevelt Bill" in the press, eventually passed and was signed into law by Governor Grover Cleveland.

Roosevelt also chaired a special committee to investigate corruption in the New York City government. Roosevelt's colleagues on the committee included two Republicans, including his good friend William O'Neil, and two sympathetic Democrats. The resolution authorizing the committee specifically targeted the Department of Public Works under Commissioner Hubert O. Thompson—the fleshy, diamond-studded wirepuller Roosevelt had noticed in Albany his first year. Under Thompson's management, the department's annual expenditure had risen 65 percent or almost $5 million from only the previous year, while taxes in the city had risen by over $3 million during the same time. The committee would meet in the Metropolitan Hotel in Manhattan, looking into other city agencies including the register and clerk's offices and the jail at Ludlow Street.

Roosevelt spent that January and February shuttling between Albany and Manhattan. This allowed him to keep an eye on his wife, Alice, pregnant with their first child. He returned to Albany on Tuesday, February 12, prepared to speak on behalf of his Aldermanic Bill the next day. On Wednesday, Roosevelt received a telegram reporting the birth of his baby girl, Alice Lee Roosevelt. With the third reading of his bill imminent, Roosevelt requested a leave of absence from the Assembly as he received the congratulations of his fellow members. He soon received a second telegram from the city, informing him that both his wife and mother lay dying. The bill was laid aside as Roosevelt caught the next train to New York. The next day, February 14, Roosevelt's mother, Mittie Bulloch, died of typhoid fever, and his wife, Alice, died of Bright's disease, an inflammation of the kidney that had gone undetected during her pregnancy. "The light has gone out of my life," Roosevelt famously wrote, marking the day in his diary with a large black "X." The double funeral was held two days later.

Within only a few days, Roosevelt was back in Albany speaking on behalf of his bill. In his speech he condemned "the aristocracy of the bad," the corrupt office holders who enriched themselves at the taxpayers' expense. A week later Roosevelt's investigating committee reconvened and heard testimony about abuses in the city jail, including extortion by the warden and guards, and jail cells being used for prostitution and selling alcohol. On March 14 the committee submitted to the Assembly its report, written by Roosevelt. It pointed to offenses in every office of city government, and took aim at the Board of Aldermen—men "who cannot be held responsible to the people for their deeds and misdeeds." Roosevelt followed the report with a series of bills to transform city government, including one to elect a president of the Board of Aldermen. Most of the bills became law, but none were as important as Roosevelt's Aldermanic Bill, signed into law on March 17, three days after the Roosevelt Committee submitted its report.

With these two major accomplishments, Roosevelt finished his Assembly career. He headed west to his ranch, making an important stop in Chicago in June for the Republican National Convention. There, in concert with a fellow reformer from Massachusetts, Henry Cabot Lodge, he made a public stand against the choice of party leaders for the presidential nomination. In 1880 Lodge and the Massachusetts men had stood against Blaine and thrown the nomination to dark horse James Garfield. In 1884, Lodge and Roosevelt tried to achieve something similar, but were not successful, and Blaine won the nomination easily. Many independent Republicans readied to bolt the party to vote for the Democratic nominee, New York Governor Grover Cleveland. Lodge and Roosevelt, however, opted for party loyalty.

Roosevelt undertook a long hunting trip to the Bighorn Mountains from August to early October. The trip was plagued by bad weather and accidents involving horses and pack ponies falling into creeks or somersaulting down cliffs. As always, Roosevelt was plagued by his own poor shooting, at one point taking six shots to bring down a blacktail buck. He usually fared better with the shotgun. Roosevelt also shot several elk and bears, including a "nearly full grown" bear cub. As he had before, Roosevelt made careful notes of the trip for his 1885 book *Hunting Trips of a Ranchman*.

While Roosevelt would later talk of the two years he spent in the West, it was really a series of trips broken up by long stays back in New York. Moreover, there was a pattern to these trips: Roosevelt made sure to be back in the city in October 1884, October 1885, and October 1886. Not only did he want to take part in the Republican campaigns, he also wanted a say in naming the delegates to the various conventions that would nominate candidates for city and state elections. In 1884 he campaigned for the Republican Party in New York and Boston. Much to the displeasure of party leaders, however, he distanced himself from Republican presidential candidate Blaine. Blaine barely lost the election, losing New York by fewer than twelve hundred votes. Had only six hundred independent Republicans in New York switched their votes from Cleveland to Blaine, Blaine would have been elected president, likely holding on to the White House for eight years. Many Republicans blamed Roosevelt and Lodge for their public revolt at the party convention. As Roosevelt headed back west for the winter, his future was very much in doubt.

Volume VIII
1884 Diary

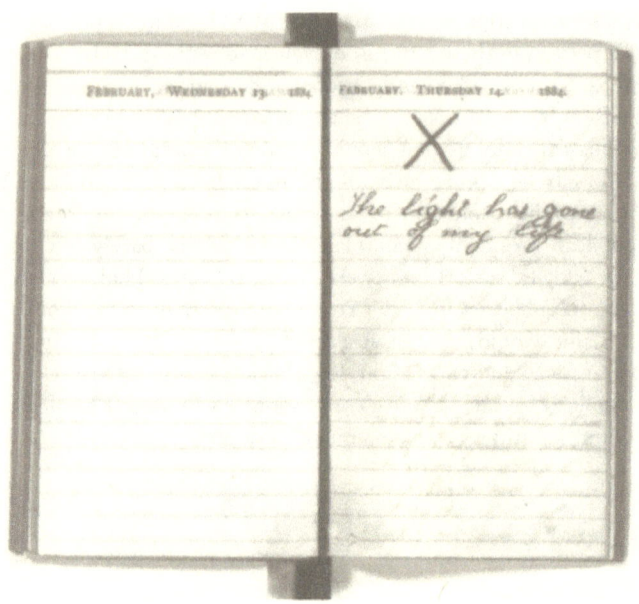

Roosevelt's diary page from February 14, 1884, the day of the deaths of his wife and mother. Theodore Roosevelt Papers at the Library of Congress. http://www.theodorerooseveltcenter.org/Research/Digital-Library/Record/ImageViewer.aspx?libID=o284449&imageNo=11. Theodore Roosevelt Digital Library. Dickinson State University.

Thursday February 14

The light has gone out of my life.

Saturday February 16

Alice Hathaway Lee. Born at Chestnut Hill, July 29th 1861. I saw her first on Oct 1878[1]; I wooed her for over a year before I won her; we were betrothed on Jan 25th 1880, and it was announced on February 16th; on Oct 27th of the

---

1. TR did not recall the date; it was October 19, 1878, on his first visit to Dick Saltonstall's home in Chestnut Hill.

same year we were married; we spent three years of happiness greater and more unalloyed than I have ever known fall to the lot of others; on Feb 12th 1884 her baby was born, and on Feb 14th she died in my arms; my mother had died in the same house, on the same day, but a few hours previously. On Feb 16th they were buried together in Greenwood.

On Feb 17th I christened the baby Alice Lee Roosevelt.

For joy or for sorrow my life has now been lived out.

Monday June 9

Arrived at my cattle ranche (Chimney Butte Ranche) on the Little Missouri.

Friday June 13

One jack rabbit, one curlew.

Both killed with double barrelled express rifle, 50 calibre 150 grains of powder.

Saturday June 14

Two curlew, one on wing, both with rifle, good shots.

Monday June 16

One badger; found out on plains away from hole, galloped up to him and killed him with revolver.

Wednesday June 18

1 buck antelope, fine horns.

A group of buck six or eight feeding together started to run across my path, while I was riding above on the prairie; I was on a first rate pony, and galloped at full speed diagonally to their course; I leaped off as they passed within twenty five yards, and gave them both barrels, killing a fine buck, shot through both shoulders.

Saturday June 21

One antelope.

On riding round a little knoll, I saw two antelope a long distance off, looking at me; I dismounted and fired off hand with careful aim, holding a foot over him and breaking his neck near the shoulder. By actual measurement the distance was three hundred yards, the best shot I ever made with the rifle.

Monday June 23

Two field plover; shot with rifle, for pot.

Wednesday June 25

One mallard drake, shot with rifle for pot.

Friday June 27

One cock pintail grouse, shot with rifle, for pot.

Trip from Little Missouri to the Bighorn Mts. [written in 1883 diary]

Saturday August 16

Have been spending a couple of weeks on my ranches, on the Little Missouri. I now intend starting out for a two months trip overland to the Bighorn Mountains. My companions are my foreman, William Merrifield,[2] who is to hunt with me, and an old french halfbreed named Lebo,[3] who is to drive the team and to cook &c. I take a light "prairie schooner"[4] with a canvass cover, drawn by two stout horses, to carry our goods, and four riding ponies for Merrifield and myself to ride. One of these is Blackie, a stout, swift rather vicious pony; Splitear, very enduring; Brownie, willing and swift, but very nervous; and Roachie, quiet and rather small. I cary [sic] a buckskin suit, sealskin chaparajos,[5] coonskin overcoat, otter fur robe to sleep in (buttoning into a bag form), oilslicker, boots and moccasins, sombrero, overalls, jersey, 2 flannel shirts, 3 suits of light, 3 of heavy underclothing, heavy socks, plenty of handkerchiefs, soap, towels, washing & shaving things, rubber blankets; flour, bacon, beans and coffee, sugar & salt, a little brandy and cholera mixture.[6] My battery consists of long 45 colt revolver, 150 cartridges; no 10 choke bore, 300 cartridges, shotgun; a 45-75 Winchester repeater, with 1000 cartridges; a 40-90 Sharps, 150 cartridges; a 50-150 double barreled Webly[7] express, 100 cartridges.

Monday August 18 [Written in August 20 entry—days of week corrected for 1884.]

Made late start. Left wagon on prairie. Merrifield & I rode on and spent the night at Langs. Out in prairie got caught in driving hail storm; Sheltered in a washout. Wind so strong could hardly stand; ponies would not face it. Our

---

2. One of the original owners from whom TR bought the Chimney Butte ranch in 1883. As president TR named him marshal of Montana. Merrifield was a presidential elector for Montana in 1904 and cast the vote for Roosevelt.

3. A Metis.

4. Wagon.

5. Chaps, to protect riders' legs from thorny bushes like the chaparral.

6. Obtained from a druggist for stomach and intestinal ailments.

7. Webley, British gun manufacturer. Still in business today.

"slickers" and chaps kept us perfectly dry in spite of the driving rain. The Winchester 45-75 shoots beautifully.

Tuesday August 19

Heavy rain storm all day. Left Langs after breakfast; stopped to kill a few mallard flappers and white belly grouse down among a lot of slews with rifle; no lunch; overtook wagon at dusk, at Lake Station on old Keogh Trail.[8] Heavy rain all night; no water except rain water from rubber blankets. Slept in wagon. Made fire of logs of old Station house; good supper—fried duck.

4 grouse 5 duck

Wednesday August 20

Lowering and cloudy. Very heavy wheeling. M. & I rode off; skirting some deep, branching brush bottomed coolies we spied a white tail buck feeding; I shot him through both shoulders at a hundred yards; good horns, but still in velvet.[9] Also 2 sage hens; all with Winchester. Camped at extremely muddy pool in dried creek early (at afternoon); we needed to dry our things; first plan to water our horses; only made 12 miles, through the deep, heavy, water soaked soil. Went through rolling prairie and then in the abruptly broken and fantastically shaped Bad Lands. No lunch.

1 white tail buck 2 sage grouse

Thursday August 21

Frost in the night. Day clear, cool and windy; wheeling much better. Early in morning a great herd of 1500 beef steers passed us; they had been bedded near us, and all night we had heard the cowboys singing and calling as they circled slowly round the herd. Our dog, a greyhound, died from wolf poison. We made about 25 miles through broken prairie; are camped by what I suppose to be the head waters of O'Fallon Creek. Saw no living game; but hundreds of buffalo skulls and old carcasses.

Lebo is a chatty, tough old plainsman, full of expedients, and ready with the wits and hands. Merrifield is a good looking fellow, who shoots and rides beautifully; a reckless, self-confident man.

Friday August 22

In the middle of the night we had a short but violent storm of wind and rain, which, as we have no tent, wet us pretty well; quite cold in morning. Wheel-

---

8. Trail between forts Lincoln and Keogh.
9. The velvety layer on growing antlers.

ing good; traveled 20 miles southwest, on a cattle trail. M. & I rode off among some foot hills of a large range of buttes, where I missed two first class shots at blacktail bucks—the only game we saw. Camped for the night near a most beautiful natural park; green sward thickly dotted over with small, steep, isolated sand cliffs, of most fantastic shape, crowned with pines.

Saturday August 23

Crossed the Little Beaver. Travelled over great rolling plains, bedded with the short, brown grass; saw several herds of cattle, which have now taken the place of the buffalo, whose carcasses can be seen everywhere; this is a breed well occupied as a cattle country. M. & I rode off among some grassy, pine clad chalk Buttes; I missed a long shot at a blacktail doe. M. missed two shots. Knocked off the heads of two young sage grouse for supper; good eating. Camped in Bad Lands of Powder River. Coyotes howling.

2 sage grouse

Sunday August 24

Spent the morning traveling down a creek through the Powder River Bad Lands; soon after lunch struck the Powder, and went on till dusk through great sage brush bottoms; made a dry camp; poor food for ponies; no sign of game. There are quite a number of cattle ranches along this river.

Monday August 25

Travelled up the Powder till we struck the mouth of the Little Powder, where we camped, just after sunset. Took the shot gun and killed for the pot six white bellies, 2 doves and 2 teals; M missed a snap shot at a cougar in a thicket. He and I made an unsuccessful hunt through the bottoms after whitetail deer; in one dense swamp or "cane break," we got very nearly mired; and in clambering among some bad lands, very broken, M's pony turned two complete somersaults down a sandy cliff some thirty feet high. Saw beaver & whippoorwills.

6 sharptail grouse   2 teal   2 dove

Tuesday August 26

Made a short days journey; not over 15 miles. In morning rode off with M. after chickens; shot 8. Met a cowboy with a fine young horse, which I purchased for a hundred dollars. Stopped overnight by the N bar ranche [sic]; thirty men and about three hundred horses preparing to start on the beef round up tomorrow. Cowboys are a jolly set; picturesque, with broad hats, loosily knotted neckerchiefs, flannel shirts, leather chaparajos.

8 sharptail grouse

Wednesday August 27

Country prettier; bottoms narrower, hemmed in by bold bluffs, with pines scattered over them. Shot a dozen sage chickens with shot gun; and late in evening while riding through a dense swamp caught sight of a yearling white tail buck, standing in a marshy openning; he was fifty yards off, and did not see me; kneeling I shot him through the heart.

1 white tail buck   10 sage grouse   2 sharptail grouse

Thursday August 28

Travelled up the Powder; crossed the river nine times; once the wagon nearly stuck in a quick sand; camped a little before coming to the mouth of Clear Creek. Country very pretty.

Friday August 29

Travelled a short distance up Clear Creek. Country very barren; broken, rolling, treeless, and covered with sage brush. Crossing steep and difficult; road crossed by deep washouts; three times the wagon stuck, and we had to help out the team by ropes hitched to the saddle trees of the riding horses. Team nearly done out.

In afternoon M. & I rode out through the cooleys.[10] Roused three blacktail bucks; shot three times with Winchester at them running, going close but a little high, finally stopping them; two stood side by side; taking careful aim I broke the backs of both with one bullet; distance 431 paces (near 400 yards) actual walking. Bests shot I ever made. Kept bullet.

2 blacktail bucks

Saturday August 30

Made some 20 miles up Clear Creek; traveling a little better, but country unchanged; large numbers of cattle (have crossed from Montana into Wyoming); passed a camp of Cheyennes. Have had a bath in the river every day lately.

Sunday August 31

Kept on up Clear Creek; camped about six miles N.W. ["E." also written] of the little town of Buffalo (before reaching it). Country still treeless, broken

---

10. Variant of "coulee," a gulch or ravine, usually dry in summer.

& rolling; many ranches, some with buttes. Have for last three days been in sight of the snow streaked Bighorn Mts. Made a good shot with the rifle at a jackrabbit, cutting him nearly in two at about 75 yds.

Monday September 1

Reached Buffalo, Wyoming; quite a frontier town.

Tuesday September 2

Went on to the sawmill on Crazy Woman creek. Here we leave our wagon and go in on pack ponies. Have seven horses, 3 to ride, 3 to pack, 1 spare, carry wagon sheet for tent; 500 cartridges for Winchester.

Wednesday September 3

The ponies proved fractious and the trail blind, so did not get off till 10; marched steadily till 5.30; slow progress as pack animals and horse ponies proved hard to drive. Camped on Willow Creek. Already pretty cold. Shot 2 blue grouse from a tree with the rifle, for supper. Still have a haunch of venison left from the two bucks. Ascent to the Bighorn Plateau was very steep. Ice formed at night.

Thursday September 4

Only made about six miles over pretty rough trail; camped by rushing mountain torrent. "Park" country; broken steep and rolling; wooded with open glades; small lakes & clear streams. M. & I went out in afternoon on foot, through cedar wooded steep hills. We separated; I found fresh tracks of a band of elk, and followed them up till I came on them; killed an old cow and a bull calf as they ran off through the woods; M afterwards killed two. No old bull in the band.

2 elk

Friday September 5

Ponies nearly done up. So made a camp to stretch hides, dry meat &c.
An old bull elk, whistling & calling, almost came into camp last night; today I went off alone on foot to trail him up; was absent all day but never saw him; shot a rabbit and a grouse on the way home. Rainy, wagon sheet makes pretty good tent.

1 red rabbit   1 blue grouse

Saturday September 6

Stormed all night; when we waked up snow covered the ground, bending down the willow bushes and loading the tall pines; rained and sleeted all day; we stayed in tent with roaring log fire in front of it. In afternoon took a three hours brisk ride on California through the mist and rain.

Our camp is a narrow valley by a brook, steep hills, some covered with pine and spruce, others bare with grass and sagebrush, broken by ravines and a few steep cliffs; some bison around us.

Sunday September 7

M. & I, on Blackie and Splitear (the two best hunting ponies), started off early in the morning, and were gone till dusk. We ride through awful ground. While hunting through a great burnt slash on foot we struck elk tracks; following them up we found three bulls; we wounded all three (I two & M. one) and went after them helter skelter running, tumbling, jumping, falling and shooting; one got away; while following it I ran across and killed a blacktail doe. One head had good horns.

2 elk 1 blacktail deer

Monday September 8

I rode out alone; saw a doe and two fawn, which I did not touch as we have more than enough meat; coming home struck a covie [sic] of grouse and killed 12, as they are good eating for a change.

Meanwhile M. ran a black bear up a tree and shot him; by bad luck I was not with him.

12 blue grouse

Tuesday September 9

Broke camp and went about six miles farther, to a branch of the Ten Sleep,[11] better camp. Snowed last night; all this afternoon it snowed at intervals, so that the country has quite a wintry look; in the moonlight at night the scenery is very beautiful.

The bear meat is very good eating; I have never been in better health. California is a superb riding horse; he is not so good a hunting pony as Blackie or Splitear.

Wednesday September 10

M. & I took a long tramp through the woods still hunting, but without success; we saw nothing except two or three deer tracks. Snow lies on the ground through the woods, and the small pools or tarns are all frozen over.

---

11. The Indian rest stop Ten Sleep, Wyoming, is so named as it was ten days' journey from Fort Laramie.

These pine and spruce forests, with their sights & sounds or more often, absence of sound, remind me of the great woods of Maine and the Adirondacs; they have a weird, melancholy fascination for me.

Thursday September 11

M. & I rode over to find the Lake; we found it, and caught about fifty trout, but only by four hours riding and six hours as hard walking as I ever had. Pretty tired, and glad to get back to camp and a first class trout supper.

Friday September 12

No game; so shifted camp to about six miles farther down towards the narrow valley with steep, wooded sides. M. & I started off on foot at three p.m. and hunted till nightfall through the woods, and hills. I got a shot at a great bull elk with magnificent antlers as he stood facing me 75 yards (81 paces off), killing him very neatly. Knocked off the heads of two grouse for supper.

1 elk 2 grouse

Saturday September 13

In morning took a four hour tramp in moccasins (I wear them walking because they make no noise); shot a spike black tail buck at forty yards through the shoulders.

In afternoon M. & I went out on foot through the woods; found a grizzly bear track in a dense forest; followed the trail noiselessly up, and found him in his bed; I shot him through the brain at 25 feet distance.

1 bear 1 blacktail deer

Sunday September 14

In the morning skinned the grizzly.

In afternoon M. & I rode out on horseback. Down to canyon; superb scenery. Emptied the Winchester at a beautiful buck; shot very badly; killed him at sixth shot. While skinning him (near dusk) saw a female grizzly and her nearly full grown cub; we ran after them on foot about a mile, over awful ground; I mortally wounded the old one; she turned to bay[12] and M. who was ahead,

---

12. To defend herself. An animal "brought to bay," or cornered, often turns and charges its pursuers.

finished her; he wounded the cub; I cut it off and finished it; the ball going clean through him from end to end.

2 bears 1 blacktail buck

Monday September 15
In morning brought in the bear.

In afternoon M. & I went out on foot again with the moccasins as usual. We found a big grizzly at the carcass of the bull elk; M. has not yet got one solely by his own gun, I made him shoot it.

Shot four blue grouse for supper.

4 blue grouse

Tuesday September 16
We all three started out on foot to beat through the woods for bears; walked all day, but saw no bear. Lebo, however, started up a bull elk, which he fired at and missed; it ran across my way, and I stood behind some trees; I could only see part of its flank, which I fired into; away it started, and, running at top speed in my light moccasins, I got another shot and broke his back.

1 elk

Wednesday September 17
Broke camp and started down the mountain. Three pack ponies heavily laden with hides and horns; progress slow; camped on Willow Creek.

Thursday September 18
Reached the saw mill where we had left the wagon; California all done up, having fallen into a creek.

Friday September 19
Went (with wagon again) to Fort McKinney. Dined at Fort.

(Doctor Tyrell, 2 soldiers 8th cavalry near Fort Wingate in New Mexico killed by Grizzly in '72)

Saturday September 20
Fair days Journey, camped above Piney Fork. Killed Jack rabbit & 2 ducks

1 Jack rabbit 2 ducks

Sunday September 21

Long days journey; camped where we lunched on August 30th, under a great Balm Tree.

Monday September 22

Went down clear creek till about six miles from Powder River; then went into camp under two huge cottonwood tree [sic], as our bear skins are rapidly spoiling and need to be fleshed and dried. Horses are not in good condition.

Tuesday September 23

Bear skins drying so did not break camp; hunted to north of creek; no game.

Wednesday September 24

Skins not yet dry; hunted to south side of creek; no game; took shot gun and killed two teal and five chickens along the river edge.

2 teal 5 sharptail grouse

Thursday September 25

Made long days journey, camped under some large cottonwoods in a bend of the Powder. Out of fresh meat, so went out shooting; shot awfully; missed three shots at whitetail; M. also missed two.

Friday September 26

Rained all night; drew wagon sheet over us, but pretty wet. Made good days journey; camped by dead Cottonwood some four miles above the N bar ranche. M. shot a whitetail doe.

Saturday September 27

Made pasture by SH ranche. Rained at night.

Sunday September 28

Went down Powder camping near Powderville[13]; shot two bluewinged teal with rifle, and eight teal and two shovellers with a right and left from shot gun.

12 ducks

---

13. Powderville, Montana.

Monday September 29

Cold rain in night, lasting all day; poor feed for ponies; traveled till night fall when we camped near White Clay Buttes; water bad, from mud hole; team nearly done out.

Tuesday September 30

Shot 7 sharptail grouse; very heavy frost last night. Hard days journey; cold and windy; road heavy; one of the team played out and we had to put split ear in the harness. It was after dark when we went into camp among the fantastic "medicine buttes"; a most picturesque camp, blazing pitch pine fire, in angle of a sandstone cliff, under pine trees.

7 sharptail grouse

Wednesday October 1

Furious hurricane blowing, with driving rain squalls. Afraid to venture on prairie so stayed in camp all day.

Thursday October 2

Still rainy; beds pretty wet; horses had strayed; could not find them till noon; then one of the team was in a mud hole; worked two horses to get her out; she could hardly stand, so had to stay in camp.

Friday October 3

Very windy; and a little rain; camped on the big sand; been out of meat for two days; went out with shot gun and killed three teal and two chickens.

3 duck 2 sharptail grouse

Saturday October 4

Clear and cold; drove to the Muddy Creek; on the way killed a jack rabbit and two sharptail grouse with the rifle; then by moonlight M. & I rode in 50 miles to the ranche, between 9 p.m. & 6 a.m.

1 jack rabbit 2 sharptail grouse

[This ends excerpt from 1883 diary.]

Sunday November 16

Reached Little Missouri, went out to Chimney Butte Ranche.

Monday November 17

Rode down (alone) to the first shack on Elkhorn Ranche; very cold; had to rustle for myself.

Tuesday November 18

Shot five sharptail grouse from trees with rifle for Breakfast. Went on to where Seawall and Dow are hewing logs for ranche house.

5 sharptail grouse

Wednesday November 19

Located ranche house.

Thursday November 20

Rode round range with Captain Robbins. Shot seven grouse.

7 sharptail grouse

Friday November 21

Rode up to Chimney Butte Ranche through snow with Seawall & Dow.

Saturday November 22

Shot six grouse. Seawall & I rode into town & back, thermometer 20° below zero.

6 sharptail grouse

Sunday November 23

Shot 5 cottontail.

5 rabbit

Monday November 24

Went out to wait for beaver. Shot 3 grouse.

3 sharptail grouse

Tuesday November 25

Seawall & I rode up to Langs.

Wednesday November 26

Rained.

Thursday November 27

Rode home.

Friday November 28

Rained.

Saturday November 29

Shot 2 sharptail grouse. Rode in town and lunched with Marquis.[14]

Sunday November 30

Sent Seawall & Dow back.

Monday December 1

Tramped all round Square Butte after deer; saw none; shot 5 grouse from tree.

5 grouse

Tuesday December 2

M. & I went all day after sheep; saw none.

Wednesday December 3

M. & I went all day after   . [Left blank.]

Feverish; so stayed in house.

Thursday December 4

Went out near house on bottom; killed a white tail doe at 40 yds with rifle and four sharptail grouse with shotgun.

1 white tail   4 grouse

Friday December 5

M. & I went out after sheep but saw none. Need meat for winter; killed 3 blacktail; a doe at 50 yards; a young buck at 120; a buck at 60.

3 blacktail

---

14. Marquis De Mores. The French marquis entered into cattle ranching in the Badlands at the same time as Roosevelt, founding the town of Medora—named after his wife—in 1883. He tried to bypass the Chicago stockyards by building a meatpacking plant in Medora, but his efforts failed and he left Medora just before the harsh winter of 1886–87.

Saturday December 6

Sylvane[15] arrived with 52 ponies, spent day breaking.

Sunday December 7

Sent for Seawall and Dow to get Elkhorn ponies.

Monday December 8

Spent day after Mountain sheep.

Tuesday December 9

Again out after mountain sheep.

Wednesday December 10

Seawall & Dow arrived.

1 cottontail rabbit

Thursday December 11

Breaking ponies.

Friday December 12

George in buckboard, Merrifield and I on horseback started on sheep hunt.

Rode and walked all day through frightfully rough ground, but saw nothing, camped in shack on Oxbow.

Saturday December 13

Tramped all over Bullion's Butte; saw nothing. Thermometer ranges from +25– –10° F.

1 sharptail grouse

Sunday December 14

Rode off three miles on horseback; then tramped a mile on foot through the roughest kind of ground; came on a Bighorn ram and shot him at about 90 yards. Came back to Chimney Butte Ranche.

1 Bighorn

---

15. Sylvane Ferris.

Monday December 15

Bitterly cold.

Tuesday December 16

Bitterly cold.

Wednesday December 17

Went out hunting in snow through brush; shot a fine white tail buck, & a prairie chicken.

1 white tail 1 grouse

Photographs

A
1   corral
2   corral
3   House & shack
4   House & shack (Fur coat)
5   Butte, snow
6   (spoiled)
7   cattle
8   cattle & cowboys
9   Merrifield, shooting
10   "   , at the ready
11 cow corral & stock
12   "   "   (better)

B
1   Joe & Wilmot
2   "   "
3   Seawall (spoiled)
4   " on horseback
5   Long Butte
6   "   "
7   Chimney Butte (spoiled)
8   "   "
9   Horses & men in corral
10   "   "   "
11 ram & elk skulls
12   "   "   "

C
1 Horseman, instantaneous
2 Sylvane on horse
3 Ram's head
4 Sylvane
5 Snowy Butte
6 Broken

INCOME ACCT 1884

Date		
Jan 1st	Dubuque & Dun	150.00
"	Dun & Dubuque	75.00
Feb 1st	Rock & Pits	150.00
Mar 1st	Putnam	91.65
" 5th	Roosevelt & Son	1912.62

Bear	Badger	Elk	Ant.	Blck	White	Hare	Sage G.	Shrp. G.	Blue G.	Duck	Curlew	Plover
	1		2			1		1		1	3	2
3		6	5	2	4	14	36	21	26			2
		Big-horn	3		1	5		32				
							1					
	1			1		1						
3	1	6	3	8	4	11		71				
			36				106			27		7

S. M. Ferris
Grand Lake
    White Cove
    Queen Co.
    New Brunswick

Express Co
St. John
    New Brunswick

"E.K.C."

Volume IX (1886)

No diary exists for 1885, which was an eventful year. In June New York Mayor William Grace offered Roosevelt the position of president of the Board of Health, seeking to replace the corrupt Alexander Shaler. Roosevelt eagerly accepted the offer, but the post never materialized, as the city was not able to remove Shaler until 1891. Still, Roosevelt remained active in New York City and State politics, despite his long absences out West. During one of his stays in New York Roosevelt became reacquainted with his youthful paramour, Edith Carow, and the two became secretly engaged. During the fall of 1885 Roosevelt rode with Long Island's Meadowbrook Hunt. When he tried to jump a stone wall, his horse tripped and both horse and rider fell, leaving Roosevelt with a broken arm. The combination of the broken arm and his relationship with Edith kept Roosevelt in New York until March 1886. With his departure looming, Roosevelt cancelled speaking engagements and spent every day with Edith the week before he left for his ranch. At seven months this would be one of Roosevelt's longest stays out West.

The winter of 1885–86 in the Bad Lands had been a hard one, and Roosevelt's ranches lost many head of cattle. Roosevelt, though, remained optimistic about his investment. "The death by loss has been wholly trifling," he wrote Anna. "Unless we have a big accident I shall get through this all right." However, it was difficult to understand how many cattle—especially cows—had been lost ahead of the next roundup, and even more difficult to measure the effects on the calving season. After being weakened by giving birth, how many cows would survive the following winter? This was the great unknown by the early spring of 1886.

Roosevelt re-entered his ranch life by going hunting. When he went with his men Sewall and Dow to retrieve four deer Dow had shot and hung up two weeks before, the group found that mountain lions had eaten them. Roosevelt immediately wanted to go after the lions, which required crossing the Little Missouri River. When the men went to retrieve the boat, they found that the rope had been cut and one of the thieves had dropped a mitten nearby. Roosevelt knew that the culprits were three hard men who lived in a shack about twenty miles away. Roosevelt had been elected chairman of the Stockmen's Association, which made him a deputy sheriff in the county. His men began building a replacement boat with which to pursue the thieves. Roosevelt and his posse captured the boat thieves a week later, turning them over to the sheriff in Dickinson. Roosevelt later recounted the pursuit and capture of the thieves in his 1888 book *Ranch Life and the Hunting Trail*.

Roosevelt spent the summer months working on his biography of Thomas Hart Benton, the Missouri senator and champion of westward expansion. Benton had encouraged Western exploration and written the first Homestead Acts granting land to those willing to work it. Roosevelt presented Benton as imbued "with the masterful, overbearing spirit of the West . . . possession of which is certainly a most healthy sign of the virile strength of a young community," and as architect of America's "Manifest Destiny"—the idea that "it was our manifest destiny to swallow up the lands of all adjoining nations who were too weak to withstand us." Roosevelt wrote these words on his Western ranch for an Eastern and largely urban audience. Here lay the importance of Roosevelt's works on the West, from his *Winning of the West* history to his personal accounts of hunting and ranching. Roosevelt wrote not as a true Westerner let alone a real cowboy. He wrote as an Easterner who could interpret and shape the West for Eastern consumption. In doing this Roosevelt acted much like fellow Ivy League-educated Easterners Frederic Remington, the great artist and sculptor of the West, and Owen Wister, author of the quintessential cowboy novel, *The Virginian*. For those back East exhausted by modern urban life—the noise, the smell, the jostling crowds—Roosevelt's writings acted as a tonic, and allowed the reader to share a small sliver of a life spent riding, ranching, and hunting. A work like *Benton* found an eager audience in a population completing its continental destiny and looking south to the Caribbean and farther west to the Pacific for further expansion.

The diary ends in July, at a point when Roosevelt was still hoping Mayor Grace would come through on his offer of a new job in New York City. With his engagement to Edith, his growing baby Alice, and all his friends and family back East, Roosevelt was strongly feeling the pull of New York. As always that late summer and early fall Roosevelt undertook a hunting trip to the Elkhorn Mountains, following much the same path he did during his 1884 trip. And as always, he returned to New York in October for election season. As Roosevelt left Dakota for one of the last times, several important events loomed on his horizon. He was about to receive the Republican nomination for mayor, and he was about to wed Edith. Finally, catastrophic winter conditions were about to hit the Upper Plains cattle country, leading Roosevelt to start making plans to get out of his ranching investment. With the combination of events at the very end of 1886, Roosevelt turned from the West to face a life and career firmly grounded in the East.

Volume IX
1886 DIARY

Friday January 1
Dinner at P.K.E.

Saturday January 2
Dinner party

Monday January 4
Opera

Tuesday January 5
Fanny Dana 2.30 p.m.; Lizzie Cary 6.30.

Wednesday January 6
Civil Service Ref[1] 12 West 31st; 8.30

Thursday January 7
Corrinne's, 7.00

Friday January 8
Dinner party at home

Saturday January 9
Amateur theatricals

Monday January 11
E.K.C. dinner.[2]

Tuesday January 12
Speak at institute.

---

1. Civil Service Reform Association.
2. Edith Kermit Carow. Roosevelt had begun seeing Edith romantically in October 1885. They became secretly engaged in November, less than two years after the death of Alice. Although his ranch desperately needed his attention during the disastrous winter of 1885–86, the romance with Edith kept him in New York until March.

Wednesday January 13
Theatre.

Thursday January 14
Authors Club 19 West 24th St.

Friday January 15
Dinner at Aunt Annie's, 7.00

Saturday January 16
Dinner party at home.

Monday January 18
Dinner Lara, West &c. Rosy.

Tuesday January 19
Astors

Wednesday January 20
Theatre party at Anna's

Thursday January 21
[Whist club—crossed out] T. evening club.

Friday January 22
Dinner to P.T. & Crokle.

Saturday January 23
Eastlake Dinner.

Sunday January 24
(Went to Chicago; cut engagements)

Monday January 25
[Speak at K.M.C.—crossed out] Whist Club

Tuesday January 26
Miss Marburys.

Wednesday January 27
Speak at Princeton

Thursday January 28
Cabot comes.[3]

Friday January 29
Dinner

Saturday January 30
Dinner at Anna's

Monday February 1
Dinner at Corinne's.

Tuesday February 2
Dinner at Lizzie's.

Wednesday February 3
Theatre party.

Thursday February 4
Dinner.

Friday February 5
Theatre party.

Saturday February 6
Century[4]

---

3. Both Henry Cabot Lodge and his wife, Nannie, visited Roosevelt in New York, cementing their increasingly close relationship. After their departure Roosevelt wrote Lodge, "I really can not say how I have missed you and your 'cara sposa' [dear wife] . . . I feel really blue when I think that it will be some nine months before I see you again." To Nannie a short time later he wrote, "You see, I never make friends at all easily; outside of my own family you two are really the only people for whom I genuinely care." TR to Lodge, 7 February 1886, Morison, I, 93–94; TR to Nannie Lodge, 19 February 1886, quoted in Putnam, 558.

4. Century Club, an exclusive private club with its clubhouse on East 15th Street.

Monday February 8
Dinner.

Tuesday February 9
Dinner at McCook's.

Wednesday February 10
Theatre with E.K.C.

Thursday February 11
Dinner at Kean.

Friday February 12
Speak at Morton Hall.[5]

Saturday February 13
Speak at O.R.

Tuesday February 16
Dinner at Whitelaw Reid's, 271 Lexington Av, 7.30.

Wednesday February 17
Dinner at home. Lizzie Cary at 4.30.

Friday February 19
McCooks.

Saturday February 20
Eastlake; cut it; E.[6]

---

5. At the Twenty-first Assembly District Republican Association, Roosevelt spoke on "Republican Professions and Republican Practices" in a continuing effort to win back to Republicans the independent vote that went to Democrat Grover Cleveland in 1884: "My experience has shown me that the man most to be feared is he who is moved by honest intentions but always manages to vote on the wrong side. In short, we must combat not alone the active hostility of the bad, but the no less deadly indifference of those who are well disposed." *New York Times,* 13 February 1886.

6. Edith.

Friday March 5
E.

Saturday March 6
Century. E.

Tuesday March 9
E.

Wednesday March 10
E.

Friday March 12
[Speak at Rep. Club.—crossed out]
E.

Sunday March 14
E; lunch; + ; Beekman Place.

Monday March 15
Started for Medora, Dakota, to spend the summer on my cattle ranches.

Tuesday March 16
Chicago

Wednesday March 17 ♂[7]
St. Pauls.

Thursday March 18
Reached Medora.

Friday March 19 ♂
Drove down to Elkhorn Ranch.

Saturday March 20
Shot 4 sharptails for supper. Ice gorge in river in front of ranch.

---

7. Symbol for Mars. Roosevelt's use of these symbols seems to indicate his nighttime observation of the planets.

Sunday March 21

Tramped across hay plateau to Tompkins ranche; very muddy.

Monday March 22 ♂

Tramped over to get deer; mountain lions had got them.

Tuesday March 23

Shot 4 prairie chicken.

Wednesday March 24

Thieves stole boat; started to build another to go after them.

Thursday March 25 ♀[8]

Went out after deer; saw nothing. Boat being built. River very high; ice piled up on banks several feet.

Friday March 26

Boat building.

Saturday March 27 ♂

Boat built. Too cold to start. Shot 4 chickens.

Sunday March 28

Bitter cold.

Monday March 29

Furious blizzard.

Tuesday March 30

Weather milder. Started in boat with Seawall & Dow down stream after thieves. Camped below Eaton. Shot 3 prairie chicken.

Wednesday March 31

Bitter cold. 4 prairie chicken.

Thursday April 1

Shot whitetail doe 75 yards; Dow shot another. Captured the three boat thieves.

---

8. Symbol for Venus.

Friday April 2

Came on with our prisoners till hung up by ice jam.

Saturday April 3

Hung up by ice.

Sunday April 4

Hung up by ice.

Monday April 5

Worked down a couple of miles till jam again stopped us.

Tuesday April 6

Worked down a couple of miles again to tail of ice jam.

Wednesday April 7

Worked down to C ♦ Ranche 2 praire chicken.

Thursday April 8

Rode to Kildeer mountain to arrange for a wagon which I hired.

Friday April 9

Walked captives to Kildeer Mountain.

Saturday April 10

Drove captives in wagon to Captain Browns ranch.

Sunday April 11

Drove captives to Dickinson & gave them to sheriff.

Monday April 12

Came to Medora.

Tuesday April 13

Stockmeeting.

Wednesday April 14

Rode down to Elkhorn ranche with Merrifield.

Thursday April 15
Rainy.

Friday April 16
Rode up to Medora.

Saturday April 17
Rode out to Chimney Butte Ranche.

Sunday April 18
Went to Miles City with Sylvane.

Monday April 19
Stockmeeting.

Tuesday April 20
Stockmeeting.

Wednesday April 21
Meeting of the Executive Committee.

Thursday April 22
Back to Medora.

[Pages April 23–June 17 torn out.]

Friday June 18
Rose up to Medora on Sorrel Joe.

Saturday June 19
Out on round up with Maltese Cross wagon.

Sunday June 20
Worked down to South Heart.

Monday June 21
Worked up to Rocky Ridge.

Tuesday June 22
Worked to Davis Creek.

Wednesday June 23
To Andrews Creek.

Thursday June 24
To Indian Creek

Friday June 25
To Bullions Creek.

Saturday June 26
Down Bullions Creek.

Sunday June 27
To Chimney Butte

Monday June 28
Rode in to Medora.

Tuesday June 29
Rode back to Elkhorn Ranche, with Merrifield.

Wednesday June 30.
Benton.[9]

Thursday July 1
Benton; rode out with Bill Rove to get and brand calves. ♀ 14th ♂ 25th

Friday July 2
Benton; rode out with Bill Rove after calves; got them into corral and branded them. Rode little black horse

Saturday July 3
Rode up to Medora on Manitou.

---

9. Roosevelt was working on his biography of Thomas Hart Benton.

Conclusion

Theodore Roosevelt's Life after 1886

It is a shame that Roosevelt's diaries end in July 1886, as his life was about to change in several important ways. In October Roosevelt again returned to New York City in time for the election season, and received the Republican nomination for mayor on October 27, his twenty-eighth birthday. He belatedly entered a three-way contest with Democrat Abram Hewitt and United Labor candidate Henry George. George was well known for writing *Progress and Poverty*, a book that advocated a land value tax to compensate for the inequality fostered by a cyclical industrialized economy. From the start, it was widely expected that Republicans would flock to Hewitt in their fear of George's election. Roosevelt accepted the nomination to help unite city Republicans still divided after the 1884 election. Election Day saw Hewitt victorious and Roosevelt come in third. He seemed to care little. Roosevelt took great joy in his friend Henry Cabot Lodge's election to Congress, and his own coming nuptials to Edith Carow.

Theodore Roosevelt and Edith were married in London on December 2, and took a long European honeymoon. When they returned to New York in March 1887, Edith was pregnant with Theodore Roosevelt Jr., the first of five children they would have together. After leaving baby Alice in the care of his sister Anna since 1884, Roosevelt readied to take up his role as husband and father. One task awaited him, however. He headed west to assess the condition of his ranch after the harsh winter of 1886–87 had devastated Western agriculture. In the Dakota Territory, farmers and cattlemen were ruined. For Roosevelt, it was the beginning of the end of his Western experiment. "I am bluer than indigo about the cattle," Roosevelt wrote Anna, "it is even worse than I feared." He wrote that he expected to lose at least half of his initial investment of $80,000. Although Roosevelt would not actually sell his two ranches until 1898, his dream of residing at least part-time in Dakota was at an end.

In the fall of 1888 Roosevelt backed Republican Benjamin Harrison for the presidency. He did good service for the party by giving speeches not only in New York, but also Minnesota, Michigan, and Harrison's home state of Indiana. When Harrison won, he rewarded Roosevelt with one of three seats on the United States Civil Service Commission. The post was a mixed blessing. Maintaining residences in both New York and Washington, D.C., was expensive, especially after Roosevelt's recent financial setback. The position was also a relatively new one, created by the passage of the Pendleton Act in 1883. Moreover, the Civil Service Commission oversaw only about 28,000 of the 140,000 federal jobs, and had only the power to investigate, and not prosecute, any malfeasance. It was also an appointed, not an elected, position, and was the first of a succession of appointed jobs until Roosevelt's election as governor of New York in 1898. In other words, Roosevelt would win no election, and hold no elected office, for fifteen long years during the prime of his life. Finally, as commissioner, Roosevelt would be investigating government officials of his own party, loyal Republicans who had in some cases been appointed by the president himself. Doing the job effectively while staying in his party's good graces would require considerable political skill.

Until he became president, Roosevelt's six years as civil service commissioner would constitute his longest tenure in any job. His time in Washington would provide him significant experience. While in the capital, he became intimate with some of the most important figures in Washington political and social circles, men like historian Henry Adams, descendant of the Adams presidents; old New York family friend John Hay; British diplomat Cecil Spring-Rice; German diplomat Speck von Sternburg; old Harvard friend Winthrop Chanler; Assistant Secretary of State William Wharton; naval intelligence officer Charles Henry Davis; and naval theorist Alfred Thayer Mahan. He solidified his friendship and political alliance with Henry Cabot Lodge. He sharpened his political and administrative skills, and showed he could navigate Washington's treacherous waters. Roosevelt even survived being the target of one of Washington's favorite career-killers, the Congressional Investigating Committee. His walks frequently took him past the White House, and it was at this time, he later admitted, that he had his first thought of becoming president. During his time as civil service commissioner, he moved his family back and forth between Washington and New York. And the family became larger, with the birth of three children during this period: Kermit in 1889, Ethel in 1891, and Archie in 1894. Roosevelt continued to write and publish, including many of his Western-themed books: *The Winning of the West*, *American Big-Game Hunting*, *The Wilderness Hunter*, and *Hunting in the Bad Lands*.

When Democrat Grover Cleveland was re-elected to the presidency in 1892, he kept Roosevelt on as civil service commissioner, indicating that it would only be for a couple more years, until 1894 or so. After so long out of New York politics, Roosevelt wanted to return to his hometown, and a chance appeared in the fall of 1894 when Roosevelt was asked once again to run for mayor of New York. Mayoral candidates were expected to contribute their own money to the campaign, something Edith indicated they could not afford. Roosevelt had yet to unload his Western ranches, and still owed money on the construction of Sagamore Hill. Roosevelt turned down the Republican nomination and immediately regretted it. That year William Strong, a reform Republican much like Roosevelt, was elected mayor.

Strong wanted Roosevelt in his administration, and first offered him the position of head of the Department of Street Cleaning. On the one hand, the issue of cleaning city streets had first brought Roosevelt into local politics in 1881. On the other hand, if he took the job, the ambitious young Roosevelt— only thirty-six years old—would be responsible for hauling away the city's garbage. To Strong, Roosevelt demurred. The mayor then offered Roosevelt a position much more to his liking, that of president of the Police Commission, responsible for overseeing the New York City Police Department.

Roosevelt began his position in May 1895, only months after the Lexow Committee, empowered to investigate the city's police force, issued its January 1895 report. The report detailed widespread corruption and brutality among police. Even during the committee's proceedings, witnesses were brought into the hall bruised and bloody from recent police beatings. The report concluded that the police themselves had become a special criminal class in New York, "a separate and highly privileged class, armed with the authority and the machinery for oppression and punishment, but practically free themselves from the operation of the criminal law."

Upon taking office, Roosevelt began to clean house. He was able to force the chief of police and other corrupt officers to resign. With his friend urban reformer Jacob Riis—a former police reporter and author of the 1890 book *How the Other Half Lives*—he began his famed midnight inspection tours, making sure police officers were on duty when and where they were supposed to be, rather than asleep, in brothels, or in saloons. Arguably, in tackling corruption among New York City's 4,000 policemen and their countless allies in the criminal and political classes, Roosevelt faced a task more vast and complex than overseeing America's federal civil service.

At the center of much of the corruption lay the weekly violation of the Sunday Excise Law, which forbade selling alcohol on the Sabbath. This state law had been backed by the rural, upstate temperance vote and imposed on the city, where it was routinely ignored. Worse, it was selectively enforced. Payoffs to the police allowed a saloon to remain open Sunday, yet police could choose to enforce closure of, say, a saloon that competed with one owned by a local political figure. Many saloonkeepers were also Tammany bosses, and their saloons often doubled as unofficial Tammany headquarters. When Roosevelt took office in early 1895, between 12,000 and 15,000 saloons were operating in New York City. Within a few months, Roosevelt had been successful in closing ninety-seven percent of them on Sundays, stopping the flow of three million glasses of beer.

As a result, by the summer of 1895 Roosevelt had become the most unpopular man in New York City. Inevitably, he was attacked by opposition politicians in the Democratic Party. But Roosevelt was also attacked by German-Americans who enjoyed a beer on Sundays and usually voted Republican. In the 1895 elections for state Assembly, German-Americans switched their votes to the Democrats, and Republican leaders blamed Roosevelt for their disastrous showing at the polls that year. Someone even sent Roosevelt a fake letter bomb that a postal clerk opened to find loaded only with sawdust. By 1896 Roosevelt was in danger of having his position legislated out of existence.

Roosevelt's hope lay with the 1896 presidential election. As he had in 1888 for Republican nominee Benjamin Harrison, Roosevelt stumped for William McKinley of Ohio. With McKinley's election, Roosevelt was awarded with a new Washington post, assistant secretary of the Navy. Roosevelt took up his new position in April 1897. While he would serve only one year, it was a momentous one. The secretary of the Navy, John D. Long of Massachusetts, was frequently out of the office, leaving Roosevelt as acting secretary. Roosevelt set about modernizing the Navy, as war with Spain appeared imminent.

By 1897 Cubans were in revolt against Spanish imperial rule of the island, only ninety miles off the coast of Florida. As Latin American revolutions stripped Spain of its holdings, the once-great empire gripped its only remaining New World colonies—Cuba and Puerto Rico—ever more tightly. This irritated a United States growing in both political and economic power, and increasingly willing to assert that power in the Western Hemisphere. By the time of the latest Cuban insurrection, Americans had invested $50 million in the island's sugar fields, while Britain and European powers increasingly bowed to American interests in the hemisphere. A Cuban junta had established offices in New York City, and fed propaganda of Spanish atrocities to the Yellow Press. By 1896, Congress had passed a resolution recognizing the Cuban belligerency. Throughout the country, Americans took up the cry of *Cuba Libre!*

Under pressure to make some sort of firm gesture toward Spain, and to ensure the safety of American lives and property in Cuba, in January 1898 President McKinley dispatched the battleship *Maine* to Havana harbor. Early the following month, William Randolph Hearst's *New York Journal* published a letter from the Spanish minister to Washington in which he criticized President McKinley. The De Lôme letter led to the minister's return to Spain and inflamed American opinion. Worse was yet to come. On February 15, the *Maine* blew up in Havana Harbor, killing over 250 American sailors. War fever gripped the Yellow Press and Americans in general. Even as McKinley tried to negotiate Cuban autonomy with Madrid, pressure on the president mounted to ask Congress for a declaration of war. On April 11, McKinley relented. By the end of the month America was at war.

Roosevelt and others like his friend Senator Henry Cabot Lodge wanted war with Spain not because of any mindless love of war, but to kick the brutal, decrepit, and Catholic Spanish Empire out of America's hemisphere. Roosevelt did his part by preparing the Navy for war, including sending orders to Commodore George Dewey to prepare the Pacific Squadron to move against the Philippines, Spain's major holding in the Far East. While still carrying out the business of the Navy Department, Roosevelt was likely distracted by other concerns. Only a week later, it was announced that Roosevelt had resigned his post to become second-in-command of the First U.S. Volunteer Cavalry. Via San Antonia, Texas, and Tampa, Florida, Roosevelt was bound for Cuba.

Thanks to the regiment's commander, career army officer and Medal of Honor winner Colonel Leonard Wood, the regiment attracted many volunteers from the American Southwest, where Wood had served. With so many cowboys and Native Americans from the Arizona, New Mexico, and Indian Territories, the press dubbed the regiment "The Rough Riders." Thanks to Roosevelt being second-in-command, the regiment also attracted many men like Roosevelt: upper class, Ivy League-educated young men who belonged to New York's top social clubs. By June 1898 the regiment had landed in Cuba and had its first skirmish at Las Guásimas on June 24, costing the lives of eight Rough Riders.

After Las Guásimas the Rough Riders settled into camp as the American high command planned the battle that would bring the war to a speedy end. The American Navy had bottled up the Spanish fleet in Santiago Harbor, while Spanish troops occupied the heights above the city. If the Americans could take the heights, they could besiege the city and make continued Spanish occupation of Cuba untenable. Roosevelt and his men were ordered to attack the San Juan Heights on July 1. Just before the battle Colonel Wood was given command of the brigade, replacing a general felled by yellow fever. This left Colonel Roosevelt in full command of the regiment. In front of the San Juan Heights sat a small hill called Kettle Hill. On Roosevelt's order his men charged up the hill, a bullet grazing Roosevelt's elbow while he shot a Spanish soldier with his revolver.

From the top of Kettle Hill Roosevelt could see American infantry making painstakingly slow progress up the San Juan Heights. Almost on instinct, Roosevelt ran to support the attack, forgetting to issue a command to the men behind him. Roosevelt turned back and shouted, "Forward march!" The Rough Riders ran up the heights as Spanish soldiers deserted their positions at the top. When Roosevelt and his men reached the crest, they could gaze down upon Santiago. Two weeks later the Santiago garrison surrendered, signaling the end to Spanish power in the Western Hemisphere. With the exploits of Roosevelt and the Rough Riders already making headlines across the country, the Battle of San Juan also signaled the beginning of a new chapter in Roosevelt's political career. Already messages were arriving in Cuba asking Roosevelt to run for governor of New York.

To run as a Republican in New York State required having the backing of the party's boss, Thomas C. Platt. Platt kept a tight grip on the party machinery and would brook no independence from a reformer like Roosevelt. Roosevelt promised not to "make war" on the machine, and to consult Platt on all matters. By doing this Roosevelt alienated many fellow reform Republicans who might have normally welcomed a Roosevelt candidacy. The result was that on November 8, 1898, Roosevelt won the governorship by a slim margin of 18,000 votes.

In his later memoirs Roosevelt would assert that he had been a radical reform governor who acted with great independence from Platt and the machine. The result, according to Roosevelt and later historians, was that Platt sought to remove the governor from New York and "shelve" him in the vice-presidency. There is little evidence to support this. By the time McKinley's vice president Garret Hobart died on November 21, 1899, Roosevelt was hoping to be renominated as the Republican candidate for governor in 1900. This meant maintaining his good relations with Platt and the party machine. At the same time, the 1899 New York City elections had shown Roosevelt's great strength among city Republicans, as he successfully bridged the divide between reform and machine Republicans. This did not illustrate Roosevelt's independence from Platt, but his ability to be, as Roosevelt himself said, "governor of the entire party" rather than of a mere faction. Moreover, Platt saw that Roosevelt's place on the national ticket with McKinley would greatly help Republicans in November 1900. Platt knew that success at the national level trickled down to the state level. On the advice of Lodge and others, Roosevelt accepted the vice-presidential nomination.

Platt was right about the effect of having a strong national ticket that included Roosevelt. The 1900 election results for New York State represented a boon for the boss. Platt successfully replaced Roosevelt as governor with a Platt lieutenant, Benjamin Odell, who secured a 110,000 vote plurality, much larger than Roosevelt's only two years earlier. In Congress, New York Republicans gained four seats. In the New York legislature, Republicans secured massive majorities, eighteen in the Senate (out of fifty seats) and sixty in the Assembly (out of 150 seats). The McKinley-Roosevelt victory of 1900 was one shared by Thomas Platt.

The Theodore Roosevelt governorship was marked by a number of progressive reforms. Roosevelt backed housing reform in New York City to make working-class tenements safer and healthier places to live. He supported a tax on public utilities. He improved labor laws and advanced forestry programs. He strengthened laws governing banking and insurance companies. Roosevelt did all this in only two years as governor, while performing a balancing act more difficult than a circus tightrope act. He continuously had to maneuver between independent and machine Republicans. Here lay his greatest success on the eve of becoming vice president of the United States. Roosevelt had championed a progressive legislative agenda as the chief executive of the largest state in the Union, and he had done so by carefully maneuvering between the hostile factions of his party. In his New York governorship were many clues of what kind of president Theodore Roosevelt might one day become. But by inauguration day in March 1901, such a possibility seemed some time in the future, as President McKinley began his second term in office.

After his wife fell ill, President McKinley rescheduled a planned June 1901 trip to the Pan-American Exposition in Buffalo to September. On September 5, McKinley addressed a crowd of about 50,000 at the exposition. The next day, the press reported, the president would visit Niagara Falls, returning to the exposition's Temple of Music to greet the public. Leon Czolgozs, inspired by anarchist Emma Goldman, approached the president in the temple with a handkerchief covering the revolver in his hand. He fired twice, hitting the president once in the abdomen. The attending doctor on the grounds of the exposition closed the wound with the bullet still inside. Roosevelt received word of the attempted assassination while camping in the Adirondacks, and immediately rushed to Buffalo. McKinley seemed to be recovering "splendidly," wrote Roosevelt, and the vice president was so unconcerned about the president's health that he made plans to see his sister Anna at the end of the month, and to make October campaign trips to Iowa and Ohio. Within a week, however, McKinley was dead.

During his seven-and-a-half years as president, Theodore Roosevelt had a tremendous impact on national and global events, and helped shape the modern presidency. When nearly a quarter of a million coal miners and related workers went on strike in spring 1902, they were met with the hostility of mine owners and managers. As the strike dragged on into a chilly fall, President Roosevelt acted to avoid millions of Americans suffering through winter without adequate heating. In an unprecedented move, the president directly mediated between labor and management, threatening to send in the U.S. Army to seize the mines and have soldiers mine the coal. Both sides agreed to abide by the decision of a five-man Coal Strike Commission, and miners went back to work by the end of October. In the end, miners received higher wages and shorter hours. Labor claimed victory, as membership in unions soared nationwide.

Never had an American president shown such sympathy with organized labor. This came into direct conflict with many conservatives who believed in a complete *laissez-faire* economy. Instead, Roosevelt believed in, as he said in his first presidential Annual Message, "proper government supervision." During Roosevelt's presidency, such belief in government oversight of commerce resulted in the Elkins and Hepburn acts that regulated railroads. Roosevelt also created a new Department of Commerce and Labor to promote economic growth and collect economic data. Most famously, the president targeted trusts as dangerous concentrations of economic power that engaged in unfair business practices. In 1902, Roosevelt had his attorney general sue the massive railroad trust North Securities under the Sherman Antitrust Act. E.H. Harriman and J.P. Morgan had formed the holding company in order to join together their railroad companies and avoid the cutthroat competition that might ruin them. In 1904, in *U.S. v. Northern Securities*, the Supreme Court affirmed that the giant trust suppressed free competition. Roosevelt had won a stunning victory against the forces of unregulated capitalism. Northern Securities was dissolved.

His political career in New York City, Albany, and Washington had taught Roosevelt the need for strong executive power, which President Roosevelt now sought to wield, from the Panama Canal to the Preservation of Antiquities Act. In Panama, he aided a revolution against Colombia to secure a zone for the proposed isthmian canal. "I took the isthmus, started the canal, and then left Congress—not to debate the canal, but to debate me," Roosevelt later stated in one of the boldest affirmations of presidential executive power in American history. Likewise, the Preservation of Antiquities Act gave Roosevelt the power, without resort to Congress, to declare national monuments and historic sites. In 1906, he championed the Pure Food and Drug Act, allowing the federal government to inspect and regulate what Americans consumed. Understanding the needs of labor, calling for the regulation of the economy, ensuring Americans would not be poisoned by tainted food and drugs, with all measures backed by strong executive power—these were the hallmarks of Roosevelt's "Square Deal" for the American people.

Roosevelt's foreign policy reflected not only an assertion of American power in the Western Hemisphere, as reflected in the Roosevelt Corollary of the Monroe Doctrine that claimed America's "police power" in the Caribbean. The worldly Roosevelt, who had traveled through the Middle East, lived in Germany, and had intimate friends in all of Europe's capitals, also understood the limits of American power and the need to work with other nations. Roosevelt made sure the United States had a presence at the Algeciras Conference of 1906, which solved the Tangier Crisis between France and Germany, when Germany objected to France's attempt to establish a protectorate over Morocco. The president personally convened the 1905 Portsmouth Conference to end the Russo-Japanese War, for which Roosevelt won the 1906 Nobel Peace Prize. He would wait to receive the medal until after his presidency, when he traveled back through Europe after undertaking an African safari.

Although no Constitutional amendment yet demanded that American presidents step down after serving two terms in office, the tradition established by George Washington remained so strong that few dared to defy it. For his successor Roosevelt tapped his secretary of war, William Howard Taft. Roosevelt had to convince fellow reformers that Taft shared Roosevelt's progressive agenda. A former U.S. solicitor-general and circuit court judge, Taft had many of the same progressive impulses as Roosevelt and a devotion to enforcing the law. As a result, in only one term the Taft Justice Department filed nearly twice as many antitrust suits as the Roosevelt administration had during two terms. But Taft was also a political naïf, having never run for office before his 1908 campaign for the presidency, and he made many moves that angered progressives. He named pro-business Republicans to his cabinet and to the Republican Party leadership. He campaigned with Republican politicians known to be pro-business, such as Joseph Foraker of Ohio. He signed into law the Payne-Aldrich Tariff Act, which kept rates high to protect American industry. Finally, Taft fired the chief of the U.S. Forest Service, Gifford Pinchot, who had been appointed to the post by Roosevelt. Pinchot had publicly criticized both Taft and the secretary of Interior, Richard Ballinger, who had restored millions of acres of forest preserves to private use. To Roosevelt and other progressive Republicans, Taft appeared to be undoing Roosevelt's reform legacy.

As Roosevelt undertook his postpresidential African safari and European tour in 1909–10, he received constant updates about Taft and his administration from friends such as Senator Henry Cabot Lodge. The fired Pinchot even visited the former president in Europe, while Roosevelt and his family took a vacation on the Italian Riviera. By the time he returned home to New York in June 1910, what to do about Taft and the Republican Party's conservative Old Guard weighed heavily upon the former president. In the summer and fall of 1910 he took an active part in the midterm elections. He toured the country giving speeches, heading as far west as Wyoming. Republican leaders urged Roosevelt to express his support of Taft as often as possible, while progressives looked to Roosevelt to endorse their positions on labor and popular rule.

As the summer progressed, Roosevelt seemed to be moving from one camp into the other. On August 31 the colonel traveled to Osawatomie, Kansas, the site of the 1856 battle where radical abolitionist John Brown tried to defend the town against pro-slavery partisans. In what became known as his "New Nationalism" speech, Roosevelt called for putting the national need before personal advantage. This would require a long list of progressive reforms: federal regulation, protection of natural resources, income and inheritance taxes, workmen's compensation, child labor laws, workplace safety laws, and a judiciary that placed individual rights over property rights. It was a radical speech that included lines such as, "Labor is prior to, and independent of, capital. Capital is only the fruit of labor, and could never have existed if labor had not first existed. Labor is the superior of capital, and deserves much the higher consideration." Roosevelt observed that such remarks could lead to his being denounced as a Communist agitator. They were not original to Roosevelt, however. The words and the sentiment were Abraham Lincoln's.

By 1911 the pressure had mounted for Roosevelt to run for the Republican nomination for the presidency. The former president's speeches since arriving back in the country had only underscored progressive Republicans' dissatisfaction with Taft. Still, Robert La Follette of Wisconsin, not Roosevelt, had long been the standard bearer among progressives and seemed the natural foil to Taft within the party. Moreover, the two-term tradition was deeply entrenched in American presidential politics. Only a virtual breakdown by La Follette in February 1912 during a speech to newspaper reporters made supporters question the Wisconsin senator's sanity and temperament. They looked to Roosevelt to pick up the progressive standard, and by early 1912 Roosevelt was in the race. In taking on the sitting president of his own party before state primaries became binding, Roosevelt was following a difficult course. Roosevelt actually beat Taft in the president's home state of Ohio, but Taft and Republican leaders still controlled the party machinery—including the delegates to the party convention in Chicago. When Roosevelt delegates were unseated in favor of Taft supporters, the Roosevelt people walked out of the convention, marched to Orchestra Hall, and founded the Progressive Party with Roosevelt at its head.

Roosevelt made the most of what would become a losing effort. In Milwaukee on October 14, 1912, that effort almost cost him his life, as thirty-six-year-old John Schrank, convinced that Roosevelt was attempting to overthrow the Constitution, shot Roosevelt in the chest with a revolver. Like something out of a bad movie, the steel eyeglasses case in Roosevelt's coat pocket stopped the bullet, a fragment of which embedded in his chest. Roosevelt lived, even as he understood he was heading for a loss on Election Day. In a four-way race, with Socialist Eugene Debs winning nearly a million votes, Roosevelt came in second and Taft third as they split the Republican vote and handed Democrat Woodrow Wilson a landslide electoral victory.

After an interlude in 1913 that found him writing his memoirs, Roosevelt and his son Kermit undertook a South American expedition down a dangerous, uncharted tributary of the Amazon River. Within days of their start, one member of the expedition had died and several canoes had been lost. When Roosevelt jumped into the water to try to save an out-of-control pontoon, he cut his leg badly on a rock. Fever set in, and he became delirious. Soon malaria and dysentery added to the misery of his infected leg. Knowing that his illness placed the rest of the expedition, including Kermit, in jeopardy, Roosevelt contemplated suicide. Rough surgery without anesthetic drained the abscess on his leg, and his condition improved. By the end of the expedition, however, the once-robust Roosevelt had lost fifty-five pounds. Arriving back in New York in May 1914, Roosevelt seemed a shadow of his former self, a spent force who would never again seriously challenge either Republicans or Democrats. In fact, the former colonel of the Rough Riders had one last fight in him.

When the European powers went to war in August 1914, Roosevelt confined himself to writing about it in an essay in *Outlook*. The essay came down firmly on the side of the Belgians, whose sovereignty and neutrality had been trampled by Germany. Roosevelt pointed out that Wilson had pledged such strict neutrality as to constrict America's ability even to protest injustice. Roosevelt wanted to use his journal article to criticize the president for his "supine inaction," but the *Outlook*'s editor cut the line. While this opening shot against Wilson may have jammed in the breach, more salvos were to come. Roosevelt became one of Wilson's fiercest critics, first calling for increased military preparedness, then for America's entry into the war. When war finally came in April 1917, Roosevelt made sure all four of his sons served. The colonel even offered his services to the War Department as a volunteer commander. The offer from the fifty-eight-year-old former Rough Rider was turned down.

His sons' efforts more than made up for Roosevelt's sitting out the war. Archie and Ted were both wounded. Quentin, the baby of the family and a pilot, was shot down in July 1918 and killed. As his diaries show, since his youth, Roosevelt had worked through moments of grief and loss by frenzied action: mad galloping through a moonless night, tramping through the Maine woods or Elkhorn Mountains, and shooting a neighbor's dog. By the time of Quentin's death, Roosevelt had lost such energy. There was only an old man, sick with grief and in constant pain from rheumatism. Talk of Roosevelt as a presidential nominee in 1920 appeared wishful thinking.

Roosevelt turned sixty on October 27, 1918, days before the armistice. By then he was barely able to walk or even sit in a chair. By December he was showing signs of a pulmonary embolism. He continued to dictate articles and editorials, but the effort sapped his strength. Suffering from pain-induced insomnia, Roosevelt was given a shot of morphine just before midnight on Sunday, January 5, 1919. His valet, John Amos, stayed in the room to monitor Roosevelt during the night. When his breathing seemed to start failing, Amos called the nurse. Edith awoke and hurried into the room at four a.m. to find her husband had passed away in his sleep. When his son Archie sent telegrams to his other brothers still serving in France, he wrote, "The Lion is dead." Roosevelt was buried in an Oyster Bay cemetery just down the road from Sagamore Hill.

Glossary of Latin Names of Wildlife Observed and Collected by Theodore Roosevelt

For birds, a handy cross-reference is Roosevelt's own *The Summer Birds of the Adirondacks*, written with Harvard chum Henry David Minot, and *Notes on Some of the Birds of Oyster Bay, Long Island*. Ever the list-maker, even while president, Theodore Roosevelt kept a list of birds observed on the White House grounds and in Washington, D.C. Note that for some of the animals the Latin name used by Roosevelt later became obsolete.

BIRDS

Accipiter cooperii: Cooper's hawk
Accipiter fuscus: Sharp-shinned hawk
Aex sponsa: Wood duck
Anas obscura: Black duck
Ardea herodias: Great blue heron
Botaurus mugitans: Bittern
Colaptes auratus: Golden-winged or northern flicker woodpecker
Colymbus torquatus: Loon
Coturniculus passerinus: Yellow-winged sparrow
Dendroica palmarum: Palm warbler
Denedroica pinus: Pine warbler
Helminthophaga chrysoptera: Swamp warbler
Helminthophaga pina: Blue-winged warbler
Loxia curvirostra: Red or common crossbill
Melospiza palustris: Swamp sparrow
Mergus serrator: Merganser

Parula americana: Warbler
Quisqualus purpureus: Crow blackbird
Tringoides macularius: Spotted sandpiper

ANIMALS

Aramochelys odoratus: Musk turtle
Arvicola riparia: Meadow mouse; also called field mouse and field vole.
Bufo americanus: Common American toad
Chrysemys picta: Painted turtle
Emys guttata: Spotted terrapin (turtle)
Eutaenia sirtalis: Common garter snake
Hesperomys leucopus: White-footed mouse
Plethodon erythronotus: Red-backed salamander
Rana damitans: Green frog
Rana halecina: Southern leopard frog
Rana palustris: Pickerel frog
Rana pipiens: Northern leopard frog
Rana temporaria: Common frog
Salamandra palustris: Common salamander

Works Consulted

MANUSCRIPT COLLECTIONS

Theodore Roosevelt Collection, Houghton Library, Harvard University [Diaries 1877 and 1886, 1882 Legislative Diary].
Theodore Roosevelt Papers, Library of Congress [Diaries 1878–1884].

BOOKS

Cowles, Anna Roosevelt. *Letters from Theodore Roosevelt to Anna Roosevelt Cowles, 1870–1918* (New York: Charles Scribner's Sons, 1924).
Dalton, Kathleen. *Theodore Roosevelt: A Strenuous Life* (New York: Vintage Books, 2004).
Dobson, John M. *Politics in the Gilded Age: A New Perspective on Reform* (New York: Praeger Publishers, 1972).
Donald, Aida. *Lion in the White House* (New York: Basic Books, 2007).
Hagedorn, Hermann. *Roosevelt in the Bad Lands*. (Boston: Houghton Mifflin Co., 1921).
Kohn, Edward P. *Heir to the Empire City: New York and the Making of Theodore Roosevelt* (New York: Basic Books, 2013).
McCullough, David. *Mornings on Horseback* (New York: Simon and Schuster, 1981).
Morison, Elting E., ed. *The Letters of Theodore Roosevelt* (Cambridge, Mass.: Harvard University Press, 1951). [Includes transcription of 1882 Legislative Diary.]
Morris, Edmund. *The Rise of Theodore Roosevelt* (New York: Coward, McCann and Geoghegan, 1979).
Putnam, Carleton. *Theodore Roosevelt: Volume I, The Formative Years, 1858–1886* (New York: Charles Scribner's Sons, 1958).
Robinson, Corinne Roosevelt. *My Brother Theodore Roosevelt* (New York: Charles Scribner's Sons, 1921).

Roosevelt, Theodore. *Theodore Roosevelt: An Autobiography* (New York: Charles Scribner's Sons, 1913) [1985 Da Capo edition].

———. *The Works of Theodore Roosevelt*, National Edition (New York: Charles Scribner's Sons, 1926). [Twenty volumes].

———. *Theodore Roosevelt's Diaries of Boyhood and Youth* (New York: Charles Scribner's Sons, 1928).

Index

Adams, Henry, 258
Adirondacks birding, 2, 6–8
African safari of TR, 266
Agassiz, Alexander Emanuel, 17
Agassiz, Louis, xi, 17
Alexander, Archie, 166
Alexander, Charley, 178, 197
Algeciras Conference (1906), 264
Allen, Freddy, 55
Alvord, Thomas G. ("Old Salt"), 209, 213, 217
American Big-Game Hunting (T. Roosevelt), 258
American Museum of Natural History (New York City), ix, 49
Amos, John, 267
Aristophanes, 19
Arthur, Chester A., 3, 206, 209, 219
Astor, Caroline, 169
Astor Library (New York City), 189
Astor, William Waldorf, 123, 167, 177

Bacon, Julia, 70, 85, 86, 88, 89, 108, 125
Bacon, Robert, 13, 18, 55, 60, 62, 74, 85
Baker, C. S., 217
Ballinger, Richard, 265
Balyies, Cornelia, 91

Bamie. *See* Roosevelt, Anna (sister; "Bamie; "Bysie")
Baumann, Hans, 196
Bayliss, Teddy, 61
Benton, Thomas Hart, 246, 256
Betrothed, The (Scott), 164
Betts, Willys, 168
Bible passages
    John 14, 23
    Psalm 19, 50
    Psalm 55, 14, 39–40
Bighorn/Elkhorn Mountains, 220, 223, 245–246. *See also* cattle operations of TR
birding
    Adirondacks, 2, 6–8
    catalogues of TR, 2, 7, 73
    Long Island, 8, 9, 73
    Massachusetts, 5
Blaine, Emmons, 115
Blaine, James G., 3, 206, 219, 226, 227
Blodgett, William Tilden ("Billy"), 16, 55
Boden, Miss, 9
Bogan (Irish Assembly clerk), 206, 214
Bonaparte, Charles Lucien, 25
"Boston Brahmins," xi–xii, 1, 56, 71, 99, 121, 125

Boston, Massachusetts. *See also* Harvard years of TR
  as cultural center, xi
  social life during Harvard years, 116, 125, 127, 129–130, 132, 136–137, 141
Briggs, Frederic Melancthon, 18
Brooks, Arthur Anderson, 10, 55
Brown, John, 265
Bulloch, Harriot Cross Foster (aunt; "Hattie"), 191
Bulloch, Irvine (uncle), 178, 191
Bulloch, James (uncle; "Jimmie"), 178, 191, 200
Bunyan, John, 41
Burr, Tucker, 56
Bushnell, Albert, 60
Butler, Benjamin, 56
Bysie. *See* Roosevelt, Anna (sister; "Bamie; "Bysie")

Campbell, Lord and Lady George, 187
Carow, Edith Kermit. *See* Roosevelt, Edith Kermit Carow (second wife)
Cassin (former Roosevelt servant), 27, 36, 42, 49, 63
cattle operations of TR
  Chimney Butte Ranch, Little Missouri, 229–230, 239, 240, 242, 255
  elected chairman of Stockmen's Association, 246
  Elkhorn Ranch, Little Missouri, 240, 252–254, 256
  investments, 220, 229–230, 245–246, 252–256, 257–258, 259
  winter of 1885–86, 245, 246–247, 248
  winter of 1886–87, 257–258
Chanler, Winthrop, 258
Chapin, Alfred C., 221, 222
Chapin, Harry Bainbridge ("Hal"), 2, 16, 30, 55, 56, 59, 63, 72, 106–107, 112, 116, 129, 136, 139, 178, 191–192
Chestnut Hill, Massachusetts
  Saltonstall home, 15, 29, 56, 60, 69
  social life, 29, 56, 61, 69–71, 73–75, 80, 82–92, 98–99, 106, 108, 109, 111, 113, 114, 116, 121–122, 125–136, 138–142, 144, 147, 149–150, 160, 169, 188
  TR wedding, 161–162

Choate, Joseph Hodges, 3, 55, 179
Cleveland, Grover, 6, 225–227, 251, 258–259
Cleveland, Stafford C., 222
Coal Strike Commission, 263
Codman, Charley, 88
Codman, Franklin, 86, 140
Colgate, Romy, 146
Columbia Law School years of TR
  decision to enter, 15, 121, 122–123
  life with mother in New York City, 122–123
  studies of TR, 166, 167, 180, 186, 187, 189, 190
Conie. *See* Roosevelt, Corinne (sister; "Pussie; "Conie")
Conkling, Roscoe, 3, 206, 209
Coolidge, Calvin, 6
Coolidge, William Williamson, 11
Cooper, James Fennimore, 46
Cornell, Alonzo, 202–203
Costello, J. J., 213, 214
Cottie, Cotty. *See* Saltonstall, Endicott Peabody ("Cottie," "Cotty")
Crane, Leroy B., 222
Cruger, Pendleton, 96–97
Cruger, Steven Van Renssalaer, 96
Cuba
  Maine explosion, 260
  revolt against Spain, 260–261
Cullum, George Washington, 199
Cutler, Arthur, xi, 50, 99–105
Czolgozs, Leon, 263

Daly, Patrick, 177
Davis, Charles Henry, 258
Davis, Charles Stevenson, 4
Debs, Eugene, 266
De Lôme Letter, 260
Democratic Party
  control of New York State Assembly, 206
  resurgence, 205–206
De Mores, Marquis, 241
Depression of 1873, 205
Dewey, George, 261
Dickens, Charles, 163
Dickey, Charles, 55, 85, 138

Dodge, Cleveland, 94
Dodge, William Earl, III, 94
Donne, John, 41
Dow, Wilmot, 14
  hunting in Bighorn/Elkhorn
    Mountains, 240–242, 245–246,
    253–256
  hunting in Maine, 50–53, 76–80,
    99–105
Dunbar, Professor, 62
Dunne, Finley Peter, 206

Eastern Railroad, 5
education of TR
  Columbia Law School. *See* Columbia
    Law School years of TR
  early years, x
  Harvard. *See* Harvard years of TR
Egger, Peter, 196
Eliot, Charles, xi
Elkhorn Mountains, 220, 223, 245–246
Elkins Act, 263
Ellie. *See* Roosevelt, Elliott (brother;
  "Ellie; "Nell")
Elliott, John (cousin; "Jack"), 6, 8, 9, 16,
  63–65, 129, 156–159, 181
Elliott, Maud (cousin), 2, 6, 16
Elliott, Susan (aunt; "Susie"), 39
Ellis, Ralph Nicholson, 10, 56
Em, Emlen. *See* Roosevelt, William
  Emlen (cousin; "Em; "Emlen")
Everett, Edward, 17
Everett, William "Piggy," 17
expeditions of TR, 1–2
  birding in Adirondacks, 2, 6–8
  birding in Massachusetts, 5
  birding on Long Island, 8, 9, 73
  fishing in Maine, 100–101
  fishing on Long Island, 8, 9
  game record (1873), 66, 171–173
  game record (1874), 66, 118, 171–173
  game record (1875), 66, 118, 171–173
  game record (1876), 66, 118, 171–173
  game record (1877), 11, 66, 118,
    171–173
  game record (1878), 65, 118, 171–173
  game record (1879), 118, 171–173
  game record (1880), 122, 171–173
  game record (1881), 173
  game record (1882), 173–174
  game record (1883), 223
  game record (1884), 244
  guns, 38, 79, 122, 155, 223, 230
  honeymoon in Europe, 178–179,
    190–201, 203–204
  horseback riding on Long Island, 34,
    36–38, 40–42, 47
  hunting in Bighorn/Elkhorn
    Mountains, 220, 223, 245–246
  hunting in Maine, 14, 49–53, 70,
    76–80, 99–105, 122
  hunting in Minnesota and Dakota
    Territory, 122, 150–159, 220
  hunting in open prairies of Illinois and
    Iowa, 151–156
  hunting on Long Island, 4, 8, 27, 30,
    34, 42–45, 58, 64, 72, 96–97, 110–111
  managing cattle operations in Dakota
    Territory, 257–258
  Matterhorn ascent, 178, 197–198
  postpresidential African safari and
    European tour, 265
  postpresidential South American trip,
    266
  rowing and sailing on Long Island
    Sound, 8–9, 14–15, 27, 35, 37, 39,
    40–46, 47–48, 58, 64–65, 70, 93–97,
    110, 146, 147

Ferris, Sylvane, 242
finances of TR
  expense and income ledgers (1877),
    66–67, 119–120
  expense and income ledgers (1878), 15,
    67, 69, 119–120, 170
  expense and income ledgers (1879), 69,
    119–120, 170
  expense and income ledgers (1880),
    122, 170
  expense and income ledgers (1881),
    203–204
  expense and income ledgers (1882),
    174–175
  expense and income ledgers (1883),
    223–224
  expense and income ledgers (1884), 244

finances of TR *(continued)*
  gifts, 69, 122, 128, 160
  inheritance from father, 15, 69
  investment in G. P. Putnam's Sons, 202, 220
  investment in land on Oyster Bay, 220
  investments in cattle operations, 220, 229–230, 245–246, 252–256, 257–258, 259
  Sagamore Hill, 220, 259
Firman, John, 182
Fish, Hamilton, 185
fishing
  Long Island, 8, 9
  Maine, 100–101
Fish, Nicholas, 178, 194
Fish, Stuyvesant, 185
Foraker, Joseph, 265

game records by year. *See* expeditions of TR
Garfield, James, xii, 122, 163, 178, 195, 206, 226
Gaston, William Alexander, 23
George, Henry, 62, 257
German-Americans, 260
Germany
  TR immersion in language and culture of, xi
  TR stay with family in Dresden, x, xi, 6
Gilded Age, xi, 11, 122–123
Goldman, Emma, 263
Goodwin, Carrie, 13, 17
Gould, Henry Eliot, 90
Gould, Jay, 123
Grace, William, 245
Gracie, Anna Bulloch (aunt; "Annie"), 8, 26, 30, 46, 72, 93, 160, 209
Gracie, James K. (uncle; "Jimmie"), 20, 26, 30, 39, 46, 72, 93, 98, 160, 187, 200, 209
Grant, Flora, 181
Grant, Ulysses S., 206, 209
Grimble, Dick, 4
Griswold, Gasper, 168
Griswold, George, 55
Guild, Harry, 108

Haddon, Harold, 82, 117, 124, 168
Haddon, Smith, 82, 124
Hagedorn, Hermann, 219–220
Hale, Matthew, 222
Half-Breeds, 205, 206, 209, 216–217, 219
Hammond, Sam, 76
Harriman, E. H., 263–264
Harrison, Benjamin, 258
Harvard years of TR
  1877, 1–11
  1878, 13–67
  1879, 69–120
  1880, 121–122, 124–145
  A.D. Club, 13, 36, 53, 54–55, 126, 129
  Art Club, 54
  boxing and wrestling, 1, 4, 10, 11, 17, 18, 19, 22, 23, 25, 54, 56, 59, 60, 61, 80
  Class Day activities, 70, 145
  college elective system, xi, 2
  decision to enter law school, 121, 122–123, 135
  Delta Kappa Epsilon (Δ K.E.), 10, 32, 54, 63, 144
  dining club, 30
  "dogcart" of TR, 69, 82, 98, 105–109, 111, 114–115
  family connections to Harvard, 1, 76
  family visits to Cambridge, 2, 6, 59, 144
  final examinations, 143–144
  Finance Club, 60, 62, 73
  Glee Club, 54, 56, 117
  grades, 6, 17, 18, 19, 23, 25, 29, 30, 45, 54, 61, 63, 73, 98, 108, 139
  graduation in 1880, 122, 145
  Harvard Athletic Association (H.A.A.), 32, 87
  Hasty Pudding Club, 74, 80, 107, 131, 139
  Mission School work, 129, 131
  Natural History Society, 107
  Porcellian Club, 13, 15, 53, 54–55, 58, 59, 61–62, 62, 107, 140
  preparation, xi
  running, 107, 116
  shooting/rifle clubs, 22, 25, 54, 85
  social life in Boston, 116, 125, 127, 129–130, 132, 136–137, 141

social life in Cambridge, 74, 80–81, 92, 107–108, 113–114, 128, 131, 133, 134, 139, 140, 144
social life in Chestnut Hill, Massachusetts, 29, 56, 61, 69–71, 73–75, 80, 82–92, 98–99, 106, 108, 109, 111, 113, 114, 116, 121–122, 125–136, 138–142, 144
social life in New York City, 26–27, 71, 73, 81–82, 111, 112, 117–118, 123–124, 137–138
social life in Oyster Bay, Long Island, 27–28, 38–49, 57–58, 72, 93–98, 109–111
Sunday School teaching by TR, xii, 4, 10, 23, 58, 81, 84, 125
thesis on political economy, 121, 135, 137
TR arrives on campus, xii
Hawthorne, Nathaniel, 41
Hayes, Rutherford B., xii, 3, 205–206, 209
Hay, John, 258
health problems of TR
  asthma, x, 1, 36, 49, 80, 154, 155
  cholera morbus, 45, 122, 148, 149, 230
  colic, 154
  malaria and dysentery, 266
  measles, 1, 4
  rheumatism, 267
Hearst, William Randolph, 260
Henry, Prince of Germany, 95
Hepburn Act, 263
Hess, Jake, 178, 204
Hewitt, Abram, 62, 257
Heywood, George, 141
History of the Conquest of Peru, A (Prescott), 139
Hobart, Garret, 262
Homestead Acts, 246
Hooker, Joseph, 209
Hooper, Arthur, 10, 16–19, 24, 55
Hooper, Bessie, 70
Hooper, Jeannie, 13, 17–19, 55, 56, 81
Hooper, Russell, 2, 5
Hooper, William ("Billy"), 4, 55, 74
House, Fred B., 222
Howe, Walter, 219–220

How the Other Half Lives (Riis), 259
hunting
  Bighorn/Elkhorn Mountains, 220, 223, 245–246
  college shooting/rifle clubs, 22, 25, 54, 85
  game records by year. *See* expeditions of TR
  guns, 38, 79, 122, 155, 223, 230
  Long Island, 4, 8, 27, 30, 34, 42–45, 58, 64, 72, 96–97, 110–111
  Maine, 14, 49–53, 70, 76–80, 99–105, 122
  Minnesota and Dakota Territory, 122, 150–159, 220
  open prairies of Illinois and Iowa, 151–156
Hunting in the Bad Lands (T. Roosevelt), 258
Hunting Trips of a Ranchman (T. Roosevelt), 220, 227
Hunt, Isaac, 219–220, 221

Illinois Central Railroad, 185
Impressionists, 192
Irish-Americans, 206, 210, 213–215, 221
Iselin, Adrian, 117
Iselin, Columbus O'Donnell ("Ike"), 82, 117, 144, 168

Jackson, Harry, 55, 60, 74
James, William, 2, 10
Jay, John, 3
Johnston, John Taylor, 188
Junior. *See* Roosevelt, Theodore, III (son; "Ted; "Junior")

Kane, Woodbury, 85
Kean, Christine, 82, 117, 187
Kean, Lucy, 82, 117
Kearney, Denis, 56–57
Kelly, John, 215
King, Percy, 184
Kingsford, Jack, 118, 145

La Follette, Robert, 265
Land and Game Birds of New England, The (H. D. Minot), 2

Lane, Kitty, 126
Lane, Lulu, 74–75, 84, 87, 88, 106, 108, 111, 115, 116
Langley, William H., 147
Lawrence, Harriet, 107, 182
Lawrence, Rosamund, 162
Learned, William Pollock, 4
Lebo, 230–244
Lee, Alice Hathaway. *See* Roosevelt, Alice Hathaway Lee (first wife)
Lee, Frank, 85, 99, 115, 127, 161
Lee, George (father-in-law), 121
Lee, Hattie, 189
Lee, Robert E., 209
Lee, Rosie (sister-in-law), 15, 56, 69–71, 70, 107, 114, 116, 124, 126, 169, 189
Lee, Tom, 74–75, 116, 161
Lexow Committee, 259
Life of Thomas Hart Benton (T. Roosevelt), 246, 256
Lincoln, Abraham, 265
Lodge, Henry Cabot, 17, 205–206, 226, 227, 250, 257, 258, 261, 265
Lodge, Nannie, 250
Long Island. *See* Oyster Bay, Long Island
Long, John D., 260
Lowell, Katie, 209
Lowell, Lulu, 128
Low, Seth, 225
Ludlow, Harriet Carnochan, 73
Ludlow, Thomas, 72, 73
Lyman, Theodore, 127

Mahan, Alfred Thayer, 258
Maine trips of TR, 14, 49–53, 70, 76–80, 99–105, 122, 148–149
Manifest Destiny, 246
Marquand, John Phillips, 116
Matterhorn ascent, 178, 197–198
McAllister, Lulu, 187
McKinley, William, 260, 262–263
Meade, George, 209
medical conditions of TR. *See* health problems of TR
Merriam, C. Hart, 7
Merrifield, William, 254
  hunting in Bighorn/Elkhorn Mountains, 230–244

Merriman, C. Hart, 2
Metropolitan Museum of Art (New York City), ix, 49
military career of TR
  assistant secretary of the Navy, 260–261
  New York National Guard Regiment, 222
  in the "Rough Riders," 206, 261
Miller, Jeff, 74
Miller, Warner, 219
Mill, John Stuart, 57
Milton, John, 41
Minot. *See* Weld, Christopher Minot ("Minot")
Minot, George, 60, 85, 88, 108, 178, 187
Minot, Grace, 126
Minot, Henry Davis ("Harry" or "Hal"), 1–2, 5, 16, 20, 111, 121–122
  birding catalogues, 2, 7
  leaves Harvard, 48–50
Minot, William, 1
Mittie. *See* Roosevelt, Martha Bulloch (mother; "Mittie"; "Muffie")
Moran, Lizzie, 82, 117, 188
Morgan, Charley, 55, 74, 89, 109
Morgan, Dick, 23, 73
Morgan, J. Pierpont, 3, 263–264
Muffie. *See* Roosevelt, Martha Bulloch (mother; "Mittie"; "Muffie")
Murray, Annie, 16, 34, 35, 38–39, 72, 82, 117, 166
Murray, Joe, 178

National Civil Service Reform League, xii
Naval War of 1812, The (T. Roosevelt), 178, 186, 189, 201, 202
Nell. *See* Roosevelt, Elliott (brother; "Ellie"; "Nell")
Newcomes, The (Thackeray), 163
"New Nationalism" speech, 265
Newsboys Lodging House (New York City), ix, x, 117, 118, 123, 124, 165, 166, 168, 180, 181, 185–187, 189, 202
New York City
  philanthropic activities of TR, 117, 118, 123, 124, 165–166, 168, 177–178, 180, 181, 185–187, 189, 190, 202

Roosevelt family homes, ix, 35, 63–64,
        122–123, 165, 209
    social life, 26–27, 71, 73, 81–82, 111,
        112, 117–118, 123–124, 137–138, 160,
        165–169, 178, 180–190, 248–252
New York City Board of Health, 245
New York City Police Department, 216,
    259–260
New York Customhouse, 3, 206, 209
New York Infant Asylum, 177–178, 186
New York Journal, 260
New York Times, 219–220
New York Tribune, 166
Nickerson, Thomas White, 4
Nilsson, Birgit, 192
noblesse oblige, xi–xii
North American Review, xi, xii
North Securities, 263–264

Odell, Benjamin, 262
O'Neil, William Thomas, 219–220, 221,
    225
Orthopedic Dispensary Hospital (New
    York City), ix, 177–178, 186, 190,
    202
Outlook, 266–267
Oyster Bay, Long Island
    Roosevelt family home, x, 27, 30,
        33–35, 36–39
    Sagamore Hill, 4, 220, 259, 267
    social life, 27–28, 38–49, 57–58, 72,
        93–98, 109–111, 146–147, 160–161
    TR honeymoon, 122–123, 162–165

Panama Canal, 264
Parish, Grace, 64, 82
Parker, Jim, 129
Pascal, Blaise, 41
Patience (Gilbert & Sullivan), 192
Patterson, Charles E., 211, 213
Payne-Aldrich Tariff Act, 265
Peabody, Endicott, 161
Peabody, Fanny, 131, 133, 136, 142, 161,
    162, 182
Peabody, Frank, 161
Peabody, Rosamina, 182
Pellew, William George, 16
Pendennis (Thackeray), 142

Pendleton Act, 258–259
Peters, Billy, 76
Peters, George Gorham, 4, 33, 55, 56
Phelps, Nellie, 117
Philippines, 261
Pinchot, Gifford, 265
Platt, Thomas C., 262
Poe, Edgar Allan, 28
political career of TR
    aldermanic bill, 207–208, 226
    aqueduct proposal, 179, 202–203,
        207–208, 212, 217
    assistant secretary of the Navy, 260–261
    attends meetings of Twenty-First
        Assembly District, New York City,
        177–178, 184
    city charter revision, 177, 186, 225
    "City Irish" and, 206, 210, 213–215, 221
    Congressional Investigating
        Committee, 258
    considered for president of New York
        City Board of Health, 245
    essay on World War I in *Outlook,*
        266–267
    governor of New York State, 258, 262
    independence from party politics,
        178–179, 207, 215, 216, 220, 221,
        226, 262
    New York City police commissioner,
        216, 259–260
    New York State Assembly, 178–179,
        179, 201–203, 205–212, 213–217,
        219–222, 225–226
    nominations for mayor of New York
        City, 257, 259
    presidency, 263–265
    presidential election of 1884, 226, 227
    Spanish-American War, 260–261
    street-cleaning bill, 177, 178, 179, 186,
        188
    supports Benjamin Harrison
        presidency, 258
    supports William McKinley
        presidency, 260
    third presidential campaign, 265–266
    United States Civil Service
        Commission, 258–259
    vice presidency, 262

Porter, Grove, 82
Portsmouth Conference (1905), 264
Post, Emily, 117, 169
Posthumous Papers of the Pickwick Club, The (Dickens), 163
Potter, Grace, 112, 117
Potter, Maria, 187
Prescott, William Hickling, 139
Preservation of Antiquities Act, 264
Progress and Poverty (George), 257
Progressive Era, 179, 207–208, 262–266
Progressive (Bull Moose) Party, 266
Puerto Rico, revolt against Spain, 260–261
Pure Food and Drug Act, 264
Pussie. *See* Roosevelt, Corinne (sister; "Pussie;" "Conie")
Putnam, Carleton, 70
Putnam's (G. P.) Sons, 202, 220

Quentin Durward (Scott), 163
Quincy, Josiah, 60

Raines, John, 216–217
Ranch Life and the Hunting Trail (T. Roosevelt), 246
Rathbone, Alice, 180
Rathbone, Grace, 125, 181
Reid, Whitelaw, 123, 166, 177, 251
Remington, Frederic, 246
Republican Party
  caucus of 1882, 205
  Half-Breeds, 205, 206, 209, 216–217, 219
  reform movement, 3, 205–206, 219–220, 225, 226, 262, 266
  Republican National Convention (1876), xi–xii, 3, 205–206
  Republican National Convention (1880), xi–xii
  Republican National Convention (1884), 207, 226, 227
  Roosevelt, Sr. activities in, 3, 179, 205–206
  Stalwarts, 205, 206, 209, 213, 216–217, 219, 221, 222
  TR independence from party politics, 178–179, 207, 215, 216, 220, 221, 226

Republican Reform Club, 3
Revere, Pauline, 13, 17, 91
Riis, Jacob, 259
Robb, Hampden, 214, 215
Robinson, Douglas (brother-in-law), 116, 146, 168, 183, 189
Robinson, Missy, 184
Roosevelt, Alfred (cousin), 16, 37, 57
Roosevelt, Alice Hathaway Lee (first wife)
  courted by TR, 56, 60, 61, 69–71, 74–75, 80–92, 98, 111, 114–115, 118, 124
  death, 226, 228–229
  death of grandmother, 138
  engagement to TR, 121–122, 127–162
  honeymoon in Europe, 178–179, 190–201, 203–204
  honeymoon in Oyster Bay, Long Island, 122–123, 162–165
  joins Presbyterian Church, 123, 165, 167, 168
  marries TR, 122–123, 161
  meets TR, 13, 15, 56
  pregnancy, 226
Roosevelt, Alice Lee (daughter), 95, 226, 229, 246, 257, 258
Roosevelt and Son, ix
Roosevelt, Anna (sister; "Bamie;" "Bysie")
  birth, ix
  death of father, 20, 24, 26, 27
  family visit to Harvard (1877), 6
  Harvard connections, 1
  health problems, x, 24
Roosevelt, Archie (son), 258, 267
Roosevelt, Corinne (sister; "Pussie;" "Conie"), 161
  birth, x
  death of father, 26, 27–28, 34
  family visit to Harvard (1877), 6
  health problems, x
  marries Douglas Robinson, 168, 183
Roosevelt, Cornelius (cousin), 48, 57
Roosevelt, Cornelius Van Schaack (grandfather), ix, 4
Roosevelt Corollary of Monroe Doctrine, 264
Roosevelt, Edith Kermit Carow (second wife)
  break-up with TR, 13, 46

children, 257, 258, 266–267
engagement to TR, 245, 246, 248–252
friendship with TR, 2, 6, 9, 16, 44–46, 70, 81, 112, 117, 178
marries TR, 257
Roosevelt, Elliott (brother; "Ellie;" "Nell")
birth, ix
death of father, 20
family visit to Harvard (1877), 6
health problems, x
hunting in Bighorn/Elkhorn Mountains, 220, 226–227, 229–244, 246–247, 252–256
hunting in Minnesota and Dakota Territory, 156–159
social life in Oyster Bay, Long Island, 94–96
Roosevelt, Ethel (daughter), 258
Roosevelt, James Alfred (uncle; "Jim"), 8, 48, 98, 109, 111, 146, 169, 180, 201–202
Roosevelt, James West (cousin; "West"), 16, 57, 129, 161, 168
hunting in Maine, 14, 50, 52–53
Roosevelt, Kermit (son), 258, 266
Roosevelt, Laura (aunt), 137
Roosevelt, Martha Bulloch (mother; "Mittie;" "Muffie")
death, 226, 229
death of husband, 25
family background, ix
pro-Confederacy sentiments, ix, 178, 191
Roosevelt, Mary West (aunt), 6
Roosevelt, O'Neil, 219–220
Roosevelt, Quentin (son), 267
Roosevelt, Samuel (cousin), 49
Roosevelt, Silas Weir (uncle), 6, 57
Roosevelt, Theodore, III (son; "Ted;" "Junior"), 257, 267
Roosevelt, Theodore, Jr. (TR)
assassination attempt, 266
begins adult diary, xii, 1
birth, ix
cattle operations. See cattle operations of TR
children, 95, 226, 229, 246, 257, 258, 266–267

death, 267
death of father, 13–14, 19–22
death of mother, 226, 229
death of wife, Alice, 226, 228–229
education. See education of TR
expeditions in nature. See expeditions of TR
family background, ix–x
family European grand tour of 1869–70, x
family European grand tour of 1872–73, x, xi
family summerhouse in Oyster Bay, Long Island, x, 4, 27, 30, 33–39. See also Oyster Bay, Long Island
family trip to Middle East and Holy Lands (1872–73), 23
female friends, 2, 6, 13, 15, 16–19, 37–39, 44–46, 56, 60–61, 69–70, 72, 74–75, 81, 85, 86, 89, 91, 106, 108, 109–110, 112, 117, 125, 126, 178
finances. See finances of TR
grief at death of father, 14, 23–29, 32, 34–40, 41, 44, 48, 57, 62–63, 64, 75, 109–110
health problems. See health problems of TR
love of the outdoors, x, xi, 2, 8. See also expeditions of TR
male friends, 1–2, 5, 13, 14, 16, 21, 30, 55–56, 63, 69–71, 73, 74–75, 81, 106–107, 129, 136, 168, 178
marriages. See Roosevelt, Alice Hathaway Lee (first wife); Roosevelt, Edith Kermit Carow (second wife)
in Meadowbrook Hunt (1886), 245
medical conditions. See health problems of TR
military career. See military career of TR
natural sciences and, x, xi, 2, 6–7, 10, 14, 17, 55, 64, 98. See also expeditions of TR
nearsightedness, 25, 38, 220
philanthropic activities, 117, 118, 123, 124, 165–166, 168, 177–178, 180, 181, 185–187, 189, 190, 202
political activities. See political career of TR

Roosevelt, Theodore, Jr. (TR) *(continued)*
  pursuit of fitness, x, xii, 1, 32, 107, 116, 126
  writing of. *See* writing of TR
Roosevelt, Theodore, Sr. (father)
  death, 13–14, 19–22
  dominance in family, x, 3
  Harvard connections, 1, 76
  health problems, 3, 11, 13–14, 16
  nomination to head New York Custom House, 3, 206
  as partner in Roosevelt and Son, ix
  philanthropic activities, ix, x, 49, 179
  pro-Union sentiments, ix
  Republican Party activities, 3, 179, 205–206
  summerhouse at Oyster Bay, Long Island, x, 4
  support for TR interest in natural sciences, 2
  TR grief at death of, 32, 34–40, 41, 44, 48, 57, 62–63, 64, 75, 109–110
Roosevelt, William Emlen (cousin; "Em;" "Emlen"), 8, 16, 64, 82, 129, 161, 168
  hunting in Maine, 14, 50–53, 99–105
Root, Elihu, 179
Rotch, Nana, 69–70, 74–75, 82, 84, 90–92, 116, 129
"Rough Riders, The," 206, 261
Rough Riders, The (T. Roosevelt), 206
Russell, Archie, 117, 168
Russo-Japanese War, 264

Sagamore Hill (TR home on Long Island), 4, 220, 259, 267
Saltonstall, Alfred, 129
Saltonstall, Endicott Peabody ("Cottie, Cotty"), 91, 142, 162, 188
Saltonstall, Mamie, 189
Saltonstall, Philip Leverett ("Phil"), 91
Saltonstall, Richard ("Dick"), 30, 59, 63, 71, 74–75, 81–82, 84, 88, 106–107, 129, 136, 161, 228. *See also* Chestnut Hill, Massachusetts
  home in Chestnut Hill, Massachusetts, 15, 29, 56, 60, 69, 121
  illness during sophomore year, 13
  returns to Harvard, 15, 53, 69

Saltonstall, Rose, 15, 56, 60, 61, 69–71, 74–75, 86, 89–91, 106, 114, 115, 161
Samson, Johnny, 55
Saxton, Billy, 60
Schrank, John, 266
Scott, Walter, 163, 164
Sedgwick, Bob, 117, 168
Sewall, William, 14
  hunting in Bighorn/Elkhorn Mountains, 240–242, 245–246, 253–256
  hunting in Maine, 50–53, 76–80, 99–105
Seward, William, 209
Shaler, Alexander, 245
Shanley, John, 216
Sharon, Frederic William, 61, 85
Sharpe, George H., 209, 213
Sharps Rifle Company, 38
Shaw, Henry Russell ("Harry"), 18, 30, 33, 53, 55, 60, 63, 74–75, 83, 84–85, 88, 91, 106–107, 115, 129, 136, 140, 178, 191–192
Sherman Antitrust Act, 263–264
Skinner, Sam, 85
Smith, Fab, 16
Smith, Fanny, 35, 81, 112, 117, 181, 186
Smith, Paul, 8
South American trip of TR, 266
Spanish-American War, 260–261
Spinney, George, 219–220
Spinola, Francis B., 215
Sprague, Charley, 81
Sprague, Dick, 76
Spring-Rice, Cecil, 258
Square Deal, 264
Stalwarts, 205, 206, 209, 213, 216–217, 219, 221, 222
St. Andrews Society of the State of New York, 123, 166
Stanley, Arthur, 192
Stratton, Sidney, 117
Strew, William, 179, 202
Strong, William, 259
Summer Birds of the Adirondacks in Franklin County, N.Y. (H. D. Minot and T. Roosevelt), 2, 7
Sunday Excise Law, 259–260

Sunday School teaching, xii, 4, 10, 23, 58, 81, 84, 125
Surratt, John, 209
Surratt, Mary, 209
Swan, Emily, 70, 97, 109–110

Taft, William Howard, 264–266
Tangier Crisis, 264
Tebbets, John Sever ("Jack"), 16, 30, 31, 33, 57, 59, 62–63, 74–75, 81, 87, 106–108, 112, 116, 124, 126, 129, 131, 136, 161
Ted. *See* Roosevelt, Theodore, III (son; "Ted; "Junior")
Teschemacher, Hubert Engelbert, 24
Thackeray, William, 142, 163
Thompson, Hubert O., 207, 215, 225
Thompson, W., 50–53
Tilden, Samuel J., 205, 211
Tophet/Topheth, 41
Townsend, Howard, 116
TR. *See* Roosevelt, Theodore, Jr. (TR)
TR, Jr. *See* Roosevelt, Theodore, III (son; "Ted; "Junior")
Trimble, Richard ("Dick"), 16, 55, 63, 74
Trimble, Walter, 161
Trimble, William, 178, 188
Tuckerman, Jeannie, 61
Tuckerman, Jenny, 192
Tuckerman, Lucy, 169, 181
Tuckerman, Mary, 81, 107
Tuckerman, Paul, 189
Tudor, William, xi
Turner, J. M. W., 192

Union League Club (New York City), 49
United States Civil Service Commission, 258–259
United States Department of Commerce and Labor, 263
Upham, George, 76

Vanderbilt, William, 123
Van Rensselaer, William Bayard, 73, 84, 88–91, 116
Vietze, Andrew, 33
Virginian, The (Wister), 246
von Sternburg, Speck, 258

Wagner Palace Car Company, 210
Wagner, Webster, 210
Ware, Charley, 55, 56, 63, 74
Washburn, Charles Grenfill ("Charley"), 16, 56, 60, 63, 75
Washburn, William, 136
Washington, George, 264
Water-Witch, The (Cooper), 46
Weeks, Freddy, 161
Weir, Julian, 183
Weld, Christopher Minot ("Minot"), 2, 5, 6–8, 16, 30, 55, 56, 59, 74–75, 81–82, 84, 86, 106–108, 109, 129, 136, 161, 178, 191–192
West, Hilborne, 209
West. *See* Roosevelt, James West (cousin; "West")
Wharton, William, 258
Wheelright, Susie, 69–70, 91
White, Helen Chanler, 73, 91
White, Octavius A., 73
Whitney, Bessie, 13, 17, 69–70, 74–75, 86–88, 90
Whitney, Ell, 74–75, 86, 117, 118
Whitney, Joe, 141
Wilcox, 151–156
Wilderness Hunter, The (T. Roosevelt), 258
Williams, Otho Holland, 62, 63, 73, 81
Wilson, Woodrow, 94, 266
Winning of the West, The (T. Roosevelt), 246, 258
Wister, Owen, 246
Wolf, Maggie, 91
Wood, Leonard, 261
World War I, 266–267
Wright, Jim, 81
writing of TR
  American Big-Game Hunting, 258
  articles on New York State Assembly, 205
  Autobiography, 21
  birding catalogues, 2, 7, 73
  essay on World War I in *Outlook*, 266–267
  Harvard thesis on political economy, 121, 135, 137
  Hunting in the Bad Lands, 258
  Hunting Trips of a Ranchman, 220, 227

writing of TR *(continued)*
   Life of Thomas Hart Benton, 246, 256
   The Naval War of 1812, 178, 186, 189, 201, 202
   Ranch Life and the Hunting Trail, 246
   The Rough Riders, 206
The Wilderness Hunter, 258
The Winning of the West, 246, 258

Yellow Press, 260
Young Men's Republican Association, 188

www.ingramcontent.com/pod-product-compliance
Lightning Source LLC
Chambersburg PA
CBHW021849230426
43671CB00006B/325